Killing Monsters

Also by Gerard Jones

Honey, I'm Home
The Comic Book Heroes (with Will Jacobs)
The Beaver Papers (with Will Jacobs)

Killing Monsters

Why Children Need
Fantasy, Super Heroes,
and Make-Believe Violence

Gerard Jones
Foreword by Dr. Lynn Ponton, M.D.

BASIC
BOOKS

A Member of the Perseus Books Group

To my son,
Nicholas Jones,
hoping to give you a slightly saner world.

Designed by Trish Wilkinson

Library of Congress Cataloging-in-Publication Data
Jones, Gerard.
   Killing monsters : why children need fantasy, super heroes and make-believe
violence /
Gerard Jones.
    p.   cm.
   Includes bibliographical references and index.
   ISBN 0-465-03695-3
   1. Mass media and children. 2. Fantasy in mass media. 3.Monsters in mass media. 4.
Heroes in mass media. 5.Violence in mass media.

P94.5.C55 J66 2002
303.6'083--dc21

                                                                          2001052667

02 03 04 / 10 9 8 7 6 5 4 3 2 1

Contents

Foreword

*J*onathan, a ten year-old boy clutching his favorite stuffed animal, a three-legged giraffe, cracks a toothless smile as he waves good-bye. He has just spent his afternoon killing people. During our hour together he has thrown hundreds of animals and soldiers from the upper tower of my toy castle, crashed a flying dragon so hard into its sturdy stone wall that a visible crack has appeared, and created a raging fire that has slaughtered all the people who were trying to save the others. He has said very little during this intense hour, only once breaking his silence when he whispered, "It's a killing world," as a mother tried to save her newborn baby from the growing flames. This week, Jonathan has been only one of several children who blew up buildings, fired up blazes, and crashed airplanes. Jonathan's therapy session with me, a child and adolescent psychiatrist, has taken place only three days after September 11, 2001.

Several months before, Jonathan had played violent games obsessively. His dad had tried to limit the activity, until I discovered that Jonathan was trying to cope with a bully at school. As he worked through that conflict, his violent play decreased. Then, after the 11th, it increased again dramatically. Jonathan told me that he was pretty scared after the terrorist activities. In fact, the only time that he wasn't scared was when he was playing scary games—then he felt okay.

Killing games gave Jonathan control over events where he and others felt none and, perhaps even more important, they gave him control over his own feelings. With these games Jonathan no longer felt as helpless. He was not as scared of others or of his own feelings.

As a psychiatrist, I see on a daily basis that frightening and violent ideas, images, and fantasies are vital parts of children's minds. The images of September 11th fueled Jonathan's fantasies and spurred his play, but they also helped him understand what had just happened in the world. Playing with violent images frightened but also soothed him, helping him feel strong enough to handle what had happened.

Killing games have much to tell us about the worlds of children and teenagers. It is important that we try to listen. Gerard Jones's book, *Killing Monsters,* helps us do just that. Listen. And it is not easy to listen to the violent stories that fill the lives of our children. It is far easier to pretend that these themes either don't exist or should be completely eliminated.

What role do violent themes and entertainment play in children's lives? What value do they have? In this powerful and important book, Jones helps us not only to listen but to ask the right questions. As a researcher of popular culture, a former comic book writer, a game maker, and equally important, a parent, he has listened to children and teens who love scary games and movies. He has run storytelling workshops with girls who idolize *Buffy the Vampire Slayer* and boys who play *Doom.* In *Killing Monsters,* he helps us discover the power and the magic that our children see in violent superheroes. He also helps us ask questions about the risks, the real risks. When do these "games" make our children more violent? Which children are at risk?

And—most important—what, if anything, can and should be done about that risk?

Gerard Jones's reassuring book offers all of us—parents, teachers, policymakers, and media critics—new ways to understand the challenges and rewards of fantasy violence in the modern imagination.

Lynn Ponton, M.D.,
Author of *The Romance of Risk:
Why Teenagers Do the Things They Do*

Acknowledgments

I've been astonished and gratified at the eagerness of so many people within the educational, medical, psychological, entertainment, and parental communities to help me make this book a reality. Each one of those experiences has reminded me of how people of the most diverse and divided opinions can be brought together by passion for children, concern for the future, and the simple joy of trying to understand how people work—and each one has reminded me of how a little empathy and honesty can knock down the greatest rhetorical and emotional barriers.

Among those who gave their time to increase my understanding were Dr. Mihaly Csikszentmihalyi of the Claremont Universities, Dr. William Damon of Stanford University, Dr. Lenore Terr of the University of California–San Francisco, Dr. Ralph DiClementi of Emory University, Dr. Donald F. Roberts of Stanford University, Dr. Stuart Fischoff of California State University–Los Angeles, Dr. Jib Fowles of the University of Houston, Dr. Edwin H. Cook of the University of Chicago, Dr. Donna Mitroff of *ABC Family*, Dr. Helen Smith of ViolentKids.com, Dr. Roben Torosyan of New School University, and Dr. Rachel Lauer, the late chief psychologist of the New York City Schools.

Dr. Lynn Ponton of the University of California, Dr. Carla Seal-Wanner of New York University and Dr. Nancy Marks were exceptionally generous in reading and critiquing chapters, as well as in sharing insights from their work and family lives. Dr. Melanie Moore gave me much help in the book's earliest stages. I'm also very grateful to the many clinical psychologists who shared with me their hard-won understandings of children, adolescents, and adults, particularly Diane Stern, Dr. Jonathon Gray, Christa Donaldson, Dr. Phyllis Shulman, Dr. Valerie Hearn, Ilene Wolf, Susan Frankel, and Eric Stein; and to the many concerned parents who've brought me their experiences and insights, especially Heidi Anderson, Leslie Fetchen, Martha Thomases, Jean Blanc, Joe Filice, Susan Stapczynski, and Gina Weinberg. Thanks to the many teachers who let me into their classrooms and talked with me about their students, with special nods to Rebecca Field, Alice Hong, and the remarkable faculty of Live Oak School; and to those who shared their early experiences with entertainment and fantasy with me, particularly Sarah Holm, Ruben Diaz, Ray Portillo, Janice Cohen, Oscar Munoz, and Mary Cotter. All the stories in this book are true, although some of my sources have asked me to change names and sometimes a biographical detail or two in the interest of privacy. Most of all, I'm grateful to the hundreds of kids and teenagers who have shared their stories, games, and fantasies with me over the past several years, both within and outside my formal workshops. Many of them asked me to use their real names; alas, out of respect to the schools, teachers, and other students I've had to hew to a policy of anonymity regarding the workshops. I encourage them all to continue with the creative pursuits that will get their names into print in even more gratifying ways.

Many people provided just the right story, insight, information, or encouragement at just the right moment: Michael Chabon, Mick LaSalle, Sam Hamm, Henry Selick, Dr. Jonathan Freedman of the University of Toronto, Dr. Craig Anderson of the University of Iowa, Dr. Henry Jenkins of the Massachusetts Institute of Technology, Dr. Jeanne Funk of the University of Toledo, Dr. James McGee of Shepard-Pratt Hospital, Dr. Thomas Brod of the University of California at Los Angeles, Marc Laidlaw of Valve Software, Lana Nichols, Will Jacobs, David Kleeman of the American Center for Children and Media, Annette Roman and Dallas Middaugh of Viz Communications, Elizabeth Thoman of the Center for Media Literacy, Dr. Hubert Jessup of MediaScope, Christopher Perrius and others from the University of Chicago Cultural Policy Center, Doug Lowenstein and Carolyn Rauch of the International Digital Software Association,

Anna Home, OBE, of the BBC and the Children's Film and Television Foundation, and the many officers and supporters of the glorious CineMagic Festival in Belfast.

Jo Ann Miller has been an extraordinary editor on a book that was never easy. With her wisdom, compassion, and a firm hand, she helped shape every page of this manuscript. Jennifer Swearingen helped enormously with the perceptivity of her copyediting. Vince Beiser of *Mother Jones* orchestrated the book's first public presentation. Carol Mann encouraged me to write this book from the moment the idea first tumbled from my mouth, and put great thought and work into making it real.

I must thank, most of all, the mentors of my own family. I grew up surrounded by dedicated public school teachers: my father, Russell Jones, my mother, Leslie Jones, and my big brother, Ray Jones. They all impressed upon me early the importance not only of teaching young people what we know, but also of respecting what young people know, want, and have to tell us. My mother hated even the most imaginary violence, but in the end her respect for people and their experiences always overwhelmed whatever preconceptions she held. We talked at length about this book all through her final battle with cancer. She died after reading only a few of my chapters, but her strength and compassion were with me through the end.

My son, Nicky Jones, was remarkably patient and enthusiastic about Daddy's all-consuming project, even when it took me away from him too many times or left me preoccupied when we were together. His storytelling, playing, explaining, and drawing were my richest source of inspiration throughout the work.

No one, however, was more valuable, more essential, to me through this demanding task than Jennie Kajiko, my friend, my partner, my reality check, my first wife and my second, the finest coparent a man could ask for. Through the most painful and wonderful growth, she has been my constant companion in this exploration of the power of honesty and empathy.

Gerard Jones, February, 2002

1

Being Strong

$\mathcal{M}$y first memory is of tearing the monster's arm off. I had crossed the sea to the hall of these warriors who were being terrorized by a nocturnal beast, boasted over mead that only I could slay it, pretended to sleep until the monster crept in to devour a warrior—and when it came to seize me I leapt up, seized its massive arm in my grip of steel, and held on as we battled through the hall, smashing the wooden walls with our fury, until at last in desperation it tore itself loose of its own limb and fled, bleeding and screaming, mortally wounded to its lair in the fens.

Quite a feat for a five-year-old.

When I was old enough to go to kindergarten, my mother went back to college to get her teaching credential. She hadn't had a lot of high culture in her own upbringing and she made sure that I was more fortunate: she tacked prints from the Metropolitan Museum to all the walls in the house and read classic literature to me at bedtime. She tried Stevenson's poems, *Gulliver's Travels,* Chaucer's *Reynard*. It all rolled off me. If I hadn't asked her about all this decades later, I'd never have known. The only one I remembered was *Beowulf,* with its pagan, barbarian monster-slayer of a hero.

He was a terrible role model. He didn't do any of the things we want our children's heroes to teach: didn't discuss solutions with the group, didn't think first of the safety of others, didn't try to catch the monster without harming it. He bragged, he bullied, he killed, and he even let his allies be devoured to further his plan. Yet, it was Beowulf I wanted to be, and Beowulf I became. I made my mom read it to me over and over, and I caught her when she tried to glide past the most gruesome parts ("The demon clutched a sleeping thane in his swift assault, tore him in pieces, bit through the bones, gulped the blood, and gobbled the flesh . . . "). I carved scenes from his battles into my Playskool blocks with a ballpoint pen and rearranged them in every possible narrative order. Running naked from the bath across the polyester carpet I thumped my skinny chest and roared, "Foe against foe, I'll fight the death!"

I was no warrior in real life. I was a mama's boy. I liked to play in the house and the backyard, liked kids who were my age but not when they got too wild. The prospect of kindergarten terrified me, and so did knowing that my mom was going to be away from home much of every day. But at home, in my own world, I could tear a pillow off the bed with a "*rrrrrrarrr!*" and see the monster Grendel fleeing in terror.

"You were an adorable barbarian," my mom said, helping me dig through a box of my childhood artwork. I found a yellowing pad covered with stick-figure warriors grimacing and flexing their muscles—loaf-like bubbles protruding from line-thin arms—at toothy monsters. I remembered striking that pose—and how strong I felt. Then, with a mock sigh, my mother added, "But I did so want you to be cultured."

As it turned out, I did grow up fairly cultured—or civilized, at least. I was as cooperative, bookish, and conscientious as my parents could have wanted. But I carried that monster-slaying hero inside me the whole time. First as fantasy: Beowulf gave way to King Kong, then Batman, then James Bond. As I outgrew fantasies, he became a scholarly interest. At one point, I quit college for a series of intensive workshops and study tours with Joseph Campbell, author of *The Hero with a Thousand Faces*. By my thirties, I was building a reputation as a historian and analyst of popular culture, and among my books was *The Comic Book Heroes*. That book excited comic book editors enough that they invited me to try writing superhero stories myself.

I did, and I turned out to be good at it. Soon I was writing for heroes like Batman, Spider-Man, and the Hulk, creating new heroes and helping adapt them into video games, cartoon series, and action figures, writing action screenplays for Warner Brothers and Fox. Apparently that hero was still alive in me.

Even in becoming a superhero writer, however, I consciously resisted what I saw as the crassness and violence of cheap entertainment. I downplayed fight scenes and stressed intellectual content. My comic books earned citations from parent councils and anti-defamation societies. I mentored kids who wanted to write and draw comics, and I worked hard to meet my readers and learn what they were getting out of my stories. That's what led me to a comics convention in Chicago in 1994 and to a conversation that turned my relationship with action heroes in a whole new direction.

The line of autograph seekers, mostly teenage boys, had finally moved through. I was leaning back for some shoptalk with the other writers at the table when I saw her. She looked about thirteen, bespectacled, plainly dressed, grimly shy, a girl I'd have expected to be reading an English fantasy novel or diving precociously into *Jane Eyre*. She was standing about thirty feet away. Staring at me.

"Can I help you?" I asked. She lurched over to me as though some invisible parent had a hand on her back. "Are you Gerard Jones?" she asked. I looked at the name tag on my chest and feigned surprise: "Well yeah—I am!" An old convention trick meant to make the kids laugh, but she kept her eyes fixed on me without a glimmer of emotion and said, "I just want to tell you that *Freex* is, in my opinion, the best comic book ever."

Freex was a writer's nightmare. Readers liked my subtle characters and challenging ideas but complained that my stories were too mild. They wanted extremes of emotion and wild fight scenes like those in *X-Men. Freex* was my effort to give them that without lowering my standards. I loved my idea: teenage runaways, cut off from the world by their deforming superpowers, who form a sort of street gang for mutual protection. I cared about teenage runaways, knew people who worked with them, wanted to capture their struggles in superheroic form. I was excited about trying to mix naturalistic teen dialogue with ferocious battles on the city streets. But my scripts just wouldn't *work*. I couldn't get the character scenes to flow smoothly into the fights. The heroes' rage felt forced. The violence felt gratuitous. I'd never devoted much thought to what makes fantasy combat work or why it spoke to me in my own youth. I was too uncomfortable with rage and violence. I couldn't feel what my Freex should feel. I began to make peace with the thought that this just wasn't a story I should have been writing. The readers seemed to agree with me: sales were dropping, and not one fan had mentioned it at the convention—until this girl said it was the best comic ever.

I asked her why, and as she talked about *Freex,* her shyness dissolved. Her name was Sharon. She lived in a small Wisconsin town with her parents, whom she loved, and she had friends, but there was no one who really shared her interests. She read a lot, both comics and real books. She insisted that her life was perfect, but I thought that she protested too much. I sensed constraint, timidity, a depressed quality, a tensely contained anger—feelings that resonated with my memories of my own thirteenth year. She loved the Freex for the variety of their personalities and their clashing emotions. I expected her favorite to be the shy Angelica, but she preferred Lewis, the charismatic jock-leader whose anger made his body lose form. I said, "It sounds like the character development scenes must be your favorites."

"No!" she said. It was the most animated I'd seen her. "It's the *fights!*"

"The *fights?*" I asked. "That's where you can see the feelings they have for each other," she said. "The way Michael goes crazy when he thinks Angela's in danger. Or Val's angry at Ray, but then she instantly turns her anger against the villain instead, so you know she really cares about him." She paused to find a word. "That's when you see their *passion*. And their passion is what really makes them powerful!"

I asked her what she felt in those scenes. "Well," she said awkwardly. "I'm *them* when I'm reading about them, right? So . . . *I'm* powerful." And that, apparently, was as deep as she wanted to go into her own feelings. She thanked me again for *Freex,* and she left.

Sharon made me take a hard look at my own biases. I'd seen fight scenes as a necessary evil to induce kids to read the more valuable contents of my stories—but now I'd made the most meaningful contact with a reader of my career *through* the fights. The characters, plots, and themes mattered, but the truly affecting, truly transformative element of the story was the violence itself. The violence had helped a timid adolescent tap into her own bottled-up emotionality and discover a feeling of personal power.

I felt uneasy with that: what message was I sending kids like Sharon? I ran the question by my friend Anne, an English professor and a widely published authority on changing images of gender and the body in mass culture.

"Look," she said. "You touched that girl's life. You gave her something that means something to her. And that's as valuable as anything you can do."

Then Anne told me about her own adolescence in the 1980s: painful home life, estranged from her parents, drinking and jail at thirteen, a suicide attempt, out on her own at fifteen, fistfights, petty crime, crashing with friends in tough inner-city neighborhoods. What spoke to her at the very worst of it was pop culture: angry punk, death metal, Goth style, violent horror movies. "Not much I'd defend now as 'good,'" she said. "But when things felt absolutely black I discovered this stuff, and it showed me I wasn't alone with these feelings. I had words, or at least images, for what I was feeling. And I found other people who were into them. When I was in a club or a movie or listening to a tape with my friends, I didn't want to kill myself any more." Some of the others in her group drifted to dead ends, but she was one of several who formed punk bands, played with Goth-inspired art and stories, and found their way to college.

"The main thing that drew me to college was the community I hoped I could find of people with similar interests," she said. "It was partly the music and the rest of the 'junk culture' that showed me there could be communities like that. I don't know where your comic book might take that girl at the convention. But that 'passion' she mentioned is part of her life now. It's in her memory. It'll always be there, and somehow it'll keep coming back, and it'll give her something."

Sharon gave me something, too: a new career. I returned to my studies of American culture, but now with a focus on what aggressive fantasies mean to young people and what roles they play in personal development. I found that shockingly little had been written about it. For all the decades of psychological research attempting to prove that entertainment violence makes children more aggressive, or desensitizes them, or distorts their views of reality, very few studies have asked why they love it or what good it might do them. Hardly any, in fact, have even asked when or why it has a negative effect or how potential negative effects might be ameliorated. Bruno Bettelheim had summed up a great deal of psychiatric research on the benefits of violent fairy tales in his *Uses of Enchantment,* but even he had dismissed mass entertainment out of hand—even though the fantasies, the themes, and the violence of that entertainment often echoed fairy tales and even though it obviously resonated powerfully with millions of modern children.

So I interviewed psychiatrists, pediatricians, family therapists, teachers, screenwriters, game designers, and parents. I read the research. I asked children and teenagers what stories, movies, songs, and games they loved and what they meant to them. I dug back through my own growing up. I watched my son as he tackled the challenges of toddlerhood, preschool, and elementary school, choosing fantasies and entertainment to help him along the way. I gathered hundreds of stories of young people who had benefited from superhero comics, action movies, cartoons, shoot-'em-up video games, and angry rap and rock songs. I found stories of kids who'd used them badly, too, and others who'd needed adult help to use them well. But mostly I found young people using fantasies of combat in order to feel stronger, to access their emotions, to take control of their anxieties, to calm themselves down in the face of real violence, to fight their way through emotional challenges and lift themselves to new developmental levels.

During those same years, however, criticisms of entertainment violence became steadily more intense. The news was replete with stories of teenage violence (even though juvenile crime rates were dropping rapidly), and many of those stories drew connections between the crimes and movies, songs, or video games. The boys who killed their classmates and themselves at Columbine High School were discovered to have loved the video game *Doom,* and its influence soon dominated speculation on what might have influenced them. Congressional committees excoriated the entertainment industry. Prominent psychologists testified that video violence had been proven harmful to children. In March 2000, the American Academy of Pediatrics urged doctors to monitor their young patients' exposure to media violence and warn parents of its dangers.

That same month, I found myself addressing a roomful of psychiatrists about *Pokémon.* I wasn't expecting to come out of it very well liked.

As adults were debating the dangers of the media, the schoolyards of America were being swept by the most intense and most universal kid craze I'd ever seen. And it was a true product of kid culture. I began hearing about this strange universe of battling pet monsters from preschoolers and middle schoolers, boys and girls, computer nerds and blossoming jocks, months before the Nintendo marketing machine caught on to what it had. I was fascinated. This new world was noisy and combative, but it was also warm and fuzzy and funny and infernally complex, and kids were weaving it into every sort of fantasy and game. When Viz Communications asked me to help adapt the Japanese *Pokémon* comic book and comic strip franchise to the American market, I jumped at the chance.

My unusual position as a creator of superheroes, an analyst of children's entertainment, and an American interpreter of that global fantasy fad landed me on NPR's *Fresh Air,* explaining the Poké-phenomenon to puzzled parents nationwide. On the basis of that interview, the Southern California Psychiatric Society invited me to deliver the keynote address at its 2000 conference on "Violence and Society." Although I'd been supported in my research by enthusiastic psychologists and psychiatrists, I was still under the impression that the mental health establishment as a whole condemned entertainment violence. Now I was about to tell a roomful of veteran mental health professionals stories illustrating the positive effects of cartoon mayhem. I braced myself for a rough question-and-answer period at the end.

One of the powers of stories, however, is to remind us that people rarely obey generalizations. We may view an abstraction—"psychiatric opinion" or "media violence"—as threatening, but stories of people wrestling with the fears, pains, and challenges of life bring us back to our own realities. Anxiety gives way to empathy, and suddenly we're not speaking in recycled newspaper headlines; we're discussing the endless individuality and unpredictability of human beings. The people at that conference, having spent their careers listening to stories, understood that well, and when my speech ended I found myself launched upon one of the most exhilarating conversations I'd ever known.

One child therapist related his own rewarding uses of Pokémon action figures with young patients. Another said that his concern was for children who didn't have the chance to talk through what they'd experienced in the media and that "what you've demonstrated here is how beneficial *any* media experience can be in the context of constructive adult attention." An especially enthusiastic psychoanalyst said, "We're so afraid of aggression in this society that we haven't been able to talk intelligently about it. You're doing for aggression what Papa Freud did for sexuality!" "You've made one little boy very happy," said a psychiatrist who'd come with her husband, another doctor. "We haven't let our son watch shows like *Pokémon,* but I think we will now."

Then Elizabeth Thoman raised her hand. President of the Center for Media Literacy in Los Angeles and a longtime critic of media violence, she, I assumed, was going to express some objections. She did have questions about whether lurid games like *Duke Nukem* could be beneficial in the same way as *Pokémon,* and I explained how they could be, depending on the young person and his reason for choosing the game. Then she said, "This way of discussing media violence in terms of individual experience could be really valuable, not just to groups like this, but to the kids themselves. You should take this into the schools."

I told her I was glad she thought so, because I already had. Beginning with my son's kindergarten class, then expanding into the higher grades at his school, I had been leading workshops in comic-strip creation in which I encouraged kids to put down their own stories and fantasies through words and pictures. As simple as they were, those workshops were sources of an astonishing wealth of juvenile imaginings and experiences. So, drawing upon the wisdom of educators, psychologists, and media literacy experts, I used those as the foundation for what I've come to call the Art and Story Workshops: programs adaptable to every level from preschool to high school that help kids pull together the images, thoughts, and emotions in their minds through individual storytelling in a comic strip–like form. I'd take over a classroom for a day or a week, get the kids talking about their ideas and passions, and challenge them to put them down on paper—in both words and pictures.

Children are usually taught to compartmentalize their communication into either linear narrative or static portraits, but storytelling that is both visual and verbal leads them to transcend the compartments, to experience their thoughts and feelings more completely. Comics also have an inherent funkiness that frees kids to express fantasies that the more adult-approved media inhibit. Visual storytelling unlocks the images they've stored up from cartoons, movies, and video games and helps them make more sense of the media-transmitted stories that fill their environments. The process gives young people a sense of authorship, of *authority* over their own emotions and the world's influences. It also reveals the way that children use fantasies, stories, and media images in building their sense of self.

What I've learned in the Art and Story Workshops has consistently reinforced my belief that the vast array of fantasies and stories that we tend to dismiss with such labels as "media violence" are used well by children. I've seen young people turn every form of imaginary aggression into sources of emotional nourishment and developmental support. But I'm startled sometimes, too. I bring in my own biases about what's beneficial and what's not. And sometimes a boy like Philip will smash them.

The theme that day was "power." When I'm working with eighth and ninth graders, I find it useful to have the class agree on an overall theme as a starting point (usually after a very boisterous discussion). After that, every kid is responsible for telling the story that excites him or her most, however silly or sentimental or horrific or tasteless others might find it. I move around the room to help unstick ideas and bolster confidence, but I make it clear that because they're doing it for *themselves,* not for the school, the teacher, or a grade, there are no grown-up restraints or expectations to observe. Philip needed no help; he dove instantly into a humorous comic strip about a wily prostitute who tricks a corrupt police officer.

"Why that?" I asked. "Because I hate hypocrisy," he said, "especially when it acts like it's supposed to be morality." "Like what else?" I asked. That's when one of the girls sitting next to him asked Philip, "Can I tell him?" He nodded, and she told me that Philip had come out as gay a month before. The boys in the class had mostly avoided him since, and his friends now all came from one clique of sensitive, politically minded girls.

As she talked, I noticed Philip and a second girl writing lines of poetry on each other's pages. I asked if they were song lyrics. "Rap lyrics," said Philip proudly, and he and the girls told me about the hip-hop tastes they shared: Dr. Dre, DMX, Snoop Dogg. But, said Philip with obvious passion, his favorite was Eminem. That was what startled me. Eminem was then at the peak of his notoriety for rageful, homophobic epithets: *"My words are like a dagger with a jagged edge that'll stab you in the head whether you're a fag or lez."* Philip noticed my reaction and forced a grin. "Don't say what my mom always says."

I asked him what that was. He nursed his thoughts for a moment, and then he poured it out: "She's being really cool about all this. Not like my dad. My dad's really making it hard, telling me it's just a phase, not letting me go to any support groups, blah blah blah. My mom's being really supportive, being there for me no matter what. But she just won't get Eminem. She calls his lyrics 'hate-mongering.' She keeps saying, 'How can you listen to that if you're gay? Why don't you listen to something that makes you feel good about yourself?' And I try to tell her why it *does.*"

"Why does it?" I asked.

"Because Eminem has the courage to say who he *is*."

It's easy to fall into the trap of thinking that young people emulate literally what they see in entertainment. That if they like a rapper who insults gays, then they must be learning hostility to gays, and if they love a movie hero who defeats villainy with a gun, then they must be learning to solve problems with violence. There is some truth in that. One of the functions of stories and games is to help children rehearse for what they'll be in later life. Anthropologists and psychologists who study play, however, have shown that there are many other functions as well—one of which is to enable children to pretend to be just what they know they'll *never* be. Exploring, in a safe and controlled context, what is impossible or too dangerous or forbidden to them is a crucial tool in accepting the limits of reality. Playing with rage is a valuable way to reduce its power. Being evil and destructive in imagination is a vital compensation for the wildness we all have to surrender on our way to being good people.

In focusing so intently on the literal, we overlook the *emotional* meaning of stories and images. The most peaceful, empathetic, conscientious children are often excited by the most aggressive entertainment. Young people who reject violence, guns, and bigotry in every form can sift through the literal contents of a movie, game, or song and still embrace the emotional power at its heart. Children need to feel strong. They need to feel powerful in the face of a scary, uncontrollable world. Superheroes, video-game warriors, rappers, and movie gunmen are symbols of strength. By pretending to be them, young people are being strong.

Adults, however, often react to violent images very differently—and in the gap between juvenile and adult reactions, some of our greatest misunderstandings and most damaging disputes are born. Soon after the terrorist attacks of September 11, 2001, many toy retailers reported sharp increases in sales of G.I. Joe and other militaristic toys. But some of those same retailers also began pulling such toys from the shelves, largely in response to parents' requests. Newspaper stories reported that many parents were forbidding violent toys and entertainment in their homes as a reaction to the tragedy. One mother said she'd hidden her son's toy soldiers because "It's bad enough that they see the Army in the airport."

Many of us worried about how we would help children deal with the terror of September 11, but when I went into the classrooms, I found that the children were far less shaken than their parents and teachers. Most of them talked about the horrific images they'd seen with a mixture of anger and excitement—and a lot of them wanted to draw pictures, tell stories, or play games involving planes destroying buildings or soldiers fighting terrorists. This isn't a failure to react appropriately to tragedy: this is how children deal with it. When something troubles them, they have to play with it until it feels safer. Rick Fitzgerald, a veteran director of the Little Red School House, the Branson School, and Live Oak School, told me that my workshops had become more important than ever: "They need to tell the violent stories that are in them now."

Adults are generally more empathetic, more attuned to the greater world, and more literalistic than children. We are more likely to feel the pain and anxiety caused by real violence when we see it in make-believe. It troubles us to see our kids having fun with something that we deplore. We fear that they are celebrating or affirming a horror that we desperately want to banish from reality. We want them to mirror our adult restraint, seriousness, compassion, and pacifism. But they can't—and shouldn't—mimic adult reactions. Play, fantasy, and emotional imagination are essential tools of the work of childhood and adolescence.

Anxiety about how our kids will turn out is an inescapable aspect of adulthood. That anxiety is always heightened in times of sudden change or general insecurity about the future. It can be a useful emotion when it helps us notice the ways in which children are using their aggressive fantasies, and when it energizes us to teach them nonviolent solutions to life's problems. It can be destructive, however, if it only heightens our children's own anxieties, or drives them away from us and deeper into a media-based reality, or keeps them from finding the fantasies they need.

In working with children, I've come up against my adult anxieties again and again. But I've also been brought back in memory to their kid's place in life, a place in which they may need precisely the images that their daily life doesn't provide, precisely the stories from which their parents have tried to protect them. For a long time, I resisted looking closely at my own adolescence. I dismissed it as simply too sheltered and assumed that superhero comics had been just a source of excitement for me. It was only when I began seriously exploring the function of aggressive fantasy in children's development that I let myself look fully at what I'd gone through in those years and began to understand why the figure of the hero kept fighting his way to such a central place in my psyche.

When I was thirteen I started cutting school. I didn't have the words to say why. We didn't talk about scary feelings in my house. My parents desperately wanted a polite and civilized home, unlike the ones they'd grown up in. My mother always seemed to be suppressing anger, my father always dodging a confrontation. They let me know in a thousand ways that they wanted a sweet little boy who didn't get angry or greedy or rebellious, and I badly wanted to be that.

They were going through a hard time; I can see that now, but then I didn't know what was happening. My mother would sit in front of the evening news drinking glass after glass of wine ("my anesthetic," she called it, although she wouldn't name the pain), telling me bitterly of a world that had mutilated her liberal ideals with assassinations, riots, war, rising crime, and racial violence, telling me as she drank how disillusioned she was as a high school teacher, how appalled she was at the new youth culture. My father would retreat into the back room with the newspaper. They barely spoke to each other and never told me why, and I could never make out their muted arguments behind closed doors.

I didn't know what to do. I hated junior high, felt threatened by what my peers were turning into. I didn't want adolescence, didn't want to have to go into that world my mother talked about. I hung out less and less with my friends, and I wouldn't tell them why. Pretty soon they stopped asking. I started faking headaches so I could stay home from school, even though home was cold and empty. My mother blamed the public school system and put me in a tiny experimental school full of misfits. I didn't protest; somehow it felt like the survival of my fragile world depended on being the nice boy who would fulfill all his parents' expectations. But by eighth grade I was cutting school to stay home all day and watch TV with the shades drawn. There was nothing on that wasteland of game shows and soap operas that spoke to me, but I kept watching, hoping for something to excite me. Sometimes late at night I would slip out of the house and take long walks alone, looking for I didn't know what.

My parents knew something was wrong, but they were lost, too. My mother tried to encourage my interests, hoping she could reignite some spark of my younger days, when I'd been so excited about everything I did. She gave me great books, and I read a lot of them. History was a pleasant place to escape to. But nothing I read moved me enough to change the way I was behaving—until a kid named Jack Baty turned in an independent study report for one of my mother's classes.

Jack was the kind of kid I think my mom wished I could be: nerdy but bright, a couple of steps off the mainstream but upbeat about his interests, always doing something creative with his gang of oddball friends. My mother probably thought that anything that excited Jack might have a positive influence on me. She must have had some doubts, though, when she saw that his report was on Marvel comic books.

I'd never really read comic books. My mom remembered the news stories in the 1950s about how experts had linked them to juvenile delinquency. By the late 1960s the news was full of expert opinion that violent TV, toys, and other pop culture was contributing to the violence in our society, and she let me know that such stuff was off-limits. But here was Jack Baty, telling her with passionate conviction that comic books, long reviled for their juvenility and violence, had matured into thought-provoking modern mythologies full of lofty messages of peace and understanding. She asked Jack to lend her a few; maybe this was something her son could get excited about. He brought them in the next day. The covers showed nothing but big guys punching each other, but she took Jack's word on the lofty messages, and she brought them home to me.

I was riveted. They spoke to me. They thrilled me more deeply than anything I'd seen in years; but not because of their lofty messages. The messages were there, dressing up the occasional plot, but I barely noticed them. The heart of the plots, what the stories were about, was *power.*

The character who entranced me, and freed me, was the Incredible Hulk: overgendered and undersocialized, half-naked and half-witted, raging against a frightened world that misunderstood and persecuted him. In normal life he was a government scientist who had to struggle desperately to maintain his altruistic self-restraint—because his own anger set off a reaction in his body that transformed him, uncontrollably, into a brute of raw, destructive power. "Mustn't . . . let myself . . . feel it!" he'd roar, and suddenly his body would explode with muscles that ripped through his clothes, and he'd hurl himself bare-chested and free through the walls around him and thoom into the sky with a mighty leap. The Hulk smashed through the walls of fear I'd been carrying inside me and freed me to feel everything I had been repressing: rage and pride and the hunger for power over my own life.

Suddenly I had a fantasy self who could show me what it felt like to be unafraid of my own desires and the world's disapproval, to be bold enough to destroy what had to be destroyed. I had my Beowulf back. And when he and I came down from the heights with an earth-shattering boom, I saw that we were on open desert beyond the narrow streets I'd been walking. "Puny boy follow Hulk!" roared my fantasy self, and I followed.

The Hulk led me on a passionate hunt for more comic books. When that wasn't enough to satisfy me, he led me to meet Jack Baty and his friends, then to call up my old friend Brian to convert him to my new devotion, then to seek out new friends, other young geeks whose inner superheroes gave meaning to their private fears, rages, and wishes. Pretty soon I was founding my own comic book club. I wrote letters to comics editors and got letters back. I went to comics conventions and met the former teenage geeks whose fantasies impelled them to write and draw the stories that gave form to my own. And when their fantasies weren't enough, I began to write my own.

After a few years I was done with comics, or so I thought. I moved on to more grown-up heroes and more sophisticated stories, established a career in writing, and resisted looking back at the painful cradle of it all. But once I began talking to kids, I could no longer ignore the Hulk standing there in the middle of my growing up. He hadn't smashed all my problems, but he'd led me to a new sense of myself. He'd helped me play through some of my deepest fears. He'd led me to the arrogant, self-exposing, self-assertive, superheroic decision to become a writer, to start writing the script of my own life.

He also gave me a new way of talking to my parents. Gerry the superhero fan wasn't the same kid as Gerry the nice boy of my mother's imagination. I began to develop fantasies and tastes that she didn't understand and didn't wholly approve of. But she trusted that anything that excited me so much must be doing me some good, and she wanted me to share it with her. My father compared my superheroes with mock disdain to the Shadow and other violent heroes of the pulp magazines he'd grown up with. They would both listen to me prattle about my favorite characters, writers, and artists. We still didn't talk openly about my angers and frustrations, but at least we talked about my fantasies of being powerful and destructive. I felt that the darker side of myself was being seen and accepted for the first time.

My mother told me years later that her anxieties had eased when she saw my love of superheroes as coming from within me, not as something that had been imposed upon me by the entertainment industry. The comic books were made by others and sold to me as a commodity, but the desire to read them was *mine*. A lot of us stumble over that as parents, blaming what our children see for making them want things, forgetting that it's our children themselves who are doing the wanting. Each child's fantasies and emotional needs are very much his own, even if he shares them with millions of other kids. When we burden those needs with our own anxieties, we can confuse and frighten children about their own feelings. Adult anxieties about the effects of entertainment are sometimes the real causes of the very effects that we fear most.

As my articles on this subject began to appear in newspapers and magazines, I heard from parents and children on the front lines of the battle between entertainment violence and its critics. A woman named Leila living in a small town in Pennsylvania contacted me about the struggles of her eighth-grade grandson. Leila's daughter was a drug addict, and her daughter's son, Jimmy, had been taken from his mother by court order at the age of five and assigned to his grandparents' care. Leila and her husband found that they had quite a job on their hands. Jimmy had intense abandonment fears and separation anxiety. He had asthma, poor eyesight, and, as they discovered after three years of struggle in grade school, dyslexia. He responded to it all with disruptive behavior, becoming a class clown. The school district assigned a paraprofessional child worker to look after him during the school day, but her duties devolved into reporting on his conduct violations.

"He's a great kid," said Leila, "but he has a lot of fears. He works those fears out through humor—a lot of it not in very good taste, and sometimes provocative, but just humor. But because he's been labeled a 'problem,' everything he does becomes a crisis." Once another kid spilled some pizza on the floor, and Jimmy said, "It looks like roadkill!" That was entered into his record as "violence" and earned him one of many confrontations with school authorities.

In junior high, Jimmy fell in love with first-person shooter games, those video games like *Doom* and *Quake* in which the player has to explore a fantasy environment and gun down the bizarre opponents who attack him. Leila supported him in his enthusiasm. "Having been responsible for raising five younger siblings my whole childhood," she said, "I grew up with a lot of stress and anger. I still remember what a huge release it was to play war and shoot up not only my siblings but the other kids in the neighborhood who had it so much easier than me. Jimmy doesn't have that, because nobody plays war in our neighborhood, and they probably wouldn't play it with him anyway. But I could see him achieving the same release in his video games. He was always calmer and more confident after spending a while with his games."

When Jimmy began talking about his hobby at school, however, the official reaction wasn't so supportive. Two teachers and the principal, on separate occasions, sat him down and told him that the games he loved would desensitize him to violence, make him believe he could kill without consequence, give him a false sense of power, make him associate bloodshed with fun. With each encounter, Leila said, he came home frightened, agitated, and more inclined to act up than before. "The poor kid has enough real fears of his own without having adults dumping their fears on him," she said. "Instead of helping him deal with the fears he has, they send the message that they're afraid of *him*—and so they make him even more afraid of *himself*."

Leila encouraged Jimmy to talk openly about what he liked, seeing that it helped him feel stronger and more in control of his life. Then a teacher called Leila into her office and told her that, under the school's "zero tolerance" policy, Jimmy was in danger of suspension for "promoting violence." She asked Leila to forbid Jimmy to play the games before that—or "something far worse"—happened.

Leila asked me whether I could provide any research on the value of shooter games that she could show the school authorities. I sent her what I'd compiled from my experiences and those of the psychologists, doctors, and educators I'd worked with and recommended that she ask school authorities to look past generalizations and do what she was doing: ask Jimmy why he loves the games he loves, show some empathy for his fantasies and feelings, trust that he's doing his best to meet his complex emotional needs, and offer help, not fear.

It made a difference, she said. The teachers didn't change their minds completely, but they listened. Tensions began to ease. Jimmy felt better about himself, if only because it seemed as though his teachers were finally thinking about who he *was* instead of what he might *do*.

When we consider children in relation to mass media and pop culture, we tend to define them as consumers, watchers, recipients, victims. But they are also *users* of that media and culture: they are choosers, interpreters, shapers, fellow players, participants, and storytellers. Viewing children as passive recipients of the media's power puts us at odds with the fantasies they've chosen, and thus with the children themselves. Viewing them as active users enables us to work with their entertainment—*any* entertainment—to help them grow. Shooter games, gangsta rap, *Pokémon* all become tools for parents and teachers to help young people feel stronger, calm their fears, and learn more about themselves.

In our anxiety to understand and control real-life violence, we've tried to reduce our children's relationships with their fantasies of combat and destruction to vast generalizations that we would never dream of applying to their fantasies about love and family and discovery and adventure. We don't usually ask whether game shows predispose our children to greed, or whether love songs increase the likelihood of getting stuck in bad relationships. But when aggression is the topic, we try to purée a million games and dreams and life stories into statistical studies. We ask absurdly sweeping questions like, What is the effect of media violence on children? as if violence were a single, simple phenomenon of which sandbox play-fights and mass murder were mere variations, as if the evening news and *Reservoir Dogs* and Daffy Duck were indistinguishable, as if children were like trees in an orchard who could all be raised to identical form by the same externalities. Many forces have been shown to contribute to aggression: religious fervor, patriotic fervor, sports rivalry, romantic rivalry, hot summer nights. Entertainment has inspired some people to violence, but so have the Bible, the Constitution, the Beatles, books about Hitler, and obsessions with TV actresses. We don't usually condemn those influences as harmful, because we understand them better, we understand why people like them and the benefits most of us draw from them. What's lacking is an understanding of aggressive fantasies and the entertainment that speaks to them.

"Narrative deals with the vicissitudes of human intentions," writes the great psychologist Jerome Bruner in *Actual Minds, Possible Worlds.* "And since there are myriad intentions and endless ways for them to run into trouble—or so it would seem—there should be endless kinds of stories." My work with kids and entertainment has been a discovery of stories. Every story of a superhero or a monster or an angry rapper—even the video game that looks so simplistic at first glance—resonates with the personal stories of its audience. And every one becomes a different story depending on the listener, the viewer, the player. A child chooses a particular movie or game because his unique story has led him there, and he weaves a new, personal narrative out of the fantasy and play it inspires.

No one has taught me more about this than my son. When Nicky was five and anxious about the end of preschool and the beginning of kindergarten, I brought him *Beowulf.* He didn't like it. So I brought him the Greek myths, and the Grimms' fairy tales, and the Dr. Dolittle novels, and Superman and King Kong and all the other stories, violent and nonviolent, that had thrilled me as a child. He didn't want any of them. He wanted *Mighty Morphin' Power Rangers.*

I don't think I enjoyed watching *Power Rangers* episodes with Nicky quite as much as my mother enjoyed reading *Beowulf* to me. I liked the goofy rubber monsters, but the road to their scenes led through the most agonizing stretches of Saturday morning teen banter. Nicky, however, loved every minute of them, and I loved watching him love them. Every commercial break he'd be running, morphing, punching, kicking, knocking fearsome monsters (usually me) to the ground—with a confidence in his body and a decisiveness in his movements that I'd rarely seen in him. I could see his excitement driving the anxiety out of him.

Then he found a new fantasy: *Teletubbies.* That show was just then invading America and finding an audience not only among toddlers and ironic adults but among countless five- and six-year-olds discovering the regressive comforts of cute baby talk and cuddly hijinks in an underground burrow. Suddenly Nicky and his friends were waddling into group hugs and squealing, "Eh-oh, LaLa" and "Where Po 'cootah?"

This, I thought, must surely be the end of the Power Rangers. But not for Nicky. When he wasn't turning into Po and asking for a hug, he'd be morphing into the Red Ranger and blasting a monster. His mom noticed that he seemed to become a Ranger when he felt more sure of himself, a Tubby when he felt a little shaky and needed more nurturing. As the end of preschool drew near, those two contradictory fantasies grew to fill more and more of his play time.

One morning I woke him up, and as we walked to the bathroom he said, "I want to see more of the Battle Show." "What's the Battle Show?" I asked. He looked at me confusedly. "We were just watching it!" he said. Then he realized: "It was a dream!" I asked him what it was like, and he laughed and told me: "The Teletubbies were playing on the grass in Tubbyland with their toys. Then these monsters were getting into Tubbyland. They looked kind of like Tyrannosauruses but they were destroying the flowers and windmill things and they were going to destroy the Tubbies' house. So Po touched something on his wrist and suddenly he morphed into the Red Ranger! Then the other Tubbies turned into Power Rangers. Only they were their own colors, so there was a Purple Ranger because of Tinky-Winky instead of a Blue Ranger or Pink Ranger. They fought the monsters and knocked them all the way out of Tubbyland, and then they morphed back into the Teletubbies!"

I asked him to draw pictures of it, but he wanted to playact it instead, and Tubby Rangers quickly became his favorite game. He took it to preschool, where he and his friends added new details: the Tubbies' underground home could rocket into space; the Nu-Nu, their vacuum cleaner with eyeballs, could morph into a Battle-Zord; the televisions on their tummies would alert them to approaching danger.

Nicky had chosen stories that embraced the extremes of his fantasy life, the most aggressive and the gentlest. Then he'd remade them into what he needed them to be. Now he'd could be as powerful and fearless as he wanted but not sacrifice his need to be comforted and protected. Red Ranger Po united the most destructive and most nurturing powers in one happy self.

Children want to be strong, secure, and happy. Their fantasies will tell us what they feel they need to attain that, if we pay attention. But we need to look beyond our adult expectations and interpretations and see them through our children's eyes. First, we need to begin disentangling the fears and preconceptions that have prevented us from doing so.

2

Seeing What We're Prepared to See

*I*n January 2001, a group of doctors at Stanford University released one of the most encouraging studies I'd seen in a long time. They found that when elementary school kids voluntarily cut back on the number of hours they watched TV and played video games, they subsequently behaved less aggressively. Everything from playground shoving matches to kids snapping, "I'm gonna kick your butt!" decreased when the kids started turning off the TV after about an hour a day. As the study's lead author, Dr. Thomas N. Robinson, commented, "What this shows is that there is something you can do in a practical way, in a real-world setting, and see the effects." That was great news to all of us who sometimes despair at our power to make the world a little saner for our kids.

The study didn't get the news coverage it deserved (probably because it was released right before the Super Bowl), but nearly every news article I saw interpreted it in a similar way. The *San Francisco Chronicle* led off its front-page story with, "Aggressive tendencies fostered in children by violent television shows and video games can be tempered if they cut back their viewing and playing, a new Stanford University study shows." What none of those news stories mentioned, however, was the fact that the study didn't distinguish among types of media content. Not only did the kids who watched the World Wrestling Federation and played *Dead on Arrival* improve their behavior when they cut back on tube time, but so apparently did the kids who watched only *Rugrats* and *Arthur,* or *Blind Date* and *Saved by the Bell.* Those results make no sense if what fostered their aggression was violent imagery.

What, then, does this study show? As with most studies, there are many possibilities. It may show that if kids get off their rear ends and go do something active for a change, they'll be less bored, less restless, and less likely to pop off out of annoyance—a finding that anyone who has spent much time with kids can endorse. In fact, in 1999, Dr. Robinson authored another study, based on the same research, suggesting that reducing TV and game time reduced kids' obesity, a finding that presumably reflects the benefits of greater physical activity more than the content of the programming.

The 2001 study may also show that kids who spend less time in mental isolation develop more effective social skills, which, as Dr. Robinson pointed out, is supported by the anecdotal evidence surrounding the study. "We had parents who said, 'This is the best thing that's happened to our family—we talk to our kids at dinnertime now.' One mother called and said her daughter used to sit at home and watch TV, and now she's found a friend down the block and they play outside every afternoon." The study also suggests that if kids take control of their leisure time instead of running on habit—if they watch or play only what they really *choose* to, whether that be *Zaboomafoo* or *Doom*— they may be able to take more control of themselves in general. Most exciting to me, it suggests that if kids are given a *purpose*—even one as simple as, "Let's cut our media consumption for a while and see what happens"—they'll feel better about themselves and use their energies more constructively. If they see adults as caring about them, trusting them to meet higher expectations, and wanting to work with them instead of just leaving them to kill the hours between school and bed and noticing them only when they act up, then they will respond.

One thing the study pointedly does *not* show is that the children became less aggressive because they saw less violence. Why, then, did nearly every news story interpret it as showing exactly that?

The reason, I believe, is that this misinterpretation has become such an integral part of our discussion of entertainment violence that we've ceased to recognize it. It's become such a habit of thought that when we hear the words "media" and "aggression" together, we go instantly back into the same looping conversation without stopping to be sure of what's been said. We expect to see evidence that violent imagery leads to violent behavior, and so we do see it. Not only do we expect it, we often *want* to see it, because it provides a reassuringly familiar answer. So we look in only one direction even when logic, personal experience, and the scientific data itself should lead us to look elsewhere.

Preconception is a powerful force. We smack up against it as individuals, professional communities, and whole societies. Once we've come to an opinion as to what the truth is (or what we want it to be), even the best trained and most conscientious of us find our thoughts flowing to fit the mold. We seize too quickly on what looks like supporting evidence and ignore evidence to the contrary. And if our preconceptions concern something as important as the health of our society or the welfare of our children, we may even angrily resist opposing information because we fear it will weaken our resolve to do what (we think) is best.

In the late nineteenth century, the standard position of the medical establishment, to paint it with a broad brush, was that sexuality was a dangerous force best left unaroused and undiscussed. Scientific research and anecdotal material were interpreted in the light of that preconception, so that sexual dysfunctions were normally explained as an excess of sexual stimulation. If a criminal were found to be a masturbator, the masturbation would be assumed to be a cause of his criminality. As the new schools of thought led by Freud and others began to convince people that the problem wasn't so much sexuality itself but our *relationship* with it, a relationship forged largely in childhood, the same body of knowledge began to look very different. The same case studies and statistics that had once seemed to point to sexual stimulation as the source of trouble and the concealment of sexuality as the best solution now began to suggest, more compellingly, that sexual repression was the greater problem and that open acceptance of sexuality was a more effective way to deal with it.

Unfortunately, many of those Freudian ideas became the bases of new preconceptions in the decades that followed. In seeking the cause of abnormal behavior in childhood maladjustment, doctors and psychiatrists fell into some dangerous misinterpretations of the evidence before them. Early research into autism looked at its possible biological origins, but then orthodoxy shifted toward blaming bad parenting. Families were torn apart, children mistreated, and years of work wasted until new generations of researchers were able to show that autism was biologically determined after all. Homosexuality was overwhelmingly considered to be a neurosis produced by skewed parent-child relationships, one that could and should be "cured" by psychoanalysis. Depression, anxiety, alcoholism, and other conditions were often approached as solely mental conditions, even when they had physiological manifestations.

Most of those preconceptions dominated the public health establishment well into the 1960s. Then, as new ideas swept through the culture at large—especially a willingness to accept and work with innate differences instead of attempting to "normalize" them—they were broadly reexamined. Not only did new research now generate revealing new data, but the old data were reinterpreted in new ways. Suddenly new views of all these aspects of human behavior became possible, and from those views new policies and treatments could be developed that have since proven to be far more helpful and humane. As Emerson wrote, "People only see what they are prepared to see."

On July 26, 2000, officers of the American Medical Association, the American Academy of Pediatrics, the American Psychiatric Association, the American Psychological Association, the American Academy of Family Physicians, and the American Academy of Child and Adolescent Psychiatry issued a "Joint Statement on the Impact of Entertainment Violence on Children," which was subsequently endorsed by both houses of the United States Congress.

At this time, well over 1,000 studies—including reports from the Surgeon General's office, the National Institute of Mental Health, and numerous studies conducted by leading figures within our medical and public health organizations—our own members—point over-

whelmingly to a causal connection between media violence and aggressive behavior in some children. The conclusion of the public
health community, based on over thirty years of research, is that viewing entertainment violence can lead to increases in aggressive attitudes, values, and behavior, particularly in children. . . .

The effect of entertainment violence on children is complex and
variable. Some children will be affected more than others. But while
duration, intensity, and extent of the impact may vary, there are several
measurable negative effects of children's exposure to violent entertainment. . . . We in no way mean to imply that entertainment violence is the sole, or even necessarily the most important factor contributing to youth aggression, anti-social attitudes, and violence. . . .
Nor are we advocating restrictions on creative activity. The purpose
of this document is descriptive, not prescriptive: we seek to lay out a
clear picture of the pathological effects of entertainment violence. But
we do hope that by articulating and releasing the consensus of the
public health community, we may encourage greater public and
parental awareness of the harms of violent entertainment, and encourage a more honest dialogue about what can be done to enhance
the health and well-being of America's children.

Clearly this was no unreasoned statement. It stood upon extensive
research, and it spoke pointedly of "some children." But the view of
children and entertainment violence it presented was broad and
simple. The impact of entertainment violence varies in "duration, intensity, and extent," but not in its essential nature or quality; its effects
are "pathological" and "negative," never beneficial. When such a
broad, simple statement is made about the infinitely complex and
mutable behavior of human beings, we need to look very hard at
what has led up to it. We need to determine whether there is in fact
a consensus of opinion among the experts, whether the research has
in fact been viewed from every angle, and whether our conclusions
are leading us to the most effective actions in the real world.

The answer to the first question is simple: there is no unity of expert opinion on the effects of entertainment violence.

Dr. Stuart Fischoff, founder of the Media Psychology lab at California State University in Los Angeles, said in his 1999 address to the American Psychological Association: "Whether we cite 100, 1,000, or 10,000 research studies which conclude that exposure to violent media produces violent behavior, 10,000 is no more persuasive or credible than 100, if the designs of the research are flawed and/or the generalizations to an external population of behaviors are patently unjustified. The current violence in society is disturbing to all of us. The current excessive, gratuitous violence in film, in video games, in music lyrics is disturbing to all of us. But because two phenomena are both disturbing and coincident in time does not make them causally connected. . . . Abhorrent as what I have to say may be, I believe that there is not a single study that is externally valid. . . . After 50 years . . . , there is, I submit, not a single research study which is even remotely predictive of [events like] the Columbine massacre."

Dr. Helen Smith is a forensic psychologist who has evaluated thousands of violent minors for law enforcement and the courts, administered a nationwide voluntary survey of violent youth, and written *The Scarred Heart: Understanding and Identifying Kids Who Kill.* "Not one young person in my experience has ever been made violent by media influence," she asserted. "Young people who are already inclined to be violent *do* feel that violent media speaks to them. A few *do* get dangerous ideas from it. But more of them find it to be a way to *deal* with their rage."

"Entertainment has the power to overexcite or present a distorted worldview to some children," reported Dr. Edwin Cook, a professor of psychiatry and pediatrics at the University of Chicago who specializes in children's developmental issues. "But for other children, the right aggressive entertainment might be the best thing they could see."

Dr. Lynn Ponton, psychiatrist, authority on adolescent behavior, and author of *The Romance of Risk* and *The Sex Lives of Teenagers,* said, "There are dangers to a young person in isolation trying to contain his or her anxieties through the habitual use of movies or video games, of any type or genre. But I don't believe the *content* of the movies or games really matters."

Although one would be hard-pressed to find a single expert asserting that physical abuse, neglectful parents, or poverty is not hurtful to children, there is a chorus of authoritative dissent from the usual condemnation of violent entertainment. Even the Surgeon General's Report on Youth Violence, released seven months after the Joint Statement, disagreed on some key points. The latter claimed that "children exposed to violent programming at a young age have a higher tendency for violent and aggressive behavior later in life." In contrast, the Surgeon General found that media violence can have a *short-term* effect (a teenager is excited by a scene in a movie or game and wants to go out and do it) but found no convincing evidence of a long-term effect. He also asserted that media is a minor factor in youth violence compared to family and peer-group issues and that the relatively few youngsters likely to be affected by it are those who are "already aggressive for some other reason."

According to Dr. Jonathan Freedman of the University of Toronto, a widely respected critic of the research literature on media violence, "the further people are from the data, the more excited they are by it." He points out, for example, that according to every meta-analysis of the research, including those conducted by supporters of the media-aggression hypothesis, there have been not 1,000 but about 200 studies, and many of those have contradicted the conclusion of the Joint Statement. It's important to remember that the doctors and administrators who author documents like the Joint Statement are rarely better versed in the media-aggression research than those of us who read about the latest study in the morning newspaper. They are so busy with their own professional duties that they are dependent on secondhand opinion and broad summaries of the research literature. AMA spokesman Edward Hill has stated that neither he nor anyone else on the AMA board was able to read the research before authoring the statement.

It's also important to consider the typical lag time in the progress of institutional thought. While one body of research is being compiled and synthesized into a shared opinion, a very different one may be developing unnoticed in its wake. The studies cited by the Joint Statement were mostly designed in the 1950s and early 1960s and executed from the 1960s to the 1980s. Since that time, as we'll see, media studies have taken a significant turn.

Finally, it's important to remember the power of preconception. Social science research is rarely launched from the position of "let's look at this and just see what we find." Common practice is for researchers to begin by declaring the results they expect to find, in order to address questions of "researcher bias." Reviewing the literature, I find in study after study that the researchers expected to find evidence of negative effects. The same preconception even determines who asks the questions and what they ask. "The conviction runs so deep in the academic and political communities that their most important mission is to warn of the dangers of media violence," said Stuart Fischoff, "that it's virtually impossible to get a large-scale study funded in this country unless it's designed to look for harmful effects."

What does the conventional research mean, then? It's a mountain of material, but like most mountains it's only intimidating when we're standing in its shadow. Once we've climbed to the top of it, it rewards us with an exhilarating new view. We can see how our preconceptions have led us into a few recurring habits of misinterpretation, and we discover that although the research may not mean what we thought, what it does mean may be more useful.

A correlation is not a cause.

The conventional research falls into three broad categories: correlative studies that compare the viewing habits of children who behave violently with those who don't; laboratory studies of the ways children behave after being exposed to violent imagery; and field studies that try to apply lab-like tests to children in the real world.

It's commonly accepted that the correlative studies have established a 10 percent correlation between media violence and heightened aggression. In fact, they vary wildly in their findings, from some that find considerably higher correlations to some that find none at all to others that find correlations between media violence and *lower* aggression. But the most famous of the early studies found approximately a 10 percent correlation, and that number has become truism in the years since.

The trouble with using such studies as evidence of media's effect on children is that a correlation is not a cause. The researchers know this well, which is why all their studies refer to a "link" or "relationship" between violence-viewing and violence-doing, but never of cause and effect. The "link" may mean only that aggressive kids are more inclined to *like* violent entertainment. We all know that starry-eyed romantics like love stories, but few would argue that early and intense exposure to sappy melodrama *causes* a romantic temperament. Young people who are more aggressive, more restless, more angry at the world, or simply more inclined to enjoy roughhousing are also more likely to want to watch action shows, listen to angry songs, or play combative video games.

These correlations may demonstrate just the opposite of the media-as-cause hypothesis. Aggressive kids may be more drawn to violent entertainment precisely because they need a compelling alternative to acting out or because they want help making sense of their own aggressive feelings. Several studies support this possibility, although conventional interpretations of the data tend to ignore it. Dr. William Belson's landmark study of violent teenage criminals is frequently cited for its discovery that those who watched violent entertainment committed a higher number of serious crimes than those who watched very little. Much less frequently mentioned is the fact that the ones who watched the *most* violence committed far *fewer* serious crimes than those who watched more moderate amounts (which may reflect a cathartic effect of violent entertainment or simply the fact that the more time a teenager spends in front of the tube the less time he has to get into trouble).

The one correlative study that has been cited again and again as support for the causal hypothesis is the famous longitudinal study that Leonard Eron conducted among a few hundred children in rural New York from 1960 to 1970. Dr. Eron found that among third-graders in 1960, the boys who liked violent TV (mainly *The Three Stooges, 77 Sunset Strip,* and assorted Westerns) accounted for about 20 percent of those considered "aggressive" by their classmates. Among those same boys in 1970, who were now out of high school, he found that the ones who had liked violent TV ten years earlier had come to account for about 30 percent of those now described by their peers as "aggressive" (hence, the famous 10 percent correlation). He concluded that watching violent television fostered an aggressiveness in children that came out in their late teens. As one reviews the literature, this particular study keeps turning up at the center of virtually every discussion of the purported long-term effect of media violence on children; it is practically the foundation of the argument that, in Dr. Eron's words, "there is a probably causative effect of watching violent television programs in early formative years on later aggression."

However, in the thirty years since the report's release, social scientists have pointed out several serious problems with it. Subsequent studies along similar lines have failed to find any such correlation. The correlation holds for the boys in the study but, inexplicably, not the girls. The nine-year-olds' viewing preferences were based not on observation or the subjects' reports but on the opinions of their mothers. Most tellingly, Dr. Eron's correlation showed up *only* when the boys were labeled "aggressive" or "nonaggressive" by peer nomination (asking classmates who they felt were the most aggressive kids in the class); when the study determined the boys' aggressiveness by two other methods, objective personality tests and self-description, no correlation was found. Peer nomination is a demonstrably unreliable means of drawing conclusions about a child's behavior. It is especially suspect in this case, in which the first peer group consisted of nine-year-olds in the macho milieu of 1960 and the second consisted of college-age adults immersed in the anti-violence ethos of 1970.

The study may support Dr. Eron's conclusion. On the other hand, it may indicate that the second peer group—those young people in 1970 who were probably already steeped in media coverage of the dangers of TV violence—were predisposed to think that the kids who loved make-believe violence *must* be more aggressive, regardless of whatever behavior they actually displayed. Research, like a computer or a mythological oracle, answers only the questions we ask of it. It doesn't tell us what we haven't thought to ask. In this case, the only question asked by Dr. Eron and most of the researchers after him was, "Do the data show that watching violence leads to later aggression?" When we ask a different question—such as, "What do the data say about the ways young people label their peers?"—we get a very different answer.

This is the kind of ambiguity that runs through the conventional research but is almost never mentioned in the popular discussion of it. The social scientists who conduct the studies know that well; they admit that they've found no explanation for the causes of violence. In 1994, amid a flurry of academic summits and government hearings at which he spoke as a leading critic of media violence, Leonard Eron himself acknowledged that his research "cannot definitely settle the issue of causal direction. . . . It's in the laboratory where you can actually show cause and effect."

Laboratory reality is not living-room reality.

Jib Fowles, a professor and researcher at the University of Houston, described the typical behavioral lab experiment from a child's point of view:

> Selected as a subject, a child would have to be brought to a strange universe. . . . The setting is institutional, with hard surfaces and angles. There are none of the textures of a home nor the school's familiar display of handwork. Other youngsters are also arriving, few of whom the child is likely to know, but all of whom are to comprise a novel social group to which the child must be aware and attuned. Around and above the children are adult strangers with clipboards who are in charge.
>
> Now in a room with other unmet children, the child may be unexpectedly frustrated or angered by the experimenters—shown toys but not allowed to touch them, perhaps, or spoken to brusquely. The child is then instructed to look at a video monitor. It would be highly unlikely that the young child would sense that this in any way resembled television viewing done at home. At home, everything is known; here, everything is unknown, demanding attentiveness. At home, the child may be prone and comfortable, and viewing is nonchalant; here, the room is overlighted, the child is seated upright, and viewing is concentrated. Most signally, at home television viewing is an entirely

voluntary activity. . . . In the behavioral laboratory, the child is com-pelled to watch and, worse, compelled to watch material not of the child's choosing and probably not to the child's liking. The essential element of the domestic television-viewing experience, that of pleas-ure, has been methodically stripped away.

The youngster then views footage quite unlike what he's seen at home: violent scenes snipped out of a show without a story to make sense of it, humor to relieve it, or the dramatic closure that ends nearly every TV show. Then he is told to play with the other kids, all strangers, all under stress, while the researchers watch. As for what to play:

There are typically only a limited number of options, all behavioral, for the young subjects. Certainly, no researcher is asking them about the meanings they may have taken from the screened violence.

In summary, laboratory experiments . . . are concocted schemes that violate all the essential stipulations of viewing in the real world and in doing so have nothing to teach about the television experience (although they may say much about the experimenters). . . . Labora-tory research has taken the viewing experience and turned it inside out so that the viewer is no longer in charge. In this manner, experi-menters have made a mockery out of the everyday act of television viewing. Distorted to this extent, laboratory viewing can be said to simulate home viewing only if one is determined to believe so.

The crux of the media-as-cause idea, the bolt that holds the argu-ment together, is that because dozens of correlative studies show that aggressive kids watch violent entertainment, and because dozens of laboratory studies show that watching violent entertainment inspires kids to behave aggressively, we can assume that real-life aggression is being caused by real-life entertainment. However, one problem with experimentation on human behavior, as critics of lab research have been pointing out for decades, is that researchers are creating an ab-normal situation and thus inducing abnormal reactions. A child choosing to watch *Dragon Ball Z* because he knows it will make him happy is having a fundamentally different experience from a child who doesn't even like *Dragon Ball Z* being told, "You have to watch this now"—and his reactions will be just as different.

That may explain the results of the famous Coates-Pusser-Goodman study, which found that preschoolers were three times more aggressive after watching a video than before—even though the video was *Mister Rogers' Neighborhood*. This led some analysts to conclude that television viewing itself, regardless of content, inspires violent behavior. It more likely means that being made by a strange adult to watch television makes a child anxious or angry. I love Fred Rogers, but I suspect if I were forced to sit in a hard plastic chair in a strange room and stare at him when I'd rather be out playing, I'd act aggressively too.

Social scientists are aware of such limitations, of course, and have tried to adjust for them in more recent tests. But, as most reviews of the literature have shown, attempts to gather evidence through more sophisticated tests have only led to more ambiguous results. As Drs. Haejung Paik and George Comstock (a pair of researchers generally sympathetic to the media-as-cause hypothesis) found in their meta-analysis of the literature in 1994, the more naturalistic a study is, the smaller the findings tend to be. For example, one research team in 1983 tried to compensate for the unpleasantness of lab conditions by treating their young subjects with extra generosity and pleasantry before showing one group a violent film, another group a nonviolent film, and a third group no film at all. Afterward, the children who watched the violent film behaved *more* altruistically and cooperatively than the children of the other groups.

When experimental methods have been taken out of the laboratory for field studies, the results have been similarly complex. Some have supported the media-as-cause argument, but there have been many like the Feshbach-Singer study, which followed boys watching TV in their own environs and found that whereas affluent boys were apparently unaffected by video violence, poor boys with records of delinquency seemed to be made *less* aggressive by it. Are such studies evidence for the cathartic power of entertainment, as some expert analyses have maintained? Or are they, when combined with all the other research, only more evidence that something as complex as children's relationship with fantasy cannot be reduced to numbers in an experiment?

All of this research is based on the idea of studying children's "exposure to violence," in the same way that we might study their "exposure" to lead or cigarette smoke. But as appealing as that medical model may be, with its promise of clear, scientific answers, it just can't tell us much about children's feelings and behavior. Entertainment isn't a chemical substance. A child's imagination doesn't behave like the cells of the body, with a predictable, somatic response. Playing a game or choosing a TV show is a conscious choice, an individual action, and part of a complex exchange between what a child needs and what the entertainment provides. If we studied the emotions of children as they were forced to kiss their loud, cigar-stinking Uncle Walters, we'd find plenty of hard, statistical data to show that kissing leads to fear, anxiety, and resentment. If we studied children as they willingly kissed their mommies good night, we'd come up with drastically different results. If we believed that kissing was harmful to children, we could surely come up with evidence to support that belief. Some psychologists, most famously John Watson, were in fact biased toward that belief in the 1920s and 1930s, and they did indeed find the evidence they were looking for. Fortunately for most of us, more compassionate views prevailed.

The correlative and laboratory data are valuable. They show us that there *is* a relationship between our children's entertainment and their behavior, a powerful relationship with many implications. It is essential, however, that we understand how to use that data to help children in the real world. This is where our determination to find a simplistic cause-and-effect relationship keeps doing us in. For, not only do we misinterpret the research by trying to find that too-simple cause, but we also neglect even to define what it is that we think is being caused.

Not all "aggression" is the same.

During the U.S. Senate's hearings on entertainment violence, Senator John McCain brought the media-as-cause argument down to its most vivid essentials. He showed footage of preschoolers playing after watching *Barney* and again after watching *Power Rangers*. After the singing and dancing of the big purple dinosaur and his grinning juvenile sidekicks, the kids played fairly quietly and cooperatively—every tired parent's dream. After the five hyped-up superheroes had finished their blasting and karate-chopping of city-smashing rubber monsters, the kids jumped up and ran around and yelled and wrestled and kicked at the air. That made it easy for Senator McCain to say, in effect, "Look how aggressive TV violence makes them!" That in turn made it easy for us to imagine those same kids beating each other up on the playground, then falling into gangs of delinquents, then opening fire on their schoolmates or mugging us on a dark street.

Except, of course, that they weren't mugging or shooting or really even fighting at all. They were playing.

The benefits of rough-and-tumble play are well documented. It can be annoying for parents, it can get out of hand and lead to head bumps, but most authorities agree that it's normal, healthy, and generally conducive to more confident kids. Profiles of violent adolescents don't generally show any exorbitant amount of aggressive play early in life and, in fact, often show the opposite: violent teenagers often had trouble bonding with peers in normal childhood play. It may be that John McCain—war hero, maverick politician, and presidential contender—spent his whole childhood playing as quietly and cooperatively as the kids who'd just finished watching *Barney* in his video clips, but I doubt it. If he was anything like the other risk takers I've known of his generation, he spent his formative years watching Hollywood gun battles and playing at least as aggressively as any modern preschooler in the wake of a *Power Rangers* episode.

Normally, when we see kids playing superhero, most of us don't see it as much of a danger. But when we fall back into anxious discussions of youth violence, we lose sight of that context. We suddenly see only a polar opposition of "aggression" and "nonaggression," and against our own better judgment we start to see all aggression as part of one destructive continuum.

The cornerstone of all media-aggression experimentation was the Albert Bandura study of 1963, which showed that children who had watched films of someone punching an inflatable clown doll subsequently punched an identical clown doll more often than a group of children who had not. Hundreds of similar experiments, with similar results, have followed over the decades since then. Clearly there's a basic truth to these experiments; we all know from experience that if kids see something exciting on TV they're likely to imitate it in play immediately afterward. But we need to step back from the interpretation put on those studies by generations of commentators, get outside the terminology that speaks of "heightened aggression," and look at what the kids are actually doing:

They're punching an *inflatable clown*.

My mother bought me one of those clowns. It was probably the same year as the Bandura study—an irony she appreciated decades later, when I reminded her of how psychological opinion had turned her against violent TV and toys later in the 1960s. I loved that clown, until I got bored with it. I loved the feeling of exploding with all my tiny strength into its springy face, knowing that no harm could come either to the clown or my hand, and watching it bounce back with a grateful smile. That clown loved being hit, I was sure of it, and the bond he and I forged over my delight in cutting loose and his in being hammered was one of the most satisfying of my life for a week or two. I felt *powerful*. Later my mother told me that I was shy about punching it hard at first, until my dad stepped in to show me how. It was the best thing he could have done.

There is no evidence to suggest that punching an inflatable clown has any connection to real-life violence. There is no evidence that kids who love to punch inflatable clowns are more prone to playground aggression or later delinquency. There *is* anecdotal evidence that clown-punching is beneficial when it has any effect at all. And yet incidents of clown-punching have been jotted down by generations of researchers as evidence of "heightened aggression."

More sophisticated experiments have attempted to isolate more antisocial, more "real," aggression by asking children what they feel, in quest of aggressive thoughts. Others have induced young adult subjects to administer electric shocks to imaginary opponents. But the results, though they disturb us, reveal no more than the clown-punching data. As Dr. Richard J. Borden demonstrated in his study of such experiments, the subjects are always led to believe that whatever they do or say is ultimately safe, fun, and approved of—even desired—by the researcher. Still others have attempted a physiological approach, gauging subjects' production of norepinephrine and other neurochemicals associated with aggression, or measuring activity in areas of the brain linked to painful or anger-inducing memories. Those too only record reactions in the stressful environment of the laboratory.

However, even if the measurements of all these tests match exactly what children experience in normal life, they may still be measuring the opposite of what the media-aggression hypothesis leads us to expect. What such experiments measure is *general arousal.* "When we are aroused," says Stuart Fischoff, "we do everything harder—talk louder, walk faster, play harder, argue more intensely—no matter what the stimulus is." All emotions are intensified; if aggression is the one we're measuring, then we'll find aggression intensified. One study found that a group of adults who watched a violent movie were more aggressive afterward than those who watched a quiet movie. But those who watched an *erotic* movie were more aggressive than those in the other two groups. Since physical action usually arouses children, it will also elevate their aggression. It will probably also make them laugh louder, jump higher, and think faster—but we're not in the habit of looking for such positive effects.

General arousal can make someone who is already inclined to be aggressive more likely to act out. When action entertainment is what someone uses to arouse himself, then that entertainment does contribute to a higher likelihood of aggression. But arousal also ebbs quickly and, in doing so, can relieve tensions and leave people more relaxed. Those experiments with clowns, questionnaires, and electrodes are frequently cited as evidence that the catharsis theory does not apply to media: if children play more aggressively after watching aggressive images, then surely the images are stimulating their aggression rather than aiding its release. But, as anyone who's paid attention to children watching TV and then playing should know, the watching and the playing aren't two separate events but steps in the same process. Catharsis requires the emotions to be stimulated before they can be released. Just *watching* a video usually won't bring about a release of tension or anger, but many times I've seen a roomful of kids get wound up over a *Pokémon* scene and then jump off the couch and reenact it physically until they're tired and relaxed. I've gone to action movies with sullen middle schoolers, seen the big-screen explosions and the seat-shaking Dolby sound effects shock them out of their funks, watched them bop around chattering happily about it afterward. Kids play through the images in their heads, try on what they've seen to make sense of the emotions, expel their energies through acts and words.

Many studies find raised norepinephrine levels in young people right after they've played violent video games. Similar conditions, however, are found in people right after playing a close tennis game or finishing a quick sprint. Relaxation comes later. Few experimental studies have bothered to look beyond the immediate aftermath of stimulation by make-believe violence, but those that have show important results. Penny Holland's recent studies at British preschools found that when kids were allowed to play with toy guns, their games became more "aggressive" in the short term but that "the atmosphere in the room was notably more relaxed later in the day."

Yet, even the question of whether a catharsis is achieved is secondary. The primary question is this: if mock-aggressive play is good for children, and if these experiments demonstrate that entertainment violence inspires children to engage in mock-aggressive play, could it be that the experiments actually demonstrate that entertainment violence is *good?*

Some field and correlative studies look only at acts of serious violence, but many cast the word "aggression" over very mild and even desirable behaviors. A report may refer to a five-year-old yelling at her friend for taking her stuffed animal as an incidence of "aggression." It *is* aggression, of course, but what meaning are we taking from this? A child yelling about an injustice may not be showing the best problem-solving skills, but surely such "aggression" is far healthier than passivity or silent resentment. I think of the "peer nomination" used in so many studies, and I wonder if some of my most successful peers would have been branded "aggressive" if our class had been interviewed as third graders.

Even if the research means just what the conventional interpretation says it does, and entertainment violence does lead to increased aggression in 10 percent of children, we still don't have a complete picture. What about the other 90 percent? Do we ignore their needs simply because they aren't becoming more aggressive? What if even the 10 percent who are experiencing heightened aggression are picking up psychological or emotional benefits along with it? What if most of them are channeling that aggression into self-assertion, healthy competition, increased energy, determination, and courage? By failing to consider the *meaning* of children's behaviors, we do worse than render the research useless. We risk reading it upside down, seeing only negatives where we should also see positives, and so taking tools from children that may be helping them deal with the very stresses that concern us. That's why arguing about the "validity" of the research will never be anything but a pointless cycle. Ask of anything powerful, "Can this be harmful sometimes?" and we'll come up with a "yes." If we ask no more than that, the answers will never take us to the whole truth.

If we keep asking the same questions, we'll keep getting the same answers. We'll keep falling back on our usual public responses, the old familiar calls to limit the quantity, explicitness, or availability of entertainment violence. Caught in our repetitive arguments, we forget that we've been here before. We seem to have forgotten, in fact, one of the most important lessons of the recent history of American popular culture.

In the late 1960s, as crime rates were rising and the war in Vietnam preoccupied us, a groundswell of sentiment against violent entertainment actually succeeded in profoundly altering the landscape of children's culture. With help from the Federal Communications Commission and the grudging cooperation of the networks, groups such as Action for Children's Television succeeded in chasing most of the violence out of kids' programming. The generation of cartoons created during the 1970s, from *The Smurfs* to *Strawberry Shortcake*, were designed to emphasize pro-social values and eschew slapstick humor and physical conflict. Even the superheroes of *Super Friends* did little more than whip up whirlwinds and discuss the importance of peaceful cooperation. Old Bugs Bunny and Tom and Jerry cartoons were edited so that kids would never see anvils hitting heads or cats slamming into doors.

Prime-time action shows like *The Incredible Hulk* and *The Dukes of Hazzard* (listed as two of the most violent shows on television in one late-1970s study) featured little action and not a single instance of bodily harm. The mighty Hulk had to content himself with tearing the bumpers off cars, smashing through doors, and sometimes knocking a bad guy into a swimming pool—and even then in only two action scenes per hour-long episode. The old generation of Westerns and cop shows dribbled away, retreated to later time slots, and curtailed their on-screen violence. Although some reruns of shows like *Star Trek* and *Wild, Wild West* continued, the grittier older programming was mostly shelved. And there were no cable channels to show anything else.

Violent movies were grown-up affairs then, the likes of *The French Connection* and *Straw Dogs.* In those early years of the Motion Picture Production Association code, violence typically brought R and even X ratings, and industry surveys found that theater managers usually enforced the ratings. Kid-oriented movies in the decade before *Star Wars* were almost religiously nonviolent. Rock music took heat for promoting sex and drugs, but in that post-flower-child era it did anything but glamorize violence. The comic book business had shrunk to almost nothing. The toy industry, which received as much anti-violence criticism as television, turned its back radically on anything suggestive of killing or warfare. Guns, swords, and even ray guns disappeared from the shelves of reputable toy dealers. G.I. Joe became a peacetime "adventurer" overnight without a weapon to his name. The Louis Marx Company, which had dominated the plastic-army-men business all through the 1960s, abruptly dropped its whole line of soldiers. "Action figures" didn't exist yet, and neither did video games.

We tend to forget now, but for about a decade not very long ago, we truly did give our children the nearly violence-free popular culture that so many critics of the media are pressing for now. "When I was a kid I thought 'action' meant Boss Hogg's car smacking into a hay bale," says Adam Veeck, a writer born into a liberal home in 1967. "Gradually I pieced together that an earlier generation of kids had had all these awesome war toys and cinematic fistfights. All I could think was what a rotten deal I'd gotten."

What happened during those years? Crime rates increased. Our national anxiety about violence, as measured by opinion polls, worsened. The kids who spent their formative years in that pop-cultural milieu became the teenagers of the mid-1980s, when juvenile crime rates rose again. The kids who spent their formative years in the 1980s, on the other hand, when action-packed movies, TV shows, video games, and combat toys seemed to be taking over kid culture, became the teenagers of the late 1990s, when those rates plummeted. Obviously, the Smurfs were no more responsible for the crime wave of the 1980s than the Teenage Mutant Ninja Turtles were for the relative calm that followed. But this does cast some doubt on the real-world value of focusing our efforts on restricting media violence.

Something else happened during those years: children's appetite for make-believe violence seemed to grow. When *Star Wars* brought fighting, blasting, killing, and the blowing up of big things back to children's media after nearly a decade without, it hit levels of success never before approximated in juvenile entertainment and launched an action-driven entertainment/toy industry vaster than anyone could have dreamed. It's almost as if the suppression of entertainment violence drove it to come back more aggressively than ever.

The Joint Statement on the Impact of Entertainment Violence on Children called for "a more honest dialogue about what can be done to enhance the health and well-being of America's children." Our children need that dialogue. They deserve it. But it can only truly begin when we come down from that mountain of old research and start asking new questions. Why do so many healthy, nonviolent children love violent stories so much? Why are so many of them excited to such happy play by make-believe combat and destruction? What do their entertainment choices say about their emotional needs? What's going wrong when they act out destructively? How can we help them make more sense of what they see?

Most fundamental of all, why do they love what they love?

3

The Magic Wand

It was the early 1970s in Greenwich Village, and the place was filling up with new moms eager to raise a more peaceful and more enlightened generation of children. They were sure that violence was bad in every form: not only the war in Vietnam, not only street crime and race riots, but also make-believe violence on TV, in toys, and in children's play. By eliminating aggression from children's consciousness at the most fundamental level, they hoped to gift the world with a new, post-violent citizenry. Toy guns were banned from homes and preschools, TVs were turned off or tuned to the least violent shows, and kids caught playing war would be directed to more peaceful pursuits.

It was Passover week. The preschool teachers told the Passover story (in a nonviolent way, without all the plagues) and distributed matzoh to the kids. One little boy, let's call him Sammy, picked up his flat, crisp matzoh and looked at it. He took a small bite, then another, and another, chomping a fairly straight line across the top. Then he took more bites, at a right angle down the edge, then a couple more, back up again, and then a few more in a line parallel to the first one. Sammy raised his now L-shaped matzoh and gazed at it with pride. What a perfect gun! Then he ran around the room shouting "pow pow pow" while his classmates squealed and pretended to fall dead and his teachers rushed toward him in horror.

The friend who told me this story said that the parents whose children passed through that preschool nearly thirty years ago still retell it—mostly with laughter now that none of their kids have turned out to be killers. I've heard dozens of stories like it. The boy who cradled the family cat in his arms, aimed its puzzled face forward, and started yelling "bam bam bam!" The one who grabbed Barbie by her legs and shot invisible bullets out of her head. The kids who were using a refrigerator box as a fort until their mother yelled, "No shooting games! Why don't you pretend the box is a spaceship?" They did so, and as she settled back into her chair, pleased that she could redirect their energies into such a noble channel, she heard them hollering, "Look out! Aliens! Shoot 'em! Bzzt! Bzzt!"

A girl named Emily sparked my curiosity in one storytelling workshop. She wasn't the only girl in her kindergarten class who used guns in her fantasies, but she used them with the most gusto. "The cat was walking through the forest when suddenly a lion tried to eat it. The cat shot it with a gun and it was gone! Then the cat found a field of flowers. The cat was walking through the field of flowers when a hunter came and tried to shoot it. The cat didn't have its gun. But it picked a flower and the flower turned into a gun. It shot a bullet out of its gun and the bullet knocked down the hunter's bullet and then it went and shot the hunter!" There was no anger, cruelty, or gore in her drawings or the way she described them to me, only humor and joy at the way guns would suddenly appear and predators would suddenly—*BANG!*—disappear. This all became even more intriguing when I talked to her mother and learned that Emily wasn't allowed to play with toy guns, a rule that had become a major power struggle in the home.

From Emily's preschool days, her mother, Cynthia, had been telling her that gun play was not allowed in their home, with lengthy explanations that real guns hurt people and that it isn't appropriate to pretend that they're fun. Within minutes, Emily would be pointing her finger and shouting, "Pchoo!" Not wanting to have to monitor and restrict Emily's every action, Cynthia settled for saying, "Not at people!" So Emily tried shooting her friends' parents, who would grab their chests and yell, "You got me!" Emily would laugh in delight. Seeing how good Emily felt at being able to provoke such dramatic reactions from adults, Cynthia let go of that restriction—but stuck to her determination to allow her no gun toys. "I just don't want her associating guns with fun and games," she said. "That's how gun cultures are made. That's how kids grow up thinking that problems should be solved with force."

But Emily would see Power Ranger blasters and foam-rubber-shooting Nerf guns at her friends' houses. Most of her friends' parents understood that she was supposed to be a gun-free kid, so they'd try to steer her away from those toys, but Emily knew the toys were there and knew she wanted them. She'd go home snapping, "Why can't I have a Power Ranger blaster? It doesn't hurt anything!" Her mother would tell her again about real guns hurting people and she'd yell, "But it's not real!" She'd make guns out of Legos and Zoobs and Toobers. She'd talk about the kinds of guns she wished she could have. She'd start bargaining: "Can I have a toy gun when I'm I'm six? When I'm seven? When I'm eight?" "By the time we give in on this gun thing," sighed Cynthia, "it's going to have to be a howitzer!"

Emily wasn't a violent kid. She loved animals and she got along well with her friends. But she was boisterous and physical. She also had to stand up to some social pressures when she kept playing with both boys and girls even as the genders began to segregate themselves in kindergarten. She was strong-willed, intense in both her joys and frustrations, and she had a temper. Transitions were tough for her, and she'd argue fiercely whenever a play date had to end or she was denied what she wanted or her parents otherwise reminded her that they held the power. Her desire for toy guns was obviously as much about the fact that they were forbidden as about the guns themselves. But guns weren't the only things she didn't get to have. Her parents put limits on her beloved Barbie accessories, too, and budgetary restraints made them say no to a whole host of toys. She didn't fight nearly as hard for those, however. Guns were what excited her imagination most.

Not long after I talked to her about Emily's fantasies, Cynthia decided that the struggle over guns was only making them more important to her, so she decided to let her have one that one of her classmates wanted to give her—not a howitzer, but a plastic ray gun that didn't actually shoot any objects. Emily was thrilled. She loved it. She shot everything in sight. She built all her play dates around it. And her parents noticed that her mood improved. She didn't turn miraculously into an easygoing child, but she picked fewer fights with her parents, and if she was allowed to do some wild shooting at the end of a play date, the transition usually went much more smoothly.

Cynthia told me later that Emily's life revolved around the gun for only a few weeks. Once she'd made shooting a part of her fantasy arsenal, it dropped down among her stuffed animals, her gypsy costumes, and her Legos as one of many things she did. Her passion shifted to cats and dogs, and what she now nagged her parents for was a pet. She announced that she wanted to be a veterinarian, and her favorite make-believe game became taking care of hurt animals. By first grade, the gun was something she brought out only for play dates with the male friends who suggested it. "I think it gave her the power she needed just then," said Cynthia, "so she didn't have to keep pushing so hard for it anymore."

Childhood gun play is universal. Ethnologists have shown that in societies where guns aren't part of the local symbology, kids play similar games with bows and arrows or spears. In every culture, children always develop some fantasy of projecting destructive power across space and knocking down a big opponent with an effortless gesture. Traditionally, such play was preparation for life: kids who grew up throwing imaginary spears would eventually be expected to throw real ones. But even in modern American society, in which only a minority of people actually use guns in real life, virtually every kid wants to pretend-shoot at least occasionally. Even in liberal, middle-class communities in which kids may never see real guns except on the hips of police officers and the message of adults is unvaryingly anti-gun, that need to shoot still arises. It isn't guns as such that the kids want. It's the power that imaginary guns contain.

Emily's magically appearing guns are by no means unique in my experience with young children's stories. Some kids like guns, some prefer magic wands, others like characters with powers that blast out of their hands, but their function within the kids' stories are identical. I've known several kids who use them interchangeably. A boy named Jeremy had his frog hero shoot the scary ghost with a gun in one picture and then, on the very next page, zap the scary devil with a "magic bullet out of his wizard staff." Guns or wands, they help children feel strong. J. K. Rowling understood this in her Harry Potter books. Her characters use magic wands to defeat their foes and defend themselves (making them much more acceptable to gun-sensitive parents), but most of the time those wands function exactly like guns in children's fantasies; Harry and his friends whip them out, aim, fire, blow up things, knock down monsters, sometimes miss or have their shots blocked or comically misfire and accidentally shoot themselves.

The "gun" of the young child's imagination is no gun at all, but a magic wand. A wand can have other functions, too, especially transformation ("Poof, you're a rabbit!"), but when the purpose is blasting a foe, most kids find the gun to be a much more exciting form of magic than the wand. The kids I've known who prefer wands tend to be a little older and more adult-focused, more often girls than boys, who seem to have internalized adult anxieties about guns and aggression and prefer to project their own fantasies into a more unreal realm. The more unfettered the child's imagination, the more likely he or she is to play "gun." After all, a gun makes an exciting "pow," it imitates the form of the shooter's own finger, it can be whipped from any pocket, and it shoots discrete little bullets of magic that focus a child's imaginary power into a single, flashing point.

But guns scare us as adults. As we try to create a less violent world, we become more and more sensitized to the dangers of real guns, and the sight of a child pretending to shoot us inevitably stirs our anxieties. A child lusting after a plastic machine gun at a toy store or gunning down aliens in a video game makes it easy to visualize him pulling a gun as an angry teenager or packing a rifle in a foreign war as a young adult. And there are real-life stories to add to our fears, stories like the six-year-old who took a real gun to school and murdered a classmate. Our fears are natural, and they stir us to think through some of the philosophical issues of modern parenting. But I believe that we burden children with something they shouldn't have to carry when we dump our adult anxieties inappropriately onto their fantasies.

I still remember an incident from the summer I turned nine. I was running around the house with a toy six-shooter and clicked off a round at my mother. She visibly stiffened and turned away from me. I lowered the gun and looked at her—I could tell I'd done something wrong, but I didn't know what. After a pause, she said, "I can't look at that without thinking of all the horror that guns have caused in the world." That horror was real: John F. Kennedy's murder was still a burning scar for her, Medgar Evers had been assassinated a year before, Freedom Riders had been shot, the war in Vietnam was escalating, and that very summer a rampage killer had taken over the evening news by shooting people at random from the University of Texas Tower. I was aware of all that horror, and it disturbed me. But that was in a different world from the one in which I was playing then, where I was probably James Bond or Napoleon Solo bringing down some shadowy foe. In that world, with my pretend gun, I felt completely confident to handle anything that came at me. My mother's reaction knocked me out of that world. I felt her disgust, knew I'd lost some of her regard and support, and took on some of her horror at my own fantasies.

When my mother and I talked about it decades later, she said, "I didn't want you growing up to think that guns were honorable. I guess that might have been an opportunity for a good talk. I wish I'd been able to do that, but I just couldn't then. Seeing you with that gun, I just felt too much conflicting emotion." I knew even at nine that real violence was bad, and with my parents' models I'm sure my ethical development would have continued even if I'd been encouraged to keep play-shooting. Still, a talk about real guns and play guns, if I'd felt safe and accepted as myself, probably would have been helpful. If nothing else, it would have given me practice talking to my parents about scary subjects. Unfortunately, that encounter closed that door. I felt both guilty at my own violent fantasies and resentful of her for taking the fun out of them. I just walked away, and later I tried to avoid showing her that side of myself. My mother, feeling so many confusing emotions about her little boy, never mentioned it again. That, and other incidents like it, only hampered communication between us and weighed down my fantasy play as I headed for my preteen years.

Many parents and teachers worry that letting children play with toy guns and watch imaginary shooting on TV will create a glamour around guns that will persist into adulthood and make them more likely to associate real guns with power and excitement. And they're right: it can.

Dr. Donald F. Roberts, a professor of communications at Stanford University who has spent more than thirty years studying children's use of media, spoke of video's power to provide mental templates. "A generation of kids grew up with the opening credit sequence of *Gunsmoke* in their minds: Matt Dillon strides heroically down the street, then draws. The camera switches to a shot between his legs, as he fires and another gunman drops in the street. Then we see his face. Now, an adult could see in his stoic expression that he really wished he hadn't had to do that—but no nine-year-old would pick up on that. He'd see the hero shooting, the bad guy falling, the hero experiencing no negative consequence. And research has shown that we experience the lack of a consequence as a *reward*. So Marshall Dillon, and the viewer, are rewarded for shooting. The child will be carrying that template forever—heroism, shooting, reward—and it will mix in with everything else he or she receives from life."

But the template can be turned in many directions. The generation of kids raised in the 1950s and early 1960s was more thoroughly indoctrinated than any other in history by images of violent, authoritarian heroism. TV Westerns, cop shows, and World War II dramas flooded into their living rooms, and when they wanted to get out of the house, they encountered a cinematic flood of more Westerns, more war epics, and horror movies in which giant monsters were destroyed by soldiers with bombs and flame throwers. And violent crime did rise with that generation. But so did the anti-war movement and, along with it, an unprecedented sweeping popular critique of violence in American society. Pacifism, the rejection of the gun culture, and opposition to military and police authority, formerly positions held only by a radical fringe, became part of the culture of a generation—the *Gunsmoke* generation. Both the crime rates and the philosophic shift, of course, can be explained by forces far more influential than TV Westerns. But those media templates were part of the mix. Maybe an angry teenage thug had Matt Dillon somewhere in the back of his mind when he went for a gun; but then so did the war protester, seeking a model for being resolute and unafraid in the face of an opposing political establishment.

"There were two rules in my house when I was growing up," related Dr. John White, neurophysiologist and family therapist. "No guns at the dinner table and don't hit your sister with a pistol." Every kid in his neighborhood played with toy guns, but none of them could rival John and his brother; the two-holstered belts with the six-shooters went on the minute they got home from school, and they stayed on, except for dinner, until bedtime. "I think our parents only outlawed them at dinner to prevent total mayhem with mashed potatoes in the middle," he said. "My brother and I could barely look at each other without one of us trying to quick-draw the other."

White grew up in a raw young suburb in Minnesota in the early 1960s. He described the bleak battle with the weather, his crazy restlessness during the endless winters, trying to find something fun to do on the frozen earth of a dead lawn. And he described being a bit of an oddball, a bright, shy Jewish kid in a neighborhood made up mostly of Lutheran and Catholic factory workers. "The gun play gave me something to do with my energy," he remembered, "and someplace to go with my frustrations, because there were constant small frustrations along the way. It toughened me—I remember feeling afraid to get shot when I was little, even though I more or less understood that it was fantasy, and I remember working up my courage to come out from behind the corner of the house and risk getting killed. That was practice for being willing to take whatever life threw at me in order to achieve what I wanted. The fury of the gun battles also whipped me into a frenzy so I could tear around without even noticing the cold, or I could fall on some frozen ground and barely get hurt."

Talking to Dr. White, I remembered what made gun play so compelling to me: it was the best tool I had, by far, for bonding with other kids. Sports segregated the kids who excelled from the kids who didn't. So did card games and complicated make-believe games, for that matter. But anyone could shoot and fall down dead. It made us equals, it put us in control of whether we'd hit or missed, it broke down our inhibitions. The biggest, scariest kid on the block could yell, "I got you!" and I could argue back, "No, you didn't!" and we could fight uninhibitedly for a few seconds before one of us started blasting the other again and we could let it drop.

"Yes!" agreed White, and suddenly there was an electricity in the air between us, two kids running out of the house with their plastic guns to see who they can find to shoot. "Early on, gunfighting was the only thing that could embolden me to yell at the top of my lungs and call attention to myself. Unless I had my guns I would tend just to disappear quietly. As I got to be known as a wild gun-fighter, though, it became easier to call attention to myself in other situations."

"So what happened to the guns?" I asked him. "I notice you're not wearing them now." He laughed: "You just can't see them." He said that he put guns aside at the end of childhood along with the rest of his plastic toys. "Apart from any loftier objections to guns I might have had in my teens, it would have felt simply *ridiculous* to want a real gun. I was a teenager. I wanted to be taken seriously in the real world. Guns were juvenile. They were the stuff of child's play and TV fantasy. The adults who tried to solve problems with guns seemed to me, as much as anything, *childish*." White went on to become a pro-gressive political activist, a neurophysiological researcher, and a fa-ther; then he left hard research to deal more with people as a family therapist and a psychologist with a free clinic. "But the memories of myself as a juvenile gunslinger are always with me," he said. "At every intimidating juncture of my life—dissertation, fatherhood, changing career direction—I remember the wild courage I could whip myself into then. It was emboldenment. Self-emboldenment."

Gun play now, of course, doesn't look the same to us as it did in 1960. More people shoot each other, for one thing, and although only a tiny fraction of young people do such things, our news indus-try turns those into a national preoccupation. For another, gory shooter video games have been added to the pop culture landscape. Stanford's Donald Roberts noted, "I talked to my son about the realities of guns when he was little, but allowed him to play with toy guns. Now, when he brings my grandchildren over with toy machine guns, I find myself thinking that I *really* wish he wouldn't let them play with those things—because now I see kids being moved from those toys to a context of shooting very human-like opponents in an arcade game, which brings it much closer to reality." But how much of that anxiety is about any real anticipation that our kids will grow up to be shooters, and how much is merely about our own, very adult discomfort at being reminded of the more realistic violence in some entertainment—and thus of the horrors of real violence? Roberts acknowledged that, too, as he laughed, "Or maybe I'm just an old guy who doesn't get it anymore!"

Lenore Terr, a psychiatrist who has specialized in children and childhood-related issues for decades, recalled, "In the '70s everybody told me I shouldn't have toy guns in my office. But I'd tell them that they need to shoot: they need to shoot each other, they need to shoot their parents, they need to shoot me. It's one of the best tools they have for dealing with their aggressions, and taking that away from them only complicates the problems that the people who want to get rid of toy guns are concerned about. Gradually the bulk of professional and popular opinion came back around to what I'd been maintaining. But there will be always be someone expressing new worries about guns, especially when there's another round of publicity about youth violence, or a new kind of media violence."

We hear alarming reports of the violence in children's entertainment today. A 1998 UCLA study has been widely quoted as showing that the average child will have seen 6,000 violent deaths on television by the time he leaves elementary school. On closer examination that figure turns out to be the number of violent deaths a child *could* see if he watched all the violent programs available to him—if he watched more hours of *Homicide* than *Rugrats*. When children's viewing habits are taken into account, we discover that most children probably see *no* violent deaths through their first six or so years, then a modest number when they start to take an interest in more adult programs and movies. Similarly, a 2001 Harvard study announced that 60 percent of video games rated "E" (for everyone) included violence. But the violence turns out to include Pac Man eating ghosts and Gex the cartoon gecko tail-whipping skeletons.

There is far more gory realism in entertainment aimed at older kids than there used to be. At the same time, especially in the little-kid market, the vast bulk of toy guns are far more fantasy-based and less realistic than those of forty years ago. Children's TV shows, although full of superheroes zapping with ray-powers, are now essentially devoid of guns. Make-believe shooting is basically the same thing it always was. The "gun" is still a magic wand. The magic it contains is still emboldenment.

Studies reveal that the vast majority of kids who take up guns in adolescence have grown up in households where guns are used or in immediate environs where guns have become part of everyday youth culture, such as gang-controlled neighborhoods. Despite the decades-long efforts of many researchers, no casual correlation has been found between actual gun use and early-childhood fondness for toy guns, finger-shooting, or gun-filled TV shows. And although parents were more permissive of gun play in the 1980s and 1990s than in the 1970s, I've seen no sign of a generational shift toward a glamorization of real guns in my work with young people. If anything, in the wake of gang wars and school shootings, it's the opposite: I've heard even the most macho, video-game-loving boys describe packing a real gun as "stupid" and "chickenshit."

When the story of the first-grader who shot and killed a classmate hit the news in 2000, many commentators tried to link it to violent media. The prosecutor on the case said that the boy "expected the victim to get back up again, just like in one of his video games." But as we learned more about the boy's life, it became clear that he didn't live in a world of imaginary guns. He did watch violent TV sometimes. But he also grew up in a crack house full of real guns, surrounded by men who used real violence to settle their disputes and expressed their anger on a daily basis with words like, "I'll kill the bitch!" He didn't have toys or video games or any other safe way to relieve his anxiety or express his aggression. He didn't have sane adult models. He didn't have a childhood. Children deserve both: an adult world of nonviolence and well-modulated aggression, and a childhood world of fantasy unburdened by adult fears.

We don't help children learn the difference between fantasy and reality when we allow their fantasies to provoke reactions from us that are more appropriate to reality. When a child is joyfully killing a friend who loves being killed, we don't make things clearer for them by responding with an anxious, "You shouldn't shoot people!" Instead we blur the very boundaries that they're trying to establish. We teach them that pretend shooting makes adults feel threatened in *reality,* and therefore their own fantasies must be more powerful and more dangerous than they thought. The result for the child is more anxiety and self-doubt, more concern over the power of violent thoughts, less sense of power over their own feelings, and less practice expressing their fantasies—a combination far more likely to lead either to behavioral problems or excessive timidity than safe self-enjoyment would be.

It's that *literal* meaning we keep stumbling over: this is a man with a gun, and a child who emulates him is practicing to become a man with a gun. But the more time I spend involved with storytelling, the more certain I am that a story's most important function is its *emotional* meaning. What matters most to a child's development is the emotional connection he or she makes with the fantasy and the way the child works it, through play and imagination, into his or her emotional life. This is the power of symbol, myth, and metaphor. Understanding a game or toy or TV show and a child's use of it is a little like dream interpretation; a cheap dream-analysis book may tell us that a gun is a "phallic symbol" or a "symbol of death," but for the dreamer to make sense of it, he needs to know whether the gun felt threatening or empowering or absurd within the dream. We could call it the *emotional template* of a fantasy. Matt Dillon is a fantasy version of ourselves who stands up against a threat, acts decisively, and dispatches it. The emotional message of that template isn't "use a gun" but "don't be afraid—and do what's right."

What draws a child to any fantasy is its emotional power. No six-year-old seizes upon a toy or TV show because he thinks it will improve him or feels it validates his taste or opinions. That's why Isaac

Bashevis Singer said that "children are the only honest readers." Every toy marketer knows that no advertising will induce a child to want something that doesn't match up with the fantasies he already has. A little girl who already yearns for the power of glamour and the chameleonesque versatility of dress-up may have her fantasies focused and intensified by a Barbie commercial. But not even a thousand viewings of that commercial will make her macho brother want a Barbie. Either children connect with a fantasy at the profoundest emotional levels or they quickly toss it aside. We often forget the intensity of their involvement with fantasy. As John Michaud, a veteran kindergarten teacher and frequent lecturer on the age group, reminds parents every year, "An eleven-year-old can learn all about tigers, but only a five-year-old can *be* one."

As adults we spend so much time taking deft steps away from our most powerful fantasies and emotions that getting whacked by the raw, visceral imagination of a child can be unsettling. Sometimes we're most disturbed by our children's appetite for the disturbing. One little boy was telling me about his imaginary world called Stuffyland. "It's where all the stuffed animals live," he said, "and the king is a hedgehog and the queen is my duck puppet and all the other ones are princes." "How sweet," I thought. "And there are no bad guys in Stuffyland, so everyone is safe," he grinned. "How *sweet!*" I thought. Then, with a huge, innocent smile, he explained, "That's because there's a machine like a trap at the edge of Stuffyland and if a bad guy ever tries to come in it *chops him right in half!*"

I don't know how vivid this boy's image of the bad-guy chopping machine was, but I know from working with other kids that they're capable of spinning out the goriest images of dismembered bodies and spurting blood with, apparently, the most casual enjoyment. To them it's a natural progression of learning what's inside the body and what can conceivably happen to it, and so a celebration of the wholeness of their own bodies. It's also practice in blowing up reality and putting it back together in their heads, an important process on the way to separating reality from fantasy.

Adults, perhaps too mired in reality, often don't know how to respond to children's fantasies. I know the smile wavered on my lips when that boy came up with his chopping machine. Decades ago, Anna Freud wrote about young children who chattered casually about cutting up their mother's bodies, which she interpreted to be expressions of the "death wish" and a genuine desire (linked in girls to the Elektra complex) to see their mothers dead. Amid her brilliant and valuable work in applying psychoanalytic principles to children, this stands out, at least to my eyes, as a rather nervous and humorless adult response to what may well have been rather joyful fantasy.

Once I saw a child's fantasies virtually blow the roof off a preschool. The director wrote in the newsletter of how disturbed she felt upon hearing a little girl mutter, as she bumped two lions together in the sandbox, "Murder Mufasa! Murder Mufasa!" She blamed this on "today's media" ("I certainly don't remember knowing the word 'murder' at that age," she wrote) and encouraged parents to keep their children away from the TV. A father named Marc Laidlaw, a science fiction writer and video-game designer with a great sensitivity to kid culture, wrote a thoughtful response for the next newsletter, acknowledging that some media influences were unhealthy for children but that the right ones, in the right circumstances, could be rewarding. He described watching the cartoon *My Neighbor Totoro* with his daughters and the conversations and fantasies they had spun from it. The response from other parents was extraordinary: hostile, accusatory, and largely anonymous. One unsigned letter read, "I have only one suggestion for the TV-loving father: Get a life." What had been a harmonious community of parents was torn apart and never quite came back together again.

We try to shelter our children from unpleasant truths, but they learn about these things. I don't know where the little girl in the sandbox learned the word "murder," although I know it wasn't used in *The Lion King* or any other little-kid media I've seen. It could have come from an adult conversation, or a big kid, or the evening news. But she heard it, as kids always will, and was probably troubled by it. By playing with the idea in the sandbox, she was trying to make sense of it in the safest way she could find. Although she may not have been directly hurt by the explosion of adult rage she unwittingly set off, she certainly wasn't helped by it. I wonder if the atmosphere at her preschool was quite as nurturing as it had been, with so many parents simmering in rage. The whole mess struck me as a microcosm of our national debate about children and the media, with so much time and energy wasted fighting over generalizations and so little effort given to communicating with the children themselves.

That was an unusually heated reaction, but an incident just a few weeks later brought home to me how reflexive it is for us to recoil from our children's reminders that they know more about the horrors of life than we wish they did. I was leading four-year-old Nicky through a crowd at Disneyland when a little boy ahead of us abruptly turned to his mother and asked, "Mom? Will you die?" His mom was visibly thrown, and her first reaction was to look for the nearest sympathetic adult face and say in embarrassment, "Typical five-year-old question!" Annoyed, I thought, "Why doesn't she just answer the kid's question respectfully instead of embarrassing him?" But then I realized that my *first* thought had been, "God, I hope Nicky didn't hear that!" I didn't want to face that reality with my little boy any more than she did. I was relieved to see that Nicky was lost in his fantasy of the moment, being a savage Tyrannosaurus. Later, though, it struck me what seemed to make Tyrannosaurus so compelling to Nicky. It was a killer, and it was extinct. He was working through his own awareness of death, at the level that was best for him.

We try to shelter children for what seem to be the kindest reasons. But their most potent fantasies are unkind and unreasonable, because even as children they gather that the world's fundamental realities are neither reasonable nor kind. The philosopher Ernest Becker argued that the driving force behind humankind's greatest endeavors is "the denial of death." Our science, art, and civilization compel us largely because they enable us to say, "I won't die—not completely—not yet." Even art that meditates directly upon death is a way of taking power over it and thus pushing it slightly away. Play is children's greatest art.

Playing with life's scariest realities continues through adolescence. Mary Pipher made the point in *Reviving Ophelia: Saving the Selves of Adolescent Girls* that girls from restricted, sheltered homes tend to be calmer and less troubled in early adolescence than girls from more permissive homes. But those same girls are more likely to fall into crises of confidence and identity in late adolescence and early adulthood. The girls she studied who were allowed to experiment, take risks, confront adult values, and face the feelings that frightened but fascinated them tended to develop a stronger sense of self and flexibility as they took on adulthood. Those who were limited to an adult standard of acceptability early on were usually less prepared to take over their own lives.

There's more to be said later in this book about the gory gun play found in shooter video games. However, my experience has been that most of the time they serve the same function for older kids that make-believe guns and gore serve for little ones. For preteens and teenagers, the fantasies they spin in their heads are far less powerful than they are for young children. They need something realistic to look at and the surprises that come from interacting with a game developed by someone else. Like a preschooler's fantasies, those games enable them to play with the realities that scare them most and to take power over them. Raps about ghetto violence, rock dirges about suicide, movies about vicious killers are the same sorts of tools. In feeling that they understand such terrors better, they also feel stronger in the face of them.

For young people to develop selves that serve them well in life, they need modeling, mentoring, guidance, communication, and limitations. But they also need to fantasize, and play, and lose themselves in stories. That's how they reorganize the world into forms they can manipulate. That's how they explore and take some control over their own thoughts and emotions. That's how they kill their monsters.

When we are at peace with our fears and angers, we are best able to love. In wanting our children to be happy and innocent we tend to view violent fantasy as one end of the spectrum and loving fantasy as the other. But I've found that the two often mingle in children's imaginations. The little boy whose Stuffyland was protected by the hideous chopping machine was able to feel safe and snug with his Stuffies, and thus able to nurture them and be nurtured by them, *because* potential threats were so vividly dispatched. This is why Bruno Bettelheim and so many other psychiatrists and psychologists have argued against the bowdlerization of fairy tales. The wolf who locks grandma in the cupboard and then runs away from the woodsman is a pleasantly comical figure, but the wolf who devours grandma and is then hacked open matches children's own imaginative and emotional power and helps them master the terrifying realities that they already know about life.

I was doing a call-in radio show out of New York when a caller asked me for advice about her sister and niece. The nine-year-old girl had made a board game of her own invention for her grandmother in the hospital; the object of the game was to help a cat eat a mouse by rolling the dice. The girl's innovation was to have the mouse devoured piecemeal: if your cat lands on a picture of its tail it eats the tail, if it lands on a leg it eats the leg, and finally it eats the head. The girl's mother had called it "depraved." I asked the caller if her niece seemed morbid or troubled in creating this game, and she said no—although the girl was upset by her mother's reaction. Nor did she ever mistreat real animals. My advice was that if the kid seemed joyous and playful in making the game, and if she wasn't acting out in any negative way, then her creation should not only be allowed but celebrated. (Whether it was an appropriate hospital gift for her grandmother was another matter, and not for me to figure out.) Not only had she invented something all her own, but she'd confronted one of the most unpleasant truths about cats with a joyous empathy. Every nine-year-old knows that kitties eat cute little animals and that the process isn't pretty. This girl's game helped her to go on loving them without having to bend her mind around a denial of their real nature.

Not every child playing at violence is doing so in a constructive way, of course. But we can't hope to understand what any child might be getting out of any fantasy until we step back from our own anxious reactions to make-believe violence. Vivian Gussin Paley, the renowned kindergarten teacher and author of many books about children, wrote eloquently in *Boys and Girls: Superheroes in the Doll Corner* of her own distaste for the violent play of little boys. The more she tried to suppress the boys' superhero battles and gun play, the more insistent their fantasy violence became—and the more they insisted that she was being unfair.

"Shooting is all about killing people," she told them. "It looks wrong in a classroom." But as the boys demanded explanations, she began to see how inconsistent that was in the light of the fairy tale play that she did allow: "Is there a difference between 'Pretend our parents are dead' and 'Pretend I'm killing you'? The children know it is all magical play. The same magic destroys and resurrects, creates an orphan or a mother—or the Green Slime. The ability to imagine is the magic; putting it into action is the play; playing it out is the safe way to discharge the idea."

Paley began to pay more attention to the details of their fantasies: bad guys killed good guys and then nursed them back to life; superheroes used their powers looking for lost friends; robbers invaded the doll corner but stayed to help take care of the babies. She concluded, finally, that violent play "is serious drama, not morbid mischief." And even when the drama turns mainly on aggression, it can embrace a child's full emotional life. She revealed that the sounds of little-boy gunfire troubled her for a long time, until she watched a group of boys play a game in which army men shot robotic Shogun Warriors and the Shogun Warriors came back to life and decided to be army men instead. "Shogun Warriors are surely brothers who love each other," she realized. "Once I recognized this fact, the shooting took on a friendlier sound."

No one ever expressed any of this more clearly than the seven-year-old son of University of Chicago psychiatrist Edwin Cook. Although Cook felt that aggressive fantasies and action-entertainment could often be constructive, he also entered parenthood with grave reservations about letting his little boy grow up with toy guns and violent cartoons. He never let guns per se into their home, but bought his son Lego Throw-Bots that fling little plastic discs as surrogates. He taught him to use hockey-style body checks instead of making fists. He tried to steer him toward nonviolent programming, and when the boy insisted on watching *Power Rangers* or *Pokémon*, Dr. Cook sat beside him and talked about the dangers of real violence. Then one day his son looked at him. "You know, Dad," he said, "you're always trying to turn me into someone who doesn't like violence. But the problem is . . . I *do* like violence!"

And so they do. Some more than others. Some for one set of reasons, some for another. Sometimes they find fantasies that help them become happier and more productive, and sometimes they find fantasies that disturb them more. But the point from which any discussion of children and violent fantasy should begin is that most of them do like violence of one kind or another, and they know it. Respecting that is where communication, guidance, and understanding start. Much has been written about the most effective responses to children's desire to play at violence. Most of them involve discussions of the reality of violence and making them aware of other kinds of play. Those aren't bad ideas. But the most essential response of all is the one the kids are looking for: grab your chest and fall down dead.

4

The Good Fight

It's hard being a kid. You struggle to learn to stand up, falling down over and over. And once you've finally got it, you try to walk—and you fall down again. You can't stop your parents from sticking you in your stroller when you want to be held or snatching you up when you want to run (although a loud explosion of rage or grief sometimes helps). As you grow up you conquer more tasks and gain more power, but you're also hit with new frustrations. You watch adults breeze through tasks with the greatest of ease, but when you try them yourself, they turn into disasters. Your parents make doors fly open by touching doorknobs that you can't reach, and then when you're finally big enough to grab one, you discover that making it work is a maddening puzzle.

Of all the challenges children face, one of the biggest is their own powerlessness. Some children face especially painful challenges: the loss of a parent, abuse, neglect, hostile schoolmates, illness, poverty, neighborhood violence. But even the best protected children, with the most supportive parents, have to wrestle every day with reminders of how small and powerless they still are. Once when Nicky was three, we took him to a park where cattails grew around a picnic table. He was running around the table, waving a cattail in his hand, laughing in joy, when suddenly his little feet turned slightly inward—and before we could grab him he'd hit the corner of the table, full speed, with his forehead. One of the happiest days of his young life had ended in pain just because he hadn't learned to run perfectly on the uneven ground yet.

No matter how many new skills we learn, life keeps throwing those picnic tables at us. Our inability to master ourselves and our world brings pain, frustration, anxiety, and fear. One of our most profound yearnings as we grow up is simply to feel powerful.

The best antidote for life's frustrations, of course, is experience; proving to ourselves that we can conquer a challenge builds optimism and resiliency for the challenges ahead. Almost as important is adult encouragement and support. But we need help along the way. Between the wanting to master something and the mastering of it can be a long trip, and sometimes what keeps us going is our ability to make ourselves believe we're strong enough. We need something to drown out that voice in our head that says we can't do it, and answer, "I can do *anything!*" When reality isn't enough, fantasy comes to our rescue.

Psychiatrist Lenore Terr, author of *Beyond Love and Work,* analyzed the myriad functions of play: exercise and relaxation, bonding and honing social skills, learning mastery, practicing for later life. Play gives children new perspectives on their frustrations: "A problem doesn't look so big when compared with what Superman or Wonder Woman can do." Fantasy play "expresses sexual and aggressive feelings, hopes, and terrible frustrations with past or present realities." It enables children to manage and defuse their feelings by displacing what they want or fear; a child who wants to punish his parents feels safer pounding on monsters as a Power Ranger. "Children have been observed for years to use their play to make themselves feel better," Terr noted, "to relieve their anxieties and unhappy moods. [By] enacting play stories with feeling, they release much of the powerful emotion that has built around their internal conflicts or their experiences with outside events."

Power fantasies can be thrilling antidotes to life's pain. I spent time with a five-year-old boy who had recently been sexually molested by a relative, and for a while afterward he spun out grandiose fantasies of his own power: "I'm so fast I can run faster than a car so he can't catch me! I'm so strong I'll hit him with those flowers and because I'm so strong the flowers will knock him out!" The fantasies would start verbally, but then he'd run wild, play them out, physically transform his fear and rage into joy. Gradually, as he began to resolve his fears with the help of his parents and a therapist, his fantasies shifted to ninjas, Spider-Man, and other more distant symbols of power. He displaced his feelings, gave himself more power over them, and rehearsed a version of himself that was strong and unafraid. "By playing out new endings, or corrections," noted Terr, "children find that there are other possibilities for next time—and, in fact, that no 'next time' may ever happen." Becoming a warrior or a superhero able to beat any bad guy is a generic but thrilling "new ending" to all the everyday stories of not being old enough or powerful enough to make things come out the way children want.

The lifelong rewards of play are flexibility, resilience, mental fortitude, courage—in short, empowerment. The more a child can view the most unpleasant situations in new ways, and the more he can manipulate and dispel his most overwhelming emotions, the stronger he feels. The stronger he feels, the more confident he will be, the less he will react from fear and anxiety, and the easier it will be for him to take control of his own life and behavior. And as Terr pointed out, no fantasy works more directly or effectively to boost a child's feeling of power than rough-and-tumble play: "Play fighting helps kids learn their own strength and how to control it. It helps them learn limits and how to observe them. It helps them function confidently in the world—they learn how to handle moderate pain and forgive friends for accidental hurts. It helps them practice being resilient in the face of the *real* aggression that they're inevitably going to encounter down the road—from schoolmates to unfair teachers, competitive coworkers, road rage."

Wrestling, roughhousing, make-believe violence acted out with the whole body smash anxieties and wrestle fears to the floor. Pretended savagery lifts kids out of shyness and knocks down barriers to closeness. Games involving chasing, pillow fighting, squirt guns, and mock combat help kids learn how to judge dangers and take appropriate risks. Jumping willingly into those pretend dangers and coming out unhurt helps kids distinguish fantasy from reality. It's hard to watch a little boy or girl becoming a kicking, tackling, body-slamming savage without wondering, "What's my baby turning into?" But it's in that *being* something—whether in the pretend of early childhood or the artificial selves of video games later—that children use fantasy best, playing with the greatest feeling and displacing their feelings most safely.

I asked Dr. Terr about the parents who tell me that they don't like their kids' aggressive fantasies becoming too physical and real. "When my son sees fighting on TV, he fights," said one. "When he doesn't, he works out his aggressions just through his toys, which is a healthier release."

"I can sympathize, but they're not doing their kids a favor," Terr said. She compares aggression to a heart: block one artery, and the same amount of blood has to pump through the remaining arteries. It can still function with the blockage, but it's healthier with every vessel open. If a child doesn't engage in play fighting, his or her aggression will probably come out in storytelling or other fantasizing. For some kids these channels may be adequate, but often they aren't; then children may have trouble letting go of their aggression, may allow it to become a bigger deal than it need be, and may express it in social relations or other less constructive ways. "That's where you may get kids who are either too aggressive," said Terr, "or so afraid of their own aggression that they turn it inward. It's best for kids to express their aggression in every safe way there is."

It's easy to get lost in the debate over whether aggression is innate or learned. It doesn't matter much in the reality of childhood. Whether we're born with aggression that needs expression or learn aggression that needs comprehension, the logic of life makes aggression inevitable. Aggression is an expression of the need to feel strong. It's an empowering response to an imperfect world. It also brings dangers with it. Children will face it, and feel it, and have to do something with it. Playing with it makes it less scary, puts them in charge.

Aggression isn't easy to control, however. Hands fly, kids get whapped, tears flow. But that can be valuable, too. "Parents often come to me very worried about children's aggression," said kindergarten teacher John Michaud, "but I tell them that if a kid doesn't conk some other kid on the head at least once during the kindergarten year, *that's* when I start to worry. An unpleasant incident is the best way for a child to see the connections between his impulses, his actions, and real consequences. If he doesn't get to practice, he may fear that his impulses are too powerful or not know how to handle stressful situations when they come along later. Working *with* children's aggression is much more useful than preventing it."

Aggression also taps into real anger, even when it starts out playfully. There is no emotion we feel so uncomfortable with in our society as anger, no other emotion that we dread more in our children. But anger can be creative, too. It can be an energizing force. It can kick us back into action after a defeat, push us through obstacles, knock our fears from our minds, double our strength. I think of kids in my workshops, scribbling and scratching out stories about people who've made them angry, starting out sullen and tense but chortling and showing off their work by the end. I think of Nicky a few hours after the picnic table hit him in the head, becoming a bloodthirsty Allosaurus and biting Jennie and me—biting us *hard*—on the legs. Pretty soon he was running around the table at home, roaring fiercely but also laughing, not afraid to run full speed again. Anger used as a weapon is destructive, anger bottled up is self-destructive, but play can turn anger to joy.

Play fighting can also turn into real fighting. A kid may not know how much damage he can do or might use roughhousing as a pretext to hurt someone. "Some kids are just too angry for it," Terr maintained. "Others have a hard time getting it right and need lots of time outs, talks, and 'you can do it again *if*' bargains before they learn. I tell parents to keep an eye on it. If kids are really picking on smaller kids, or hurting pets, or causing intentional damage of some sort, then intervene. But I also tell them to *encourage* play fighting—as long as it remains play."

Nicky turned our home into a laboratory for play fighting. He created what he called "the war game," in which he and I would battle through the whole house, running, hiding, ambushing, tackling, hitting, kicking, shooting Nerf guns, throwing Toobers and Zots. He invited his friends, boys and girls, to join us, and during kindergarten and first grade it became the one event that everyone demanded of a play date at Nicky's house. Each of them brought his or her own fears, desires, and sensitivities into the war. Some liked to hit hard and blow off real anger. Some just liked to scream and hide. Some would hit the floor and bounce back up like inflatable clowns, others would bawl over a toe stub. Nicky himself was reticent about too much mayhem, liked to structure the games with rules, and was a little too sensitive to his friends' anger or disagreement.

But in every game we learned to adjust. Angry kids learned some control and fragile kids some resiliency. Nicky learned some things about not taking other kids' feelings too personally and not having to maintain so much control. The wild, tension-shattering fun of the war game enabled them all to expand their emotional and social capabilities even in the midst of explosive emotions like anger and pain. They learned to accept each other in their vast range of abilities, fragilities, and temperaments and work out ways to function together. Nicky's war game made for great play dates and helped him strengthen some good friendships.

Much of the power of play fighting comes from the fantasies that support it. It isn't enough to say, "I'm a six-year-old running around!" Much of the immersion, displacement, and expression of children's play is dependent on *being* something: superheroes, monsters, army men. TV shows, movies, video games, and toys can nourish those fantasies. They provide symbols of power—powerful beings they can *become*—that their usual experiences cannot. We may be happier when our kids become dinosaurs or knights or something else that hasn't been trademarked by a corporation, and they very often do. But there is a special power inherent in cartoon characters and action figures: they are individualized and yet universal, human and yet superhuman, unique visual symbols that can be held clearly in the mind's eye and are instantly recognized by everyone. For a child seeking a more expansive sense of self, a less generic and more individualized bigness, sometimes only Pikachu or Darth Maul will do. Especially at around age four or five, as children become more conscious of themselves as individuals, trademarked superheroes can be the perfect surrogate selves.

Those superheroes can also inspire kids to play. Rough-and-tumble play requires effort and sometimes a defiance of adult restraints. It can take a shot of fantasy from the TV or the toy box to rev a kid up enough. But that shot may not be welcomed by adults who don't quite trust play fighting. It disrupts our homes and classrooms and requires our anxious vigilance. It reminds us of real violence. We might respect it when it flows from our children's own innocent ideas and high spirits, but it's suspect when it seems injected into them from outside. Especially when it's from loud, plastic trash marketed to them by some corporation. We already dread our children being controlled by that corrupt world. To see them being turned *violent* by it is too much. How much anxiety is contained in that one mother's line, "When he sees fighting on TV he fights"?

In *Boys and Girls,* teacher and author Vivian Gussin Paley described the "near-riot conditions" that erupted in her kindergarten classroom when one boy brought his *Star Wars* record for rhythm period: "The moment it went on, the boys' inhibitions were released. . . . Suddenly the boys turn on one another, leaping and screaming, 'You're dead!' 'I killed you first!' Robots run into spaceships, rockets destroy TIE fighters, storm troopers shoot at everyone. Each boy is fighting every other boy. Even Teddy is pulling someone down." She immediately took the record off and started reading *Charlotte's Web.* The kids quieted down quickly. "Such events," she noted "cause teachers to outlaw superhero play forever."

But, she concluded, the value of the mayhem to the children is worth too much to outlaw it. "The pleasurable aspects of the play help reduce tensions, which then build up again if make-believe aggression appears too real to the child or the teacher. . . . Certainly there is a wider variety of violence pictured today in stories and play, but not more actual fighting. The increase in mock-aggressive fantasy play may even lessen the need for real combat." When kids played Spider-Man, trapping and shooting each other, they argued far less than when they played "workmen." "Perhaps when you pretend to fight, you don't really need to fight. Or maybe a superhero doesn't

need to prove he is powerful; his label tells the story. A builder, confronted by a collapsed block structure, has no such sustaining symbol
of competence."

There are dangers to commercial entertainment's influence. Kids
take in commercials and commercial values along with their symbols
of power. Some kids are seduced into sitting and watching instead of
jumping up and playing. The stories can be so formulaic and the toys
so clichéd that they may not inspire the expansion of imagination
that less popularized products can. It's important that we counterbal-
ance all that with other values. But those "sustaining symbols" are
real to children. When I run story workshops with young children,
they bring in fantasies of being princesses and kittens, crocodiles and
pirates—and of being Pokémon, Wolverine, Harry Potter, and obnoxious TV wrestlers. All are equally important to them. Each is
suited to what that boy or girl seems to want to be at that time:
glamorous, nurtured, predatory, invincible, all-destroying.

Aggression is fun, but it's also scary, and not just to adults. Emotions come suddenly upon kids and make them do things they never
wanted to do. Aggression can make them hit too hard, hurt themselves, hurt their friends, break their toys. It can make parents tense or
embarrassed or angry. It looms large in kids' minds but defies understanding or control.

No wonder they lock instantly onto action scenes in cartoons and
TV shows. Those cartooned images of fighting encourage their own
aggressive fantasies, but without pulling them into any real conflict
or danger. They reassure kids that even aggression can be made
harmless and fun. Play based on those well-contained fantasies will
seem safer as a consequence, especially since popular culture also
gives children a common language of symbols for organizing play-
fights with their friends. Several times I've seen the most aggressive
kids try to take over a game until a worried player will reign it in
with a line like, "That's not how you do Power Rangers!" Superhero
play has unstated but inherent structure and rules that can keep the
aggression from flying out of control.

One of the joys of my work on children and fantasy was meeting
Dr. Donna Mitroff. We were both on an "Ethics in Broadcasting"

panel at a KidScreen conference and were expected to be antagonists. We differed on some specifics but happily agreed on the basics. Mitroff is a child development specialist and former elementary school teacher who had served as a public television producer and educational consultant before Fox Kids Network hired her to set up a socially conscious Standards and Practices unit and help keep their programming in line with FCC requirements. She arrived expecting to have endless battles about Fox's *Power Rangers*, but she found instead that the struggle was to set standards that didn't permit unacceptable images or storylines—while still allowing kids to build the healthy stories and fantasies that made the series so important to them.

"This is why we need to break out of the old dialogue," she asserted. "People keep wanting everything black or white: is it violence or nonviolence, is 'violence' harmful or not? We can't really discuss these matters until we can at least distinguish between *violence* and *action*. Action that inspires rough-and-tumble play can be profoundly beneficial, and there's a real loss when it's excised or banned as "violence." Children have a deep need, an almost physical need, for these archetypes of power and heroism."

The art of life is the building of a self that serves us well: a weaving together of caution and optimism, toughness and openness, love and boundaries, self-interest and empathy. Aggression has to be part of that self. It can be destructive, but it can also be directed into assertiveness, decisiveness, healthy competition, and altruism. It helps us protect ourselves and what we believe in, inspires us to show off and make the best of ourselves. And as any kid in the middle of a wild X-Men game or an athlete in the moment of triumph or a writer coming out on top of a challenging chapter can attest, there is no joy sweeter and no satisfaction more unassailable than healthy aggression channeled toward a creative end.

We learn to channel it mostly from reality: parents, peers, self-understanding, life experience. But play helps, too. Most of our fundamental learning is in childhood, and play is an important part of any childhood work. A child learning to enjoy and play with his aggression is working toward his or her eventual wholeness.

One of the virtues of media entertainment is that it enables young people to play long after the normally sanctioned age of fantasy is past. "Our culture is very hard on play," said Lenore Terr. "There always has to be a point, developmentally, where the play principle has to make way for the reality principle. But our culture insists on it earlier and more completely than a lot of cultures, and it seems to do it earlier all the time." Far too early we tell children to get serious, get down to working on their test scores, good conduct, fashion accessories. By the third grade we're usually taking away most of their unstructured time with planned activities and academics. We give them the message that they shouldn't play pretend or silly games. Kids who roughhouse make us nervous by the time they hit the first grade. By preschool we may already be urging them into organized athletics, which is another good place for kids to play with aggression and power, but not a substitute for the egalitarianism, freedom, and individuality of wild play. They internalize all that, and by the middle of elementary school they may already feel that child's play is beneath them.

Entertainment can make aggressive play feel acceptable to older kids. Television wrestling mimics roughhousing in many ways. Those absurdly brawny men picking up their opponents and slamming them into the mat, or bouncing off the ropes and flying fist-first through the air, are exactly what roughhousing little children see themselves doing in their minds. It's even make-believe; most of the wrestling fans I've talked to over the age of nine know that it's choreographed, or say, "I don't care" (which means they know but don't want to pop the bubble by saying it out loud). Many of the younger ones think those "Atomic Piledrivers" and "Undertaker Drops" are real blows, but even they have learned that the wrestlers are never seriously hurt and that the more likable one nearly always wins. Unlike real sports, which carry with them too much grown-up anxiety for many fantasy-craving kids, professional wrestling is rough-and-tumble play.

It's far more vicious, of course. Its emphasis on pain, rage, and willful injury makes it exactly what children's fantasy play isn't. But that's the point. That gives it a quality of seriousness, of "reality," that makes it more legitimate to kids going through the awkward stage of disdaining child's play but still yearning for it. Even if kids only appreciate it as fans or as collectors of the cards and action figures, they're revisiting the fantasies of play fighting. And some kids are inspired to imitate their favorite wrestlers in physical play. It's much cooler for a ten-year-old to pay homage to Stone Cold Steve Austin than it is for him to be a Power Ranger.

Interestingly, wrestling has had three moments of popularity on television: the late 1940s and early 1950s, the late 1960s and early 1970s, and the mid- to late 1990s. The first was in the wake of a world war, when violence was vividly remembered but being forcefully rejected, and the new style of family was suburban civility and tranquillity. The others were both times when crime rates had recently soared, adult anxiety about violence was intense, and raising kids to be nonviolent was a dominant concern. In all of them, violence was a concern of young people but one they were discouraged from exploring. Millions of them became fascinated with a publicly enacted game of roughhousing.

Video games lack the physicality and freedom of play fighting, but they retain much of the fantasy. Even the goriest shooter games are essentially variations on a kindergartner's war game. When we look beyond the bloody special effects that shock adults—and give the games their "coolness" to older kids—we can see the player scampering, hiding, peeking out, blasting away, being blasted, "dying," and getting back up. Gamers don't get to throw each other to the floor, but they almost make up for it by whooping about their wins and chattering excitedly about their favorite features. When Nicky first got into *Spyro,* at the age of eight, he'd bounce around on the couch as he fought his battles, then run through the house yelling, "I beat Ripto! I beat Ripto!" Most of his friends had already lost interest in playing the war game by then, and even he was developing a selfconsciousness when we tried it. *Spyro* gave him some of that back.

In one of my Art and Story Workshops, two bright, slightly geeky eighth-grade boys created humorous comic strips about video games. They obviously loved gaming, but they were making fun of it, too, thus making sure it was known that they were cooler than their passion for fight games might make them seem. They created a martial arts game about "the evil Cygon" and "the ninja of pain." From the enthusiasm they put into the fight scenes I could tell that it wasn't just the gaming they loved, but the fantasy heart of the fighting itself. They finished early, and I showed their pages to the rest of the class. The boys were proud but embarrassed and started getting squirrelly as the other kids were finishing up. Suddenly they got up and started to act out a ninja fight in the back of the room. "I am Cygon, master of the universe, and shall not be defeated!" "Feel my fingers of absolute destruction, evil Cygon!" They were grinning self-consciously, glancing to see who was watching, obviously enacting a "parody" of games to show their superiority to them. But they kicked and punched the air with commitment, too. They were excited. They were using every big-kid method they had to preserve their dignity, but they were having a play fight, right there in an eighth-grade classroom.

Entertainment violence embraces far more than the superhero fantasies of early childhood, takes more problematic forms and plays more complex roles. But at heart, it's about the joy of feeling big and strong, the freedom of being able to survive anything and to overcome any obstacle. It's about action, power, and mastering life.

Martha Breen is an artist who knows both tradition and creativity: she was trained as an archaeologist and creates Judaica and children's books with a unique humor and humanity. She and her husband had both grown up watching Loony Toons but debated whether they would be right for their young son. When he was three, they decided to let him watch the Roadrunner. "I can see Lenny's pleasure in stories with violent twists," she said. "I watch him and I can literally see how dangerous conflict energizes his body. It fills him with a kind of enthusiasm. The enthusiasm makes him feel alive. And, well, life loves itself."

5

Girl Power

Superheroes, fight scenes, and gun toys have traditionally been assigned to what we think of as "boy culture." Parents of
girls often assume they'll never have to deal with violent fantasies or
play. But their girls may surprise them—and the current generation
of girls is surprising them more than any previous one. The more I
study and work with children, the more instances I see of girls using
make-believe violence for as many developmental purposes as boys.
They often use it in different ways, and for slightly different purposes, but it can be just as important to them as to their brothers.

In early childhood, the play of boys and girls is more similar than
different. Both are likely to be rough-and-tumble dinosaurs and then
quiet down by playing mommy-and-baby. But toward the end of the
preschool years, they begin to diverge. "Kindergarten," wrote Vivian
Gussin Paley, "is a triumph of sexual self-stereotyping." Girls tend to
pull away from play fighting by the end of preschool, often dramatically, and sometimes with a strong disapproval of the roughness of
boys. Paley described the daily complaints of girls about boys who, as
superheroes or robbers, invade and disrupt the quiet doll corner.

The phenomenon is almost universal across eras and cultures. Even
the girls of the San, a group of Kalahari Bushmen with a culture
quite unlike our own, tend to withdraw from rough-and-tumble play
by about the age of six. Authorities offer various possible explana-

tions, including biological disposition, but they also point to pervasive cultural factors. In our culture, dads tend not to wrestle their daughters to the floor as they do their sons; we place more emphasis on how girls look; we make a bigger deal of girls' pains and injuries. Paley stressed the importance to children of labeling themselves "boy" or "girl" as their social selves become more complex, which includes demarcating whole spheres of behavior as un-boy-like or un-girl-like.

Whatever its origins, the shift is deeply internalized and usually lasting. I've seen the alarm and outrage of girls running to the nearest adult yelling, "The boys are fighting again!" and it strikes me as the same alarm and outrage of the many mothers I've known who ask, "How do I stop my sons from *fighting?*" In one study, the great play researcher Brian Sutton-Smith and his colleagues showed groups of preschoolers and young adults video tapes of preschoolers play fighting. The preschoolers of both sexes declared, on average, that two of the fourteen tapes showed real fighting and twelve play fighting. Adult men classified them in almost precisely the same way. Adult women, on the other hand, thought, on average, that eight of the fourteen showed real fighting.

Although I'm generally suspicious of lab studies, this one fits well with what I've observed. When mothers respond to my ideas with, "But when my son sees violent cartoons, he fights," I ask, "But is it real fighting or play fighting?" And I find that the question itself is difficult for some mothers. Many mothers have no trouble making the distinction, but some are caught in the black-and-white dualism of "fighting is bad" and "quiet is good." On one hand, they are perpetuating one of the traditional functions of women: to soften the brutishness of male culture and protect the gentler aspects of civilization. Or, as Lynn Ponton put it, "Mothers have always seen one of their sacred duties as keeping boys from killing each other." On the other hand, they may still be fighting that grade-school battle with the boys.

The need for aggressive play continues in girls, however, although it changes to function within their developing social identities. From the end of preschool onward, girls' play tends to be increasingly about relationships. Violent fantasies about mindless brutes battling or spaceships clashing usually leave them cold, but if those fantasies are built around social constructs or relationships between sentient characters, then even the most feminine girls are likely to connect to them.

Once I was helping shepherd Nicky's kindergarten class back from a field trip, and while we were waiting for the streetcar, Nicky started body slamming me playfully. One of his classmates, Haley, who normally played quiet games with girls and didn't mix much with the boys, saw this, drifted toward us, and then, looking me intently in the eyes, punched me gently in the chest. I pretended that she'd almost knocked me down. She smiled and hit me harder. I played along, she smiled wider and hit me harder. A couple of the boys jumped in, keeping their heads down, pounding me on the sides and legs. Haley kept going for a good two dozen punches, until I had a nice bruise on my sternum to show for it—and the whole time she kept her eyes locked on mine. I wasn't just a grown-up body to pummel but someone whose reactions were to be tested and recorded.

Among Nicky's kindergarten classmates, I quickly gained a reputation as a dad who would wrestle and play fight. Every boy and girl who came over wanted to play Nicky's "war game." For the boys, it was mostly about firing accurately with Nerf guns and hitting me with pillows. Sometimes they'd hide and ambush me, but the hiding was brief and the ambush savage. The girls loved the Nerf guns and pillows, too, but they preferred to conspire with Nicky on whispered strategies, lie in wait, watch me hunt for them, tease me with a false attack, run away laughing, and look back at my reaction. When they did shoot me at close range or pound on me, though, they did so as gleefully as any boy.

Violence for the girls was more a punctuation for a complex web of manipulations and suspense, whereas for the boys it was likely to be the whole point. But I could see how joyful and liberating that violent punctuation was, and I sensed that the girls didn't get enough of it in their normal lives. Early in Nicky's kindergarten year, I was talking to the father of a girl named Maritte, one of the most rambunctious players of the war game. He said, "It must be so different having a boy. You know, it's true, as much as we fight the stereotypes, that girls really are made of sugar and spice and everything nice." I resisted the temptation to ask, "Jim, have you *met* Maritte?" Soon enough, Jim heard about the war games and told me he appreciated how exhausted and relaxed his daughter was after her play dates with Nicky. The mock violence served the relationship, too: Nicky and Maritte remained close even as the boys and girls in their class segregated themselves in the second and third grades.

When girls don't feel free to play at open aggression, their desires to play with power and conflict don't go away but take other forms. Lenore Terr noted, "After they've abandoned rough-and-tumble play, girls' social play can become extremely aggressive. Games about inclusion and exclusion, social competition and defeat, express a great deal of aggression. You see it in fantasy play with Barbie dolls, and you see it in the very serious social maneuverings of little girls, too." While boys run around wildly, playing battle games, crashing into each other, sometimes stepping over the line into real fights, girls draw into fierce little cliques, testing their power and one another's emotional toughness with daily battles about who's in, who's out, who's speaking to whom. This is why Terr thinks girls would benefit from more encouragement to engage in rough-and-tumble play, which can help them feel tougher and stronger as individuals and therefore less at the mercy of peer approval and matters of appearance and dress. It can also help them to master their anger and tensions in playful ways, making them less likely to take their feelings out on one another or themselves.

The popular culture of girls usually masks its violent side, but girls find that side when they need it. Barbie is frequently criticized as a model for passivity, consumerism, and obsession with appearance, one role she does play. In the actual play of little girls, however, she also functions remarkably often as an action heroine. Sandra Hume, a writer and editor now in her late twenties, told me about a wide range of violent fantasies she played out with Barbie from preschool to her preteen years: "My parents split up when I was four, which unleashed a tremendous amount of rage between them for a while. During the same time my Barbies would slap each other around over the one Ken in my collection, try to horde all the shoes and then fight viciously over those. Or sometimes they'd bond together to defend one of their sisters from the attacking Ken." She attributed some of those images to watching *Wonder Woman,* others to *Dallas* and *Dynasty,* which she watched with her mother, and others to her attempts to make sense of the adult life around her.

Over the next several years, Sandra's conflicts became more complex, and so did her Barbie play. Her mother went through three relationships with men, and with each new partner the dynamics of the family changed unpredictably. Sandra described her household as "highly sexualized," as her mother rode the waves of falling in love and breaking up repeatedly. Her feelings of rage and fear were closely bound up with gender roles and sex. She made friends with Lana, another girl from a turbulent home, and together they concocted vast adventures drawn from Greek mythology, *Wonder Woman, Star Wars,* and fantasy novels. "Tribes of Amazon Barbies with aluminum-foil swords would slaughter invading armies of Kens," said Sandra. "Heads would roll. Literally—we had these Kens whose heads had fallen off, so we'd use them for victims."

When they finally put Barbie aside, Sandra and Lana turned to adolescent fantasy entertainment: Gothic and death-rock music, role-playing games, comic books like the violent, savagely satirical *Preacher.* Much of it was alarming to the adults around them and certainly looked drastically different from Barbie, but Sandra said, "It was still the same basic feelings we were working through, just at a more sophisticated level." She maintained that her fantasies and play, from Barbie through *Preacher,* gave her a feeling of "power over the forces that kept throwing my life into upheaval. They got me used to doing something with my emotions first before I just acted out, and they gave me a continuity that real life wasn't giving me. And I've been a lot stabler in my life and relationships than my mom."

Even now, when female action figures have become so much more common than in Sandra's childhood, I see little girls pitting Barbie against ferocious stuffed animals and burying Ken under mountains of wooden blocks from which Barbie has to dig him out by sheer strength. Almost never, though, do I see or hear about girls pitting

Barbie against a Power Ranger doll or introducing Barbie into action-figure play with boys. Girls above the age of four or so tend to compartmentalize Barbie into the realm of girlishness, but within that realm, they explore fantasies far more complex and powerful than what Mattel's packaging and advertising would suggest.

Girls have long shown a remarkable ability to identify with male fantasy figures when they aren't provided with adequate female models. In writing comic books I found that although girls welcomed strong and interesting superheroines, they could identify just as easily with a male hero as long as he was psychologically complex or involved in intriguing relationships with other characters. Sharon, the girl who loved my *Freex* so much, made it clear that she identified with Angela, the shy female character whom she most resembled, but also with Lewis, the volatile leader of the group, whom Angela loved. Devin Kalile Grayson, one of the most successful female writers in comics, told me that she first fell in love with comics through Batman and Robin. Batman, in fact, has turned out to be one of the most popular fantasy-selves for superhero-loving girls, mainly because his stories are as much about relationships—with Robin, with Catwoman, with the world of his own alter ego, Bruce Wayne—as about action.

In the desire to sustain their self- and social images of femininity, however, most school-age girls will pointedly show no interest in subjects like superhero comics, which they still tend to label "boy stuff"; when they do seek action heroes from the media, they often cloak their passion in what they consider more appropriately girlish behavior. When I talk to women who grew up on the *Star Wars* and *Indiana Jones* series, they invariably tell me that they identified less with Princess Leia or any of Indy's female friends than with Luke Skywalker, Han Solo, and Professor Jones himself. A physician named Janice Cohen told me: "We'd always start by talking about how cute Mark Hamill and Harrison Ford were. It was important that adults saw us as being infatuated with Indiana Jones, and it was important that we saw *ourselves* as being infatuated with Indiana Jones, but when the movie started to roll, and when I rolled it over and over again in my memory and my conversations with friends, I *was* Indiana Jones." He was a perfect fantasy for Janice as she worked hard to be a good girl and a good student, while also yearning to charge off, risk dangers, and make things happen. "Indy sort of played the 'good girl' himself, in his professor identity, and then tossed off the restrictive clothes, grabbed the whip, and came alive."

A great deal was made in the movies of Jones's female students being in love with him in his classroom role. "That validated us," said Dr. Cohen. "But when he left the classroom, he left them behind—and he took *us* with him. He picked up a female sidekick, but she was everything we thought a girl shouldn't be—foulmouthed, drinking, obnoxious, horning in on the fantasy. When he finally showed her up and had to save her, that was *me* in my absolute fantasy ideal, showing that I was better than any of the girls who didn't act like girls. Indy was a perfect model for being a good girl, good student, good citizen, and yet still being powerful and proactive—which, in a sense, is what I wanted for myself all the way into college."

The pattern continues with the current generation of girls. In my storytelling workshops I've encountered many Harry Potter fantasies, from kids ranging in age from kindergarten to high school, but nearly always from girls. The Potter books have sold astonishingly well among boys too, but it's the girls who engage more passionately with the fantasy, and they identify more strongly with Harry himself. Most of them express some sort of fond annoyance for Harry's female friend, Hermione; with her obsessive study and rule-following, and somewhat impaired senses of humor and adventure, she represents everything that the girls find restrictive about traditional girlhood, a set of traits that Harry consistently has to rebel against in order to slip free into the realms of battle and power. The girls also enjoy, with amused condescension, the character of Ginny Weasley, the younger and sillier girl struck mute by her infatuation with Harry, whereas young male readers tell me they find her annoying. Ginny speaks to girls' fascination with emotions and relationships. I suspect that Ginny, like Indiana Jones's students, enables girls to feel a little safer in identifying with Harry by allowing them also to view him as an object of romantic love. The author of the Potter books, J. K. Rowling, is a woman, and I wonder if any male fantasist could have intuited the emotional needs of young female readers half as well.

Girls show a greater flexibility and complexity in their fantasizing than boys. Young girls are far more accustomed than boys to viewing a fantasy character simultaneously as a *subject* of identification and as an *object* seen from the outside. A boy might be Indiana Jones, but a girl can identify with both Indiana Jones and the female sidekick in love with him. That's an imaginative strength, but it's also, of course, an effect of the self-diminishment that girls have traditionally been taught from early childhood. If a woman is expected to glory not in her own accomplishments but in her husband's, then girlhood requires learning to admire the accomplishments of heroes without openly wanting to be them.

Children's entertainment supported those expectations for most of the twentieth century. The most popular model of female physical power for little girls, Wonder Woman, pointedly stood outside the traditional duality of girlishness and boyishness: a lone visitor from a lost island of Amazons, she was always a naive *other,* disconnected from normal, human women. As her young fans became more socially sophisticated, they generally understood that Wonder Woman was a fantasy to enjoy from a distance, not a model to aspire to. The producers of her TV show in the 1970s found that her appeal was strong among preschool and kindergarten girls, but then rapidly evaporated. By the time her fans had reached middle childhood, they were in love with, and pretending to be, Luke Skywalker. Over the past decade, however, the entertainment industry has been far more helpful in supplying young girls with female power symbols, and girls have responded eagerly—especially when the creators place their superheroines in a context of vivid social and emotional relationships.

When I was reading superhero comics in the early 1970s, it was an almost entirely male preserve, and no matter how many female heroines the writers and artists tried, no girls seemed interested. When I began noticing comics again as an adult, a decade later, the situation had changed noticeably: boys still made up the bulk of the fans, but the number of preteen and teenage girl readers was growing rapidly, and their tastes had changed the way superhero stories were told. At the end of the 1970s, the creative team on *X-Men*, the writer Chris Claremont and artists Dave Cockrum and John Byrne, had taken a new approach to superheroines, emphasizing not what they looked like or what their powers were so much as which teammates they were friends with, who they were angry with, who they admired, and who they felt they should protect. They included some romances, but unlike the simple frustrations of Superman and Lois Lane, these were more complex and tangled with issues of friendship and loyalty. They were, in short, more like the real crushes of early adolescence, which are less interesting as love relationships than as complications to female alliances. Girls began to read *X-Men,* and sales began to rise. Other comics began to follow suit, and more and more girls and young women found fantasies in comics that spoke to them. That was one reason comics rose from near death in the late 1970s to attain an unprecedented vitality and universality a decade later.

Female members of superheroic teams had never been successful with young kids. The teams aimed at little kids in the 1980s, from He-Man and the Masters of the Universe to the Teenage Mutant Ninja Turtles, were almost entirely male in composition. In the early 1990s, on the other hand, the five Power Rangers included two females, judging by market research, who were comparable in popularity to their male cohorts. The female Rangers were successful with kids partly because girls were becoming more comfortable with superhero fantasies and boys were becoming more comfortable with powerful females having a place in their fantasies—but also because of the nature of the group.

The Power Rangers' stories emphasized teamwork above all else. The Rangers hung out together constantly in their civilian forms, transformed simultaneously into their super-forms, and could defeat their opponents only through coordinated assaults by the whole team. In order to defeat their greatest foes they had to link their vehicles, their "Zords," into "Mega-Zords," which wouldn't work if even one member was absent. Power Ranger toys reflect that: Zords and weapons snapped together into bigger, more powerful forms. Watching Nicky and his friends play Power Rangers, I often saw them express feelings of incompleteness until they had all the

Rangers together for an action-figure battle. When they pretended to be Power Rangers themselves, they usually worked hard to make sure that each color of Ranger was accounted for, even if that meant a boy playing the Pink or Yellow Ranger, or a girl playing the Red, Blue, or Green. Unity, togetherness, the group identity was as important to the mystique of the Power Rangers as their powers and their colors, and that made it a powerful fantasy for girls as well as boys.

The Power Rangers, however, remained solidly in the "boy" camp as the sexes segregated themselves around kindergarten. As essential as the female Rangers were to the group, the fact that their hair and faces were concealed by helmets and visors and their bodies were sheathed in the tights associated with the boyish world of super-heroes de-emphasized their femaleness. They were girls whose femaleness didn't matter, which may have made them appealing to parents who hoped to raise their daughters to be free of gender stereotypes, but not to girls whose femaleness was becoming more and more important to their increasingly complex systems of identity. By kindergarten, a girl's drawings of girls usually focus on wide eyes, hair, and frilly dresses as markers of femininity—even if the artist herself wears jeans nearly every day. Pink uniform and breasts aside, the eyeless, hairless, muscular Power Rangers were quite the opposite of what girls read as female models; they came to see the female Rangers as girls who were made more like boys by their participation in physical power.

Dr. Carla Seal-Wanner, a developmental psychologist and educator who specializes in children's media, related the case of Amanda, who in preschool was the most enthusiastic of all the Power Rangers fans in her class and played at being a Ranger with more aggressive rambunctiousness than any of the boys. At first her parents were thrilled; here was a girl rejecting stereotypical femininity and proudly taking on physical power. But Amanda continued playing out her rough-and-tumble Ranger fantasies not only as the other girls in the class rejected them but even as the boys began to outgrow them. Her Ranger play took on a particularly repetitive, frustrated, angry quality, until even the wilder boys were complaining that "Amanda's too rough."

When Amanda finally abandoned the Power Rangers in first grade she continued to seek the company of boys and to engage in aggressive play, but she also began to behave with ferocious verbal and social aggression to both boys and girls. By the fourth grade, when it became apparent that she was denying herself food in order to keep herself flesh-and-bones skinny, some of the adults in her life realized that Amanda might feel acute confusion and anger about her gender. She didn't like being a girl, resented girlishness in general, and overplayed what she thought of as boyish fantasies in an effort to ease her anxieties and mask the very sensitive isolated child within. The Power Rangers had been a helpful fantasy for her for a while, but as the sexual landscape of childhood had become more complex, her adherence to them had probably made it harder for her to mature in more constructive ways.

A far more inclusive fantasy of power appeared a few years later in the form of *Pokémon*. Among many factors in the enormous success of the Poké-phenomenon in the summer and fall of 1999 was the fact that it spoke to nearly every sort of kid, with every sort of fantasy. Although its first and most fervid fans were boys, especially those who loved Game Boy and collecting cards, the craze, at its peak, seized girls, even grade-school girls, in remarkable numbers. No action cartoon had ever sold plush toys and pink lunch boxes like *Pokémon*. Although the craze soon faded, many girls remained loyal, continuing to sustain products like the girl-oriented comic book, *Magical Pokémon Journey*.

I heard from many mothers who were startled to see their little girls falling so in love with a franchise that came out of video games and centered on violent fights between bizarre monsters. But it was no surprise to those of us viewing the phenomenon from within. For one thing, the whole Pokémon universe is founded upon relationships; human trainers catch and care for the monsters called Pokémon, teaching them to use their powers in battle as the monsters teach their trainers the virtues of patience, empathy, and nurturance. The trainers are linked by intricate affiliations with various gymnasiums, teachers, tournaments, and secret organizations, and the Pokémon evolve from one form to another as they master their skills, so that Pichu, Pikachu, and Raichu aren't just different creatures to memorize but siblings and symbols of the process of growing up.

For another, every sort of character can be found among the Pokémon, from savage dragons to impishly cute rodents to cuddly balloon creatures to loyal canines. Kids who loved fish could become the silly Goldeen, kids who fantasized about taking care of babies could carry a plush toy of the infantile, egg-shaped Togepi. And any relationship or emotion could be embodied and exaggerated through Poké play: the fiercest battles, the most gentle nurturing, the silliest acting up, the fiercest declarations of loyalty made sense as some part of the mythology.

Pokémon also included a human heroine who appealed to most girls as much as, or even more than, the male protagonist. Misty was very girlish, and fashionably so, with her ponytail, bare midriff, scrawny limbs, and unspoken crush on the oblivious Ash. She exhibited the frailties that girls identify with femininity: a sentimental adoration of anything cute and streaks of vanity, squeamishness, and self-absorption. She liked pretty water Pokémon best of all, and she took on most of the maternal responsibilities for the baby Togepi. She also possessed a trait that American popular culture has rarely allowed in fictional girls, though girls know very well it can be a part of their emotional makeup: an explosive, screaming rage, which could knock poor Ash off his feet. At the same time, she was as tough and eager for combat as any Pokémon trainer and at crunch time was as physically potent and passionate as Ash.

An old saw of the entertainment industry, which dates back at least to the movie studios of the 1920s, maintains that a story has to include action to appeal to boys and men, characters and romance to appeal to girls and women. But girls respond to action just as powerfully as boys if the context is meaningful to them. *Pokémon* fans laughed as Misty's rage knocked Ash to the ground and jumped up in excitement as Ash won a savage battle against a superior opponent because he and his Pikachu had formed a profound personal bond. Cartoons, comics, video games, cartoony live-action like *Power Rangers* are all about exaggerations of emotions and situations to make them clearer and more powerful to children. Make-believe violence, in that sense, is a *cartoon* of conflict: a cartoon of anger, exasperation, loyalty, betrayal, and love. The violence in little girls' fantasies doesn't stand apart from or in opposition to the human relationships in those fantasies. It's a vivid, exciting, and sometimes wholly satisfying expression of the relationships.

Annette Roman, an editor at Viz Comics, said that she fell in love with the *Pokémon* projects she worked on after having generally had little enthusiasm for action comics: "Part of that was seeing how excited it made my nieces and the daughters of my friends, an excitement I'd never seen any pop-culture phenomenon inspire in so many girls before. Then, as I really began to let myself connect with it, I saw how much I would have benefited from a fantasy like this as a girl. This was a fantasy world that allowed girls to be *complete*. They didn't have to keep their anger and aggression in like good little girls, but they didn't have to act like little boys either. They could be cute, funny, loving, charming, and then be destructive little terrors too."

Significantly, both *Power Rangers* and *Pokémon* were originally Japanese creations. Even though Americans have spent far more time and energy in discussions of gender images in the media, we have been dismal at creating heroic figures for little girls. My experience in the comics and animation industries has been that creators of superheroes feel that male characters are the most living and legitimate, but that they are "supposed to" include strong females, and so they stitch female characters together from tired old archetypes and a few feminist clichés. Even George Lucas, who produced the most powerful children's symbols of the last several decades, was never able to create a female character who connected powerfully with children. A few women who grew up on *Star Wars* have told me that they tried to like Princess Leia, but her obnoxiousness and unbelievability wore them down; ultimately they found her interesting only in respect to her relationships with Luke and Han. The only real success was Wonder Woman, and she was created by a psychologist, Dr. William Maulton-Marston, who understood little girls' need for powerful symbols during the sex-role confusion of World War II.

Japanese culture stresses traditional sex roles to a much greater extent than modern American culture. At the same time, the Japanese have generally been far less worried about the social or ideological implications of children's entertainment; they have been more willing than Americans to let its content be dictated by children's tastes rather than adult concerns about what it "should" contain. Japanese culture has always been especially tolerant of fantasy elements, and its highest art forms and spiritual disciplines have been refreshingly free of literalism. Even the indigenous religion, Shinto, is founded upon what the mythologist Joseph Campbell lovingly described as "pure fairy tale stuff," like the legend of the sun goddess who hides in a cave and has to be tricked out by a noisy party thrown by her brother, which no modern worshipper feels a need to believe literally. Zen is all about play and suggestion, not doctrine. The "Floating World" school of classical Japanese art is an evocation of life as a dream. Perhaps living in close proximity in such a small area, constrained by powerful social codes, has taught the Japanese the value of an inner life. Americans, with our polyglot, mobile, conflictive society, are much more wary of others' thoughts and emotions.

Japanese children's entertainment provides more complex and all-inclusive fantasies than our own, and American children respond enthusiastically to it. Hollywood invented the giant-radioactive-monster-attacks-the-city genre with *The Beast from 20,000 Fathoms* in 1951, but its creations invariably ended with the adult-pleasing destruction of the monster by the police or military. Japanese producers followed the formula with the first *Godzilla* in 1954, but then they noticed what Hollywood failed or refused to see: kids loved the *monsters,* not the authorities. And not only Japanese kids: my son cried his eyes out when he first saw *Beast from 2000 Fathoms,* and for a year afterward he wouldn't watch another monster movie unless I promised him that the creature would survive at the end. By the beginning of the 1960s, Japanese monsters were becoming increasingly admirable, sympathetic, even lovable, and they always survived at the end. American producers kept killing their monsters until they ran the genre into the ground, but the Japanese created an internationally popular product that's still going strong today.

Speed Racer, Astro Boy, and *Kimba* did well on independent TV stations as American network children's programming abandoned physical action. More recently, *Power Rangers, Pokémon,* and *Dragon Ball Z* have seized American kids' imaginations with types of adventure and heroism that domestic productions aren't providing. The entertainment that appeals to girls' imaginations provides images of female power that speak to the complexity and scariness of gender roles in a time of social change. The male producers and video-game designers in Japan who created *Power Rangers* and *Pokémon* drew from their experiences of what female fans responded to in games and cartoons, and they created symbols that reveal a great deal about what girls worldwide are craving from their fantasy lives today.

Girls very much want personal power and to be equal participants in a world that includes both sexes. But they want to go on developing their identities as girls at the same time, which in grade school requires that they keep their separate girl culture intact. They may not have their life agendas mapped out yet, but in fantasy they know that they want to step into a world of power and equality but still bring with them the qualities that they've come to understand as feminine. One American industry that has been more responsive to those fantasies than action entertainment is the pop music business. It has produced some of the images of female power that are most compelling to girls today—and most unnerving to their parents.

When we last saw Emily, the girl who had finally talked her mother into letting her play with toy guns, she was in the second grade, putting down violent fantasies and deciding she wanted to be a veterinarian. Cynthia, her mother, had made peace with her gun fantasies, but she was also pleased to see them fading away. As she told me later, her daughter still played with boys fairly often, was still a physically adventurous kid, but was now working harder on building friendships with girls. She was, in general, pleased with her daughter's development and no longer worried much about her media interests or fantasy life. Then Emily discovered Britney Spears.

Nearly all of the girls in Emily's class were into Spears that year. Although Emily wasn't among the first to discover her, once she did, she seized upon the singer more aggressively than any of her friends. She initiated games: "Let's pretend that I'm Britney and you're her friends." "But I want to be Britney!" "So do I!" "Then we can all be

Britney. And some animals are caught in a fire at the zoo and we have to come save them." She wanted to dress like Britney—not the slinky Britney of the awards shows but the cool-teen Britney of the videos on Nickelodeon. She found friends who got to listen to Britney's songs and memorized all the lyrics before Cynthia could make up her mind about whether to allow the songs to be played in the house. She even had Britney dreams: "She came into my room and woke me up, then she carried me out through the window and took me to this huge house full of dogs and cats."

Cynthia found herself going through agonies even more intense than the guns had inspired. She didn't want her little girl being taught stereotypical gender roles by the media, she didn't want her being sexualized in grade school, she didn't want her growing up thinking that looking pretty and manipulating boys were a girl's only source of power. What did it mean that she was in love with Britney Spears, all of whose songs were about boys, whose entire image was built on exaggerated gender traits, and whose first hit had horrified parents with its title line, *"Hit me, baby, one more time"*?

When she told me about her anxieties I tended to agree. My sense of pop singers like Spears was that they were sex objects marketed to children who didn't know what they were buying into. Then I asked the question I've always asked in this research. Not, "What does this look like to my grown-up eyes?" but, "Why do they love what they love?" I talked to kids, including Emily, about Britney Spears and started watching her videos through the eyes of a little girl whose previous fantasies showed that she craved images of personal, physical power. And it made sense. Spears *was* presented as an object of prettiness and sexuality, her songs *were* all about winning over boys, but her most vivid actions were symbols of physical power.

Pop singers have always been symbols of power, merely by the fact that they command the microphone, the camera, and the attention of a crowd. Even Tiffany and Olivia Newton-John seemed powerful to girls of the late 1970s, and young women who now find them dreadfully bland took some inspiration from pretending to be them when they were much younger. As gender roles have evolved, as girls have come to crave more overt symbols of power, their tastes have created a market for a more aggressive, more confrontational style of pop performance. Britney Spears's trademark dance move was to raise her fist and pump her forearm in a sweeping line across her torso. She also thrust her fists at the air, she jumped, she stomped, she spun, and she kicked—a combination of stage dancing, gymnastics, and fight-scene moves that click with any kid's imagination as images of action and power. She also did pelvic thrusts, which unnerve parents with their unquestionable sexual implications but which are also extraordinarily powerful and liberating moves for anyone who can unlock his or her torso enough to do them. And whenever Spears kicked or punched or thrust, her fictional world responded dramatically. The music pumped, the background dancers went flying, the camera zoomed in, the crowd cheered.

Spears was as powerful a cartoon of individual physical action taking over reality and knocking the world into a new shape as *Power Rangers* or *Pokémon*. Even her much-maligned lyrics contained some exciting images of power. Their narratives may all have been about boys, but when little girls sang the refrains of "Crazy," "Stronger Than Yesterday," or "Oops I Did It Again," they celebrated acting up, toughening up, and strutting their power to shake up other people's lives. Even "(Hit Me Baby) One More Time" turned out to be a song about wanting *action*, a demand for a clear statement of affection from a boyfriend. As in card games, as in sports, the "hit" is a playful metaphor for quick, exciting satisfaction. To demand a "hit" is an act of assertiveness, not passivity. To hear it as an invitation to physical abuse is to hear our own fears instead of our children's reality.

Critics and parenting experts have warned of the messages little girls learn when they bop around like Britney Spears and win attention by doing so. They have a point: if the only approval and attention girls ever get is for acting like a pop star they may not find much reason to develop their other strengths. It's important to be conscious of the sexual and consumeristic imagery of entertainment and keep our conversations with children open to discussing them. But it's even more important to respect the power that girls feel when they thrust and jump and sing.

Emily had a lot of social information to process: she was a head-strong girl who liked boys' games, even as some of her best female friends were refusing to play with boys; she had no adult male figure in her home life at an age when she and her friends were becoming increasingly interested in male-female pairings; her single parent encouraged her gender-transcending behavior and expressed anxiety about socially coded femininity, even as the girls around her were expressing their femininity more and more rigidly. Emily wanted her power and her individuality, but she wanted to feel a full mastery of girlishness at the same time. Enter Britney Spears, every inch the living Barbie doll, but pumping her fists, strutting the stage, blasting out her pop-powered lyrics about hitting and strength, dominating videos full of leaping bodies and flashing explosions by the sheer force of her physical, sexual, cartoony presence.

I told Cynthia something I'd heard from another mother, Rachel, who resisted buying her daughter a Barbie doll in order to protect her from the messages about gender that Barbie embodied. The more she resisted, however, the more the little girl wanted it, and the more worried she became about *why* she couldn't have it—was it something wrong with *her?* "Finally," said Rachel, "I realized that my daughter needed my approval more than my protection." Barbie, Britney Spears, guns, Pokémon, they all come down to the same dilemma for parents: are these products teaching my children exaggerated gender traits and negative behavior, or are they allowing them to play with concerns that real life has already given them?

The woman who invented the Barbie doll in the 1950s, Ruth Handler, has said that watching her daughter play convinced her that girls were inevitably curious and worried about female adulthood and its obvious signifiers and that they craved ways to help them play through their feelings. "I realized that experimenting with the future from a safe distance through pretend play was a very important part of growing up," she said. "I believed it was important to a little girl's self-esteem to play with a doll that has breasts." Thus, it is not Barbie who inspires body-issue concerns in little girls, as so many of her critics have maintained, but the real bodies and the real behavior of the adult women in their lives. Barbie gives them a way to take power over those concerns. However, watching a little girl play with a Barbie, or imitate Britney Spears, does induce anxiety about what sort of person she might become. We think that taking away the symbol of her anxieties might dispel her anxieties, as well as our own, but it may leave her with no way to make herself feel powerful in the face of them.

Cynthia chose approval, too. "It's scary enough for Emily to negotiate all the power-tripping and politicking of the girls in the second grade without me telling her that it's dangerous for her to see if she can play the role of a girl successfully. When she's Britney she's high on herself. When I tell her not to be Britney she's worried or angry. I want her to know that she can be anything she wants to be. How do I do that unless I let her prove to herself that she can be Britney Spears, too, if she wants to be?"

Britney Spears CDs and videos entered Cynthia's house. Cynthia didn't like any of them, but she liked seeing Emily having fun, and she liked the conversations they sparked about which songs she liked and why. Then, just like the gun passion, the Britney passion began to cool. She and a friend got into their parents' Beatles CDs, which gratified Cynthia, although, she said, "less than it would have a while ago. I've been letting go of the idea that her fantasies are supposed to validate my values. I don't know that my fantasies at her age had anything to do with the values I ended up with, and I don't see why she should have the same fantasies to deal with her world that I had in a very different world."

Life for girls has changed drastically over the past few decades, and it goes on changing. They are shown more opportunities than ever by the adult world, but they also face higher expectations to perform academically, athletically, and personally. They no longer expect to marry and be supported while raising a family, but rather to work as hard as any man and still raise a family, often without much help. They know that adults are worried about their emotional health, self-esteem, eating habits, and the countless unnamed dangers that lie ahead in adolescence. Adults tell them that looks, popularity, trendiness, pleasing boys don't matter—but the real life of children's society shows them that they *do* matter, whether adults want them to or not.

And observing adult behavior shows them that such things matter far more to adults than they will admit. Then, when girls find entertainment that helps them play with those frightening realities, adults focus their anxiety on the entertainment instead of the reality and turn the girls' fantasies into another source of tension.

As girlhood changes, girls' fantasies are changing. As their fantasies change, the entertainment industry scrambles to create stories that will speak to them. Its motives may be nothing more than profit, but in trying to find stories and images that will sell, it discovers girls' most powerful yearnings. Right now, girls are yearning for more power, while trying to weave it, in many different ways, into a new kind of female self. We can help them with that if we let them follow their fantasies and play their games, while we also go on teaching them that they can be anything they want to be.

As the world changes, popular culture changes in ways that force us to reconsider our preconceptions. As the next chapter shows, we sometimes find that power fantasies don't always follow familiar forms and that fantasies of aggression don't always serve the emotional functions we expect.

6

Calming the Storm

$\mathcal{T}$here is a correlation between violent crime rates and intense entertainment violence, but the correlation is the opposite of what the usual hypotheses would suggest. The entertainment industry's bloodiest peaks come *after* real crime has come to dominate the news media and national conversation.

The late 1920s saw a rise in crime and the newspapers' preoccupation with bootlegger wars. By 1930, public opinion polls showed that "lawlessness" had become the leading concern of Americans. That same year, a low-budget entry in the minor genre of gangster movies, *Little Caesar,* became an unexpected box-office smash. Over the next few years, the public devoured a cycle of ever more brutal crime movies with an appetite that the Hollywood factory was barely able to meet. In 1931, the surprise success of *Dracula* and *Frankenstein* launched another violent, lurid genre. Many psychologists, politicians, and religious leaders blamed the movies for inspiring the lawlessness, but crime rates began dropping after 1933, when crime and horror movies were still going strong. Those movies began losing box-office steam only after the majority of Americans had begun calming down about crime.

Thirty years later, rising crime rates, assassinations, and the war in Vietnam were raising public fears of violence to unprecedented levels—and then intensely violent, horrific movies like *Bonnie and*

97

Clyde, The Wild Bunch, and *Rosemary's Baby* outstripped all box-office expectations. The crime genre had never been strong in TV ratings, but the viewing audience turned late-1960s shows like *Mannix* and *Hawaii 5-0* , full of fistfights, shoot-outs, and wild chases, into hits. During the 1970s, the nightly news and the public began to display a fascination with serial murderers and other bizarre violence. Gory horror movies rose steadily in popularity from 1976 *(The Texas Chainsaw Massacre)* to 1980 *(Friday the 13th),* when they became an established genre.

Beginning in the mid-1980s, the crack-gang wars inspired another wave of anxiety about violent crime. In 1989, gangster rap suddenly discovered a wide audience. From 1992 to 1995, Hollywood hit its bloodiest period ever, as everything from summer blockbusters to independents seemed to focus on murder and destruction: *T 2, Reservoir Dogs, Pulp Fiction, Natural Born Killers.* TV violence hit an alarming peak of popularity, from the chair-throwing of daytime talk shows to professional wrestling. Again, many people blamed the entertainment for causing the reality, but by the time violent entertainment reached its peak, real crime was decreasing. As opinion polls showed Americans worrying less about real violence, the popularity of violent movies and TV shows declined.

Other types of violent news can inspire similar audience responses. For each of the six weeks after the terrorist attacks of September 11, 2001, the top box-office movies had violent, and fairly gruesome, themes—an unusual circumstance for autumn. It's when people are most anxious about real violence that they most want to see it in make-believe.

We often hear that entertainment violence will make children more frightened of real violence, or numb them to its horror, or make them believe that the world is meaner that it is. In fact, *reality* can have those effects—especially the distorted version of reality shown to us by the commercial news media. Fantasy provides an antidote. It can help people take control of their fears and approach life's scarier aspects more realistically.

Few public incidents have had as strong an impact on young people as the school shootings of the late 1990s. For weeks, the TV news and adult conversations dwelled on the horror, the unpredictability, the commonplace locations of the shootings. Parents, teachers, and school administrators, especially after the Columbine High School shootings, reacted with a fearful vigilance that emphasized to every child the possibility of violence exploding in any classroom at any moment. For teenage boys, the knowledge that many adults suddenly saw them as potential killers added to their tensions. A lot of them wanted games that helped them turn their tensions into play. Shooter video games like *Doom, Quake,* and *Castle Wolfenstein,* with fantastical settings and opponents, had been popular before, but in the year after Columbine, games with more realistic settings and human opponents, like *Soldier of Fortune* and *Unreal Tournament,* began to take off.

I worked with a sixth-grader named Andrew whose parents were concerned about his sudden interest in violent movies, TV, and video games. He'd had little interest in violence until the spring of fifth grade—when the Columbine murders hit the news. For weeks the incident dominated the TV programs he watched and the conversations he heard. He thought about it a lot. He became intensely curious about the violent media that had been implicated in the murders, and he discovered that he liked it. Shooter video games and action movies filled his afternoons and weekends. His parents tried to restrict him to the most age-appropriate material, but in the summer before sixth grade, he discovered *Natural Born Killers* at a friend's house. He'd heard that movie named as a possible inspiration to more than one school shooting, and he was intent on seeing it. Over the span of a few weeks, he and his friend watched it again and again and again.

"That kind of, like, made it real," he said. "Then I got kind of used to it." I asked him what happened then. He shrugged. "Then I stopped thinking about it so much." He continued to enjoy violent movies and games fairly often, but the intensity of his interest and his need for repeated exposure diminished sharply. He and his friend started playing *Mario Tennis* again instead of watching *Natural Born Killers.* Andrew started hanging out with his old friends again. His anxious preoccupation about school shootings diminished.

Andrew had been oversensitized to violence and danger. Exposing himself repeatedly to video violence until he "got used to it" helped him to ease his sensitivity down to a more realistic level. When he "made it real," he was taking away some of the power it held over his imagination.

The adolescent psychiatrist Lynn Ponton has often seen young people containing their anxieties through entertainment. Their anxieties usually aren't as specific as Andrew's. If they feel generally troubled about social competition, they might watch *Ten Things I Hate About You* dozens of times; if they're angry or feel physically vulnerable, they might choose an action or horror movie. Whatever their worries, these young people find it soothing to immerse themselves in familiar or predictable portrayals of unreal people going through an exaggerated version of what troubles them. They don't usually return repeatedly to stories that are very believable or emotionally affecting. They may be powerfully moved by those stories, but to soothe their anxieties, they usually need their entertainment to be cartoony, intense, and unreal.

This can be problematic, warned Ponton. Young people whose conflicts are too serious and who don't have any other help resolving them can fall into habitual media use that keeps them spinning in their anxieties without alleviating them. Their entertainment may not exacerbate their problems, but it can hold them trapped. For most young people, however, entertainment can be a great help in easing the tensions of real life.

Younger children were shaken by Columbine, too, and over the subsequent months, hard-hitting action cartoons—*Pokémon, Dragon Ball Z, Digimon, Monster Rancher*—soared to an unprecedented height of popularity. *Pokémon* had begun its rise before Columbine and, as I noted earlier, owed its success to a whole complex of factors. But in writing *Pokémon* material, playing with my son as he went through his own Poké-obsession, and running my workshops through the peak of the phenomenon, I sensed a deep connection between children's moods and the sudden urgency of the fad. Kids were jittery that spring. Even those who'd been sheltered from the details knew that something terrible had happened at a school. I'd never seen so much explosive, nervous energy in classrooms. The stories they wrote for me were more violent than usual. And right then, *Pokémon* vaulted unexpectedly out of cultish popularity among Game Boy players and card collectors and into the imaginations of nearly every kid in America. Violence in *Pokémon* was loud, flashy, angry, repetitive, but it was also bloodless, no one died, and it always ended happily. It centered on kids who sometimes seemed out of their league against older opponents but who stood up to danger and always came through unscathed. Suddenly millions of kids wanted to immerse themselves in that world—and they wanted it with a frantic need that few kid crazes had ever inspired.

Pokémon served many needs, but I believe that those safe, endlessly repeated trips into fantasy violence played a role in helping a nation of anxious children work through their fears. And I believe that's one reason they were able to drop the fad so suddenly, once they, and their parents, relaxed a bit and moved on.

These are some of the essential functions of play. It "explodes" tensions through emotional arousal and make-believe aggression. It provides correctives, happy endings, that help children to believe that what frightens them can be overcome. It helps them navigate their concerns through structures and rules that they can learn and predict and so feel they've mastered. It allows them to manipulate troubling ideas until those ideas become familiar and lose their power. Entertainment performs those same functions when young people build it into their fantasies or work it into their social lives or play with it as a video game.

Children crave fantasy violence for many reasons, but one reason they so often crave it raw, loud, and angry is that they need it to be strong enough to match and master their anxiety and anger. Entertainment violence has become far more intense and explicitly gory over the past forty years because the reality with which we confront young people has become so much more intensely and explicitly violent. What television news programs are willing to show, what parents are willing to discuss within earshot of their children, gives young people thoughts and images to grapple with that demand fantasy images just as potent. Being shocked by an image within the safe

confines of fantasy can help them learn not to be so shocked in reality. That's one of the reasons older kids teach themselves and each
other that the most hideous gore is "cool." Thoughts of real brutality
trouble them; by calming themselves down in the face of an imaginary version of it, they can take more control of those thoughts.

Correlative studies on media effects tend to support this, although
the results have often been misinterpreted, and many vital questions
have never been asked. In addition to asserting that viewing entertainment violence leads to real violence, the Joint Statement on the
Impact of Entertainment Violence on Children issued in July 2000
stated, "Entertainment violence feeds a perception that the world is a
violent and mean place . . . [and] increases fear of becoming a victim
of violence, with a resultant increase in self-protective behaviors and
a mistrust of others." Those words are taken almost verbatim from
the work of George Gerbner, who focused attention on this "victim
effect," or what other psychologists have called the "mean world syndrome," by comparing people's stated perceptions of crime rates with
the amount of television they watched: people who watched more
television tended to believe that crime rates were higher than they
were in reality.

Subsequent studies have backed up some of Gerbner's findings, but
with significantly different implications. Other researchers have
pointed out that he failed to take socioeconomic and other demographic factors into account. The people who watch the most TV, on
average, are poor people, and among poor people the heaviest watchers are black people. Elderly people watch more than young adults.
Since poor people are more likely to live in high-crime neighborhoods, and poor black people are more likely to live in neighborhoods with the highest rates of crime, and elderly people have reason
to feel especially vulnerable, those groups' higher-than-average concern about crime is reflective not of television's unrealistic view of a
"mean world" but of a *realistic* concern about the environments they
live in. A more significant flaw of the Gerbner studies is that they
failed to characterize the subjects' viewing habits. Were these people
watching crime shows, soap operas, sitcoms, cartoons, or the evening
news? This is a common problem in studies of "media violence";

they often don't distinguish between fictional entertainment and television's version of "reality." The lurid, alarmist, "if it bleeds it leads" commercial news—presented as reality, and usually *local* reality—has the power to make people think that the world is far meaner than it is. Entertainment's power is the opposite. More detailed studies in the wake of Gerbner's have shown that people who worry about crime do tend to be fond of police and detective shows. But those shows always end with virtue triumphant and the heroes safe, a soothing counterpoint to the worldview promoted by the news.

If young people grew up in a society less preoccupied with violence and horror, they might crave less entertainment gore. They might be better off, too. But it's unreasonable to ask them to be satisfied with make-believe that is more sanitized than their reality. Taking away the entertainment that enables them to grapple with reality won't make their reality better but may only leave them more defenseless against it.

There's no question that many people are disturbed by violence, both real and fictional. Children under the ages of seven or eight, who are still working through the distinction between fantasy and reality, can find realistic images of negative emotion and powerful evocations of suspense painful. Older children and adults who are especially sensitive to others' pain or squeamish about gore may find their anxieties more heightened than relieved by a Hollywood image. The evidence shows, however, that even the youngest children generally try to avoid looking at what disturbs them; when a troubling video is playing on a TV in the same room, a preschooler will typically turn away or distract himself with a toy. We need to be sensitive about exposing children to powerful material that they haven't been prepared for or haven't shown an interest in. At the same time, we need to be sensitive to the fact that when they *want* to see entertainment that echoes their anxieties, then it's probably bringing them some comfort. And often when they are confronted by the harshest realities, they need the harshest fantasies to help them through it.

Mary Cotter is a former criminal-justice researcher for the Soros Foundation and now an administrator with God's Love We Deliver, a charity serving AIDS sufferers in New York. She grew up in a working-class part of the Bronx and entered adolescence in the early 1970s at the peak of New York's crime wave and the nadir of its economic and civic despair. The news was full of bloodshed, terror, and apocalyptic fears. Then, in her fourteenth summer, the Son of Sam killings terrorized the city. She was haunted for years by fears of insane, random violence.

At fifteen Mary suffered a terrible personal blow: her father died suddenly. Her mother was barely able to keep herself together, and Mary spent her adolescence trying to take care of herself, vulnerable and angry, in a very mean world. Among the things she found to help her through it were angry punk music, underground comic books—and slasher movies.

Sadistically gory horror movies had been around since the early 1960s, but they'd been far from the entertainment mainstream, mostly confined to a small audience of low-income males, until the mid-1970s, when they began to find an audience among teenagers and young adults of both sexes and every class. Hollywood studios started producing and distributing them. Social commentators, critics, and parents were appalled; the movies were misogynistic, prurient, and very possibly incitements to violence against women. "I was savvy enough to be aware of those themes in the movies," said Cotter, "and I remember being uncomfortable with them. But the images were so powerful that I was willing to put up with it. It was like the worst thing I imagined, and I could see it and feel it over and over again. Every time it would inflame all my fears while it was going on, but then I'd come down from it and be a little less troubled by it."

When *Friday the 13th* came out in 1980, with its tough, smart heroine who defeats the killer at the end, Cotter was thrilled. "Now I had a heroine I could bond with and root for, but I still had the gore to take me through those visceral feelings." Millions of other members of her generation seemed to feel the same; *Friday* became the breakthrough hit of the slasher genre and spawned a gore industry that prospered through the 1980s. "The heroine went through all my worst nightmares and survived. It was such a *release!* Seeing it with friends made it even more powerful—more people to share the fears with, more of a release."

Cotter says that the popular culture she immersed herself in during adolescence changed the course of her life. "It may not have been the biggest piece, but it was a piece in calming down my fears and anger enough that I could *think* about them, which in turn made it more possible for me to empathize with and understand people in pain and turmoil rather than just reacting to them from my own fears. You can never say exactly why you ended up where you did, but I have no doubt that entertainment, *violent* entertainment, played some role in leading me into a career working with people who have been profoundly affected by violence and trauma."

Like the boy named Andrew, Mary Cotter had been oversensitized to violence. That made it harder for her to function in the world and connect to other people. By desensitizing herself somewhat through entertainment, she helped herself open up and grow.

Desensitization has become a scary word. The Joint Statement on the Impact of Entertainment Violence on Children asserted, "Viewing violence can lead to emotional desensitization toward violence in real life. It can decrease the likelihood that one will take action on behalf of a victim when violence occurs." There are extreme forms of desensitization that are dangerous for individuals and society. "I've worked with children from neighborhoods in which violence is so common that they grow up seeing body bags as just part of their surroundings," said Lynn Ponton. "They'll talk about going down and playing by the body bags as if they were the sandbox. It will be hard for those children even to conceive a world without violence." However, there is no real-world evidence, either anecdotal or scientific, to link the viewing of media violence of any sort to indifference in the face of real violence.

As with many stubborn preconceptions, the media-desensitization hypothesis began as an effort to make sense of a real horror. In 1964, in a placid lower-middle-class neighborhood in New York, a young woman named Kitty Genovese was stabbed to death as her neighbors ignored her cries for help. Thirty-eight people listened to her screaming for more than half an hour before any of them did so much as call the police. It was an appalling and incomprehensible incident that made every concerned citizen wonder what we were becoming and why. Some psychologists and sociologists argued that we were becoming desensitized to violence and the sufferings of others and that the relatively new medium of television must be at least partly to blame.

Time has debunked the idea. The Genovese incident wasn't a symptom of a trend but a terrible fluke. After decades of violent media, good samaritanism and everyday heroism haven't declined. Thousands of images of explosions and death did not dull anyone's horror at the realities of September 11, 2001. A thirteen-year-old boy in one of my workshops said the opposite was true for him: "I kept seeing the video of the plane hitting the tower, and it looked like something out of a video game or a movie. And I'm thinking, I've seen this millions of times, only now it's *real*. And looking like something that's supposed to be fun or exciting just made it *worse*."

Later studies of the Genovese case found that her neighbors were not at all desensitized to violence. In fact, they were mostly very nervous about crime, at least partly because of the tremendous attention that the news media were giving to New York's rising crime rate. In their nervousness, they "didn't want to get involved" and convinced themselves that nothing terrible was really happening or that someone else must surely have taken care of it. What Kitty Genovese needed was not more sensitized neighbors but calmer and more confident ones. The people who are best able to act in the face of violence are those who are least horrified by it. Police officers wouldn't be as effective if they were as sensitive to violence as the rest of us. A certain desensitization to gore makes a better surgeon. An ability to dissociate a bit from pain makes a better social worker.

Although the reasons for believing in the idea of media desensitization have fallen away, the fear has continued to haunt us. Several researchers have attempted to find the cause of the "bystander effect" in video violence. The most widely cited desensitization experiments are those of Drs. Ronald Drabman, Margaret Thomas, Fred Molitor, and Kenneth Hirsch. In the most recent of these, by Molitor and Hirsch in 1988, two groups of ten-year-olds were put in front of video monitors showing kindergartners playing and were told to call a grown-up if the little kids began misbehaving. The ten-year-olds who had just watched a fight scene from *The Karate Kid* tended to wait a little longer after the kindergartners started snatching toys from each other before calling an adult than those who had watched scenes from the Olympics instead.

It's easy to interpret their results as evidence that violent media numbs children's desire to help others. When we hear a researcher report a "delay in seeking adult intervention," especially when we've been told that we're about to hear evidence of the desensitization hypothesis, we immediately visualize children sitting passively and uncaring as something bad unfolds before them—a frightening fore-shadowing of the bystander effect. If we apply some empathy and sensible values to their behavior, however, we'll see that the children may have been manifesting a much healthier set of emotions.

The children who had watched the karate scene were slightly slower at calling in the adults, but they by no means waited until any real danger was imminent to the kindergartners in their charge. In fact, no such dangers were *ever* imminent, because the children they were "supervising" were actually appearing in a staged videotape in which nothing but very safe misbehaviors occurred. As anyone who has refereed a play date can attest, the child who comes running to the nearest adult at the first instigation, yelling, "Make him quit it!" is usually not the most socially conscious, the most caring, or the bravest child but the most nervous. The researchers made no effort to understand the motivations of any of the children in calling for adult help when they did. Nor did they question for a moment that calling for adult intervention at the first sign of aggression might not have been the wisest course. Based on what the children saw on their monitors, I'd say the subjects who waited longer displayed better parenting skills.

It's possible, as many analysts of the data have pointed out, that the children who waited longer had experienced a catharsis and so felt less anxious and more trusting. It's possible that they were *over*sensitized by the stressful laboratory environment, and so a bit of "positive desensitization" was just what they needed. From my own experiences with both kids and entertainment I would add another possibility. Follow-up interviews of the subjects revealed that of the children who were shown the *Karate Kid* film clip, every last one had already seen the movie, some of them as many as ten times. To them, the clip they watched wasn't simply a context-free image of punches and kicks, as it would have seemed to the researchers, but a reminder of a story that the kids knew well—a story about a boy who learns to master aggression, take command of his own life, and defeat the bad guys through his own resources rather than running for help.

What children seek in images of entertainment isn't desensitization to real suffering but images of violence rendered safe and unreal. Not only has no evidence ever convincingly linked entertainment violence to indifference to real violence, but observations of children suggest that it usually doesn't even numb them to more humanly affecting entertainment. When they are drawn to sympathetic or believable portrayals of human suffering, they typically want to feel the feelings the stories evoke, and they don't usually watch them repeatedly. Young people may like their violence high-impact and gory, but they also like it bigger than life and well separated from emotional reality.

Diane Stern, a family therapist with two sons, told me about her older boy, Sam. He had loved action entertainment since his preschool days: *Power Rangers*, then James Bond, then martial arts video games, whatever had fights and explosions. As he entered middle school, he began to sample more grown-up entertainment: *The Matrix*, rap music, shooter games, Stephen King novels. He loved all of it.

One evening, though, Sam tried to watch the movie *Traffic* with his parents. He had long ago ceased to be troubled by any typical Hollywood bloodshed and mayhem. But here was a scene of a drug dealer being tortured, physically and psychologically, by a rival. He was a loathsome character, utterly unsympathetic, but he was naked, trapped, vulnerable, and suffering. "Mom, I can't watch this," said Sam, and he left the room to play one of his violent computer games. When she asked him about it, Sam said it was "too real." He loved to watch bad guys being blown up by James Bond, and when Diane would express her queasiness he'd respond, "Mom, he's a bad guy! He's *there* to get killed!" But he couldn't stand seeing even a "bad guy" suffer in a realistic, human way.

We want our children to be sensitive to violence. It's reassuring that a boy like Sam can still be appalled by cruelty in a movie. We might wish that he would react to all violence that way, that he wouldn't compartmentalize a human character as someone who is "*there* to get killed." We're afraid that images of violence will make real violence *less* real to him. But we also don't want our children to be crippled by fear of violence But make our children's environments as safe from violence as we can, and so it's disturbing when images of violence come pouring into their living rooms and bedrooms through television and video games. When a boy like Andrew prefers the horrors of *Natural Born Killers* to the safe lawns of his neighborhood, we're afraid it's making violence *too* real to him.

Entertainment violence, however, can help children make sense of that distinction between the real and the unreal. In calming children's fears about violence and making them more comfortable with the images of violence that inevitably enter their minds, entertainment violence can help them see what's just a fear and what really needs to be dealt with.

I was able to see this process at work in a context very different from those I usually experience when I was invited to participate in a global conference on youth and media in conjunction with the CineMagic International Film Festival in Belfast. Northern Ireland was quite a place to talk about violence: the cease-fire that had ended thirty years of civil war in the region was still in place then, but shaky. Riots had erupted just a few months before between Protestant youths from the Shankill neighborhood and Catholic youths from the Falls Road area. I ran a seminar with Declan Croghan, a youth worker and writer for the BBC, on filmmaking and other forms of storytelling as ways for disadvantaged young people to tell their own stories and draw some notice from the adult world. There were teenagers from CineMagic's Belfast Outreach program there, including some boys who'd been caught up in the summer's riots and been dismissed as hoods by their neighbors. With the program's help, they'd regained some community respect, and self-respect, by making a rap CD and a pair of videos about their experiences.

In the audience was a young man named Richard. He stood out from the crowd: skinny, quiet, and conservatively dressed, grave beyond his nineteen or twenty years. He asked some very earnest questions about developing programs through youth centers that would use the media to bring Catholic and Protestant teens together. It turned out that he helped run a youth center for the Society of Friends in Shankill, where the cease-fire was less welcomed than resented, where twenty-foot "peace walls" still stood between Catholic and Protestant blocks, where murals of hooded assassins with machine guns covered the walls of the local Kentucky Fried Chicken. Richard's goal was to help poor, angry teenagers see the benefits of peace; his competitors were paramilitary gangs that wooed those boys daily with promises of guns and uniforms and the license to kill. Thugs of the Ulster Volunteer Army and the Ulster Defense Force would troop through his youth center in full regalia, provoking the young men who went there to play darts and talk, testing the courage of the volunteer staff. But Richard's faith in God and the Quaker creed kept him going to the center and opening its doors every day.

After the seminar I saw him heading into the multimedia arena of the conference center, where computers were available to all the young attendees. I hurried to catch up. I praised him for his work, told him about my own family's involvement with the Civil Rights Movement in Mississippi and the fitful, incomplete, but heartening progress Americans have made in our own sectarian disputes. He was intent on the computers around him, but as he chose one and began to operate it, he talked to me about Belfast and its struggles and his obligation as a Christian to continue the good work whether he could see an end in sight or not. As he talked, I suddenly became aware of the computer game he was playing. It was *Quake 3*, the latest version of one of the most popular first-person shooter games of the 1990s.

The mere presence of the game surprised me. No American conference on children, dominated by youth workers and educators, would have made bloody video games available to its young attendees. But in Belfast, where violence is a much more immediate reality than it is for most Americans and a more realistic view of its causes prevails, a piece of make-believe violence wasn't so alarming. I was even more surprised, however, by the fact that a pacifist activist chose that game from among many less violent alternatives.

Richard was talking about a man involved in his mission who'd been "butchered by terrorists," who struggled to embrace the Christian ethos of forgiveness even as his gut and memories told him to hate his attackers. As he talked his fingers played over the controls so that his game-self sneaked around corners, surveyed for enemies, and then—BAM BAM BAM—blew them apart.

"You're good at this game," I said.

"I've played it since I was a kid," he said.

I watched him a minute (BAM BAM SPLAT). Then I had to ask. "You don't see any conflict between this and your pacifist beliefs?"

"It's just a game," he said. For a second he wasn't with me as he popped out of a corridor and found himself face to face with two monstrous opponents at once. I resisted making a joke about "a *Quake*-playing Quaker" and instead asked him how he felt when he played it. He killed both foes with a deft stutter of fingers on the buttons and said, "It's exciting. I'm on guard. But I'm in control."

I couldn't quite handle the mingling of the violent imagery on screen with the stories of butchery and rage I'd been listening to, so I turned away from the screen and looked at him. I told him I was researching the many ways young people use violent stories and games.

"Games are good," he said, still intent on the screen. "They give kids something to do with their energies." Then he added, "I'd like to get one of these for the center. It'd give a lot more kids a reason to come."

"Would you use *Quake*?" I asked. "There are less violent games, too."

Richard finally looked at me. Impatiently. Almost disdainfully. He said, "They wouldn't play *those*."

People want to play with what matters to them, what excites or fascinates or scares them. That may be something they've imagined, something they've seen on TV, or something they've lived. For Richard, playing *Quake* was a power fantasy, but the power was to remain calm in a frightening reality. When he came out of the fantasy of the game into his difficult reality, he would feel refreshed for the struggle. He wanted the angry, frightened boys at his youth center to have the same fantasy world in which they could kill their own monsters. We aren't made better people by fear and worry. We're made better by courage, confidence, and calm. The more realistically and courageously we can face violence and suffering, the more effective we will be against them.

In order for children to use their fantasy play to master their fears, they must be able to view it fully as fantasy. To help them differentiate between fantasy and reality sometimes requires that we learn a little about the difference ourselves.

7

Fantasy and Reality

$\mathcal{W}$hen Harrison was very little, we took him to the circus, and he wanted one of those light-up swords they sell there," Gina Weinberg related. "We said no, but he really wanted it. And he wanted to know *why* he couldn't have it. It was the first time Allen and I had encountered this situation, but we'd been discussing how we would respond to it since before he was born. We said, 'Because swords are for hurting people, and we're afraid that playing with one will teach you to *really* hurt people.'"

Gina was a public school teacher before she quit to become a full-time mother. In both roles she always strove to be as thoughtful and conscientious as she could be. She described herself and her husband as "like any new parents, insecure and not having a clue, relying on what society says is the right way to raise a child. And every message I was getting from society and the experts was that violent play and violent media would teach children to be violent. So our rule was no swords, no guns, no TV shows or cartoons that showed anyone hurting anyone else."

They also feared that aggressive play would exacerbate Harrison's trouble in modulating his anger. He felt emotions very strongly and tended to feel almost every negative emotion—sadness, fear, embarrassment—as anger. He'd yell, throw things, slam doors. Gina and Allen could see that Harrison was troubled by his own inability to control his impulses. He enjoyed helping enforce the no-violence rule at first. Gina would take him shopping for Lego sets and he'd say, "Wait, mom! We can't get this one! You see that little knight in the back? He's got a sword!" Denying his own desire for toy weapons seemed to give him a feeling of strength.

The situation changed as Harrison's little brother, Joseph, grew older. By the time Joseph was three, when Harrison was six, he was displaying a passion for swords. "I don't even know where he got the idea!" Gina told me. "Suddenly everything he touched became a sword!" At first she tried taking them away from him, but there would always be another toy broom or pencil to turn into a weapon. She and her husband started calling them "the long things" ("heaven forbid we should call them 'swords'") and telling Joseph that he could play with them only if he used them like a magic wand. He tried, but the "long things" kept turning back into swords. "Finally," Gina said, "I realized that this little guy *needed* to have sword fights. I couldn't articulate why. But as a mother I could just see that he *needed* them."

Soon after Gina and Allen relaxed the sword rule, the Columbine shooting occurred. Gina felt bombarded by the news media and other parents with the message that those two boys had been turned into killers by video games and movies. Harrison's school teacher felt that violent play led to violent reality; not only did she forbid combat-related toys of any kind, but whenever a child acted out aggressively she'd draw the parents aside and ask what he was being allowed to watch or play with at home. Gina wondered if she was making a terrible mistake by allowing toy weapons. Allen disagreed. He'd had a typical sixties boyhood, loved toy guns and war movies, but had grown up to be a pacifist. "I told him what I was hearing all around me," Gina said, "that the world is more violent now, media violence is worse now, and so all this stuff is riskier."

By that time, I had encountered Harrison's imagination myself. He was in the same kindergarten class as my son, and was clearly one of the most boisterous and imaginative kids in the class. I ran a comic strip workshop in the classroom, and of all the stories, many of them filled with action and combat, his stood out among the rest for its joyful, explosive, fantastical violence. His protagonist was a fire-bellied toad, being pursued by a gang of "froggie killers," who jumped through a series of deadly traps outfitted with whirling knives and hammers to squash his opponents flat. As he walked me through the huge, colorful images of flashing blades and flattened bad guys, his face was split in a huge grin, he glowed with excitement over his comical mayhem—but he checked my reaction a lot, too, more often and more intently than most of the kids. The more I liked it, the more he glowed.

I made a point of keeping tabs on Harrison's imaginings. Later I learned that some of them had become the bases for the class's favorite recess games; the kids, both boys and girls, would divide into teams of "froggies" and "froggie killers" and run around having ferocious wars. Under slightly altered forms, like the "nature savers" versus the "nature killers," those games continued even into the second grade. His character "Superfrog" became a classroom legend as he squashed, devoured, and burned up villains to "keep the classroom safe." Outside the house, Harrison consistently generated his peer group's most thrilling, and happiest, fantasies of bloodshed, combat, and superheroism.

Inside the house, meanwhile, Harrison and Joseph were increasing the pressure on their parents to make a decision about violent play. Harrison's difficulty with anger became more complex. As he became more self-aware, his anxiety over his inability to control his reactions intensified. He began swinging to the opposite extreme and behaving regressively. If he was disappointed, the only way he could keep himself from going to excessive anger was to pretend to be a baby and make cutesy crying noises. His parents tried to help him find a middle ground between the extremes, but it was difficult.

Joseph was another intense kid, but he handled his anger better than his brother had at the same age. "We noticed that both of them did better when they played together," Gina told me, "and they usually did best when the play was about some sort of power or fight fantasy. The more we saw that working, the more we relaxed our rules. We even bought this little toy that flings foam darts—as close to a real gun as I could allow myself."

Then Allen started sharing his love of military vehicles and equipment with Harrison. Gina asked him, "Don't you think that might glorify war for him, or make him want to join the military someday?" Allen just laughed. "Gina, are you nuts? Trust me. I've loved this stuff my whole life. Nothing *ever* made me want to join the military. Not for an *instant.*"

Next he started playing a police game with the kids. Harrison loved arresting and handcuffing Allen. "That's when the lights started to go on for me," said Gina. "All these games made him feel *powerful.* We're so afraid of kids getting out of control, or going in some direction that we can't control, that we forget how little control they have. Harrison feels like he can't control his own emotional reactions, he can't control his brother or the anger that his brother brings up in him, he can't *really* control his own parents, or household, or life. Of course he needs to feel powerful!"

By the time Harrison reached the second grade, Gina wanted to lift all her restrictions against make-believe violence, but she still felt afraid. She decided to consult a psychologist: Eric Stein, a therapist who works with both children and adults and has a particular interest in play and fantasy. Gina discovered to her surprise that he also let his young clients play with toy guns in his office. She asked him what she might be teaching her children by allowing them to play at violence.

His answer was very simple, she said, but it was a revelation. He said that one of the biggest challenges children face is distinguishing between fantasy and reality. One of our most important tasks as adults is to help them make that distinction. The way to do that is to let them *have* their fantasies.

"All of a sudden," said Gina, "it hit me that all this time *I* had been confusing fantasy and reality! This is a little boy with a plastic sword, and I'm telling him, 'This might make you into a violent person.' Think how confusing that must be when you're little. Instead of hearing a parent say, that's a toy, that's fantasy, there's no *real* danger in it, *you* have complete power over it, he's hearing you say, that scares me, that's more powerful than you are, that's going to turn *you* into a killer!"

Gina told me that she wants her sons to understand that they can imagine anything, pretend anything, want anything. They can be as mad at someone in their minds as they want, pretend they're shooting them, squashing them with a steam roller, anything. They just shouldn't *do* it. "Teaching them the difference between *thinking* and *doing* is my main job, and if my fears send the message that what they play or see on some TV show is equivalent to *real* violence, that just completely blows it out of the water." She caught herself and laughed. "Blows it out of the water. Is that a violent image or *what?*"

This is the essence of helping children make sense of violent entertainment, toys, and games: differentiating between what they mean to the children and what they mean to us. We have to let them have fantasy *as* fantasy, while teaching them about reality. We also have to see our own fantasies *as* fantasies, our own fears simply *as* fears, and distinguish them clearly from the reality of our children's relationship with violence.

Gina still limits the amount of television her boys watch, but more because of the limitations of the medium, not its violent content. She still keeps their entertainment to what she considers age-appropriate levels, and she tries not to let their play get so wild that anyone is hurt. But she leaves the rest up to their own tastes and fantasies. Harrison still has some trouble modulating his emotions, but now he far more often finds that middle ground that his parents hoped he would.

"The change I see," Gina said, "is that when he's playing policeman or soldier now, or when he's showing me his drawings of Superfrog being strafed by an F-16 or whatever, I see a Harrison that I never saw enough of before. He's an *eight-year-old!* Just a happy, confident, playful boy who isn't afraid of his own feelings—like he should be. I can see the worry about whether he can handle his impulses lifting from him. And I can see that that in itself gives him more power over them."

This is only one story. But what Gina has revealed reflects the problem that our society has in dealing with issues of violence in a realistic way. Our own worries about the effect of make-believe violence reinforce the difficulty our children have in separating reality from fantasy. There are other stories, more painful to hear.

"Violence in our house was a huge no-no," Kristin Kinkel said in an interview. She described how her parents, two high school teachers in a small Oregon town, tried to do what most enlightened parents thought was right in the early 1980s: they forbade their children from watching any sort of action shows on TV, playing with any toy weapons, or indulging in any play fighting. That wasn't a hard rule for Kristin to follow, but it was harder for her younger brother, Kipland. "He had been interested in guns from as far as I can remember," she said, "from a little, little boy. And he was not allowed to have soldiers. He was not allowed to have any toy that had any kind of violent anything." That would become a running conflict in the household.

Every report of Kip Kinkel's upbringing has stressed that growing conflict with his parents. His older sister was an academic whiz and a natural athlete who had no behavior problems. Kip, dyslexic, less well coordinated, inclined to be disruptive when he wanted attention, soon became the "problem kid" of the family. Their dad, Bill, has been consistently described as genuinely concerned but authoritarian, competitive, and appearance conscious, with a great deal of his own self-image invested in Kip's success. He wasn't good at accepting his children's foibles or skilled at give-and-take. He reportedly never had a complaint about his first child, but with his second he fell into a pattern of pressure, criticism, and conflict. Kip's mother tried to act as a conciliator, but with little effectiveness, leaving Kip to feel at the mercy of his father. Stories of his childhood emphasize his tremendous efforts to please and his powerlessness to change himself or win his father's approval. Everyone who knew Kip has agreed that he was an angry kid, with legitimate reason, but that his anger wasn't received well at home. He had no way to express or experiment with that anger until middle school, when he fell in with some tough kids and started on an escalating path of delinquency.

Kip went on the Internet and discovered instructions for building explosives. Millions of kids look for forbidden knowledge on the Internet and play with it in fantasy, but for Kip it wasn't enough just to read and pretend. His angry fantasies had become part of a real conflict at home. He'd been taught to see those fantasies as a real problem. He made real bombs and started setting them off in the woods. Then he started studying guns and hounding his parents to buy one for him. He wouldn't let up, believing perhaps that the only relief for his anger lay in the real power of a deadly weapon. His parents were troubled enough to send him to a psychologist. The psychologist's report described Kip's rage and included a quote from the boy that showed how damned he felt in his father's eyes: "My mom thinks I'm a good kid with bad habits. My dad thinks I'm a bad kid with bad habits."

Fantasy and reality had become dangerously blurred for the Kinkels. Not only had Kip reached his teens unable to think of any way to express his rage except through the use of real weapons, but his father was apparently unable to separate his son's feelings and fantasies from a judgment of his son as a whole. Neither of them was able to say, "These are my thoughts, and I can control them." Everything was real. "I have to have a gun." "My son is bad." Their emotional conflict was evolving into a symbolic battle over bombs and guns that had little to do with the real roots of their conflict.

The psychologist suggested that Kip and his dad buy a real pistol and take a gun safety course together. It would be a chance to create a safe, shared reality in which they might be able to get outside their rage and learn to communicate better. They did so, and it seemed to work. Kip's behavior improved, his mother expressed optimism, and the psychologist suggested that Kip could terminate therapy. But the plan somehow broke down. Bill stopped practicing marksmanship with Kip. He let Kip keep the gun, though. He began buying more guns for him, increasingly powerful guns, but spent less and less time with him. Afterward, acquaintances described Bill as saying he'd "given up" on his son. Sometimes he justified the weapons purchases as the only way to contain his son's obsession. He behaved like a man who had fled into a fantasy, one in which Kip's emotional needs would take care of themselves, so that he didn't have to tangle with a terrifying reality.

Kip, meanwhile, pushed his fantasies closer and closer to reality. The news was full of school shootings. That reality—presented luridly and made more sensational than it should have been by the news media—connected powerfully with his fantasies of rage and revenge. He talked about how *he* would perpetrate a school shooting. He wrote murderously angry stories for class assignments. No one talked to him about any of it. He put the lyrics to a Marilyn Manson song on his wall, which asserted that there could be "no salvation." His sister reported that it was unlikely that anyone at home ever asked him why those words meant so much to him. Finally Kip was caught buying an illegal handgun at school. He was arrested and expelled from high school. His father showed up at the jail to take him home, ashamed and enraged. Kip had finally turned his fantasies into a very clear-cut reality.

No one knows exactly what happened next, but Kristin Kinkel has speculated that her father and brother must have had a furious argument and that Kip's obsession with guns must have been the focus. Whatever was said, Kip responded by shooting his father in the head. When his mother came home, he shot her. Then he went back to his school and started shooting wildly at classmates until another boy wrestled him down. As soon as he dropped the gun, Kip said to him, "Kill me now."

The story of Kipland Kinkel is obviously exceptional. Millions of kids are kept from violent media and play. Many of them, surely, must also have hostile relationships with a parent and don't receive enough help with their anger. But they don't shoot anyone. Some of the other kids who have acted out their anger in rampage shootings were kept from violent media and play early on; others were not. Some, like the boys who did the shooting at Columbine, were given messages by their families or schools that their interest in violent entertainment was scary or sick, others were not.

But Kip Kinkel's story dramatizes, in its most horrible form, the cost of investing fantasies with too much reality. It seems likely that anyone who shoots other people as a way of expressing obsessive rage has somewhere along the way failed to grasp the difference between reality and fantasy. We all have at least flashes of thought about destroying someone who has made us suffer, but most of us can take those thoughts out of fantasy and view them in the light of reality, where we can see that acting on them would make everything worse and not better. Not everyone learns that skill.

Dr. Helen Smith, a forensic psychologist who has evaluated thousands of violent teenagers, noted that most young people who turn to violence are poor and act from utilitarian motives involving money, drugs, or turf. But those who act out of an obsessive rage almost always have trouble putting their thoughts and feelings in perspective. "They tend to feel powerless, much more powerless than is realistic, so they'll reach for the first thing that they expect to make them powerful. Or their self-esteem is inflated but very fragile, so they'll take any attack on that as being a real threat. They perceive things incorrectly but haven't learned to see their own perceptions *as* perceptions. They confuse their own emotional reactions with reality. It's very much a problem of distinguishing reality from fantasy."

According to Dr. Smith, part of the trouble is due to a lack of problem-solving and critical-thinking instruction in childhood. Another part is related to our general fear of violence. "People are always asking me why our society is so violent, but in some ways I don't think it's violent *enough*. These kids don't grow up understanding their own aggression. Teachers and parents say, sit still, be nice, cooperate, and they don't give kids any opportunity to play with the aggressive feelings that come up for them. Dads are afraid to wrestle their sons to the ground, kids aren't allowed to pretend to kill each other, and they're certainly not taught to fight in any sort of controlled way, or even to stand up to someone who's giving them trouble. With all the emphasis in our schools now on getting kids in touch with their feelings, the scary feelings like anger are just kind of wished away. A kid says, 'I feel like I love you' and we say, 'Awww.' He says, 'I feel like I want to kill you' and we say, 'No you don't!' So a kid runs into some real conflict in life and he feels this rage coming up in him and he doesn't know what to do with it."

What if Kip Kinkel had been allowed to play with make-believe guns and bombs from the first moment he wanted to? What if he had been helped throughout his life to say, "This is my rage, these are my fantasies, and over here is the world that I can actually affect"? What if he'd been allowed to play at being powerful, and so at least learn to take power over his own fantasies—instead of being told that his fantasies were too powerful for him to be allowed to play with?

There was a boy named Dan in one of my eighth-grade workshops. He turned in a speculative autobiographical comic strip, describing an angry middle-schooler who succeeds academically but feels like an outcast among his peers; he has fantasies of bringing a gun to school and gunning down his classmates, but instead throws his rage into the success track and becomes a rich, unscrupulous lawyer. Most of the images on the page were drawn competently but perfunctorily, but one was etched with a stunning precision and passion: the protagonist's fantasied shooting spree. The wounds and staring eyes of the dead kids on the ground, the horror in the faces of the survivors, the stony rage of the shooter, the details of his gun were carved into the page with a clear and rageful love. I couldn't take my eyes off it. I couldn't take it calmly, either. This was May 1999, barely a month after Columbine.

I usually showed the best or most heartfelt stories to every class and discussed them at the end of the workshop, but this one I brought to Dan's teacher first. She told me that he had no record of delinquency or preoccupation with violence. He behaved sensibly, kept his grades high, and looked likely to be accepted into the best high school in town. However, he also had a tense, sometimes hostile, relationship with a father who pushed him hard to succeed. He tended to dissociate himself from his classmates and disappear into dark preoccupation. His teacher was as unnerved by the image as I was, but she agreed with me that we should neither pretend it wasn't there nor make too much of it.

I showed Dan's page to the class along with several other kids' work. Dan was slouched low in his seat with adolescent cool, but his eyes were watching me intently. I praised him for his evident passion and honesty. "This is the kind of thing that scares grown-ups," I said, and he gave me a stoic nod. "But it's an important thing to say, because I suspect it's on a lot of people's minds." He said, "Thanks." He kept his emotions tightly bottled, but he sat up a little, and he looked as animated as I'd seen him in three days of work. I passed the pages out to the class, and the one the other students were in the greatest hurry to read was Dan's. Some found it too spooky and moved quickly on, but several others, both boys and girls, stared at that one image for a long time. I watched them soaking it up, and I watched Dan watching them, too.

I asked Dan what the process had meant to him. At first I couldn't get much more than, "It was a nice break from reading *Our Town*." I had a feeling there was more to be learned from him, though, and checked in again with him several months later, after he'd become settled in high school. This time he was willing to reflect a bit more. He told me how Columbine had been on his mind constantly then. He wasn't the only one. Another boy in his class started wearing black trench coats to school and loved it when some of the parents complained. Yet another boy kept making Columbine jokes until a group of classmates got scared and threatened to report him. Dan kept his thoughts bottled up, but he couldn't escape them. "I kept thinking, I'm the profile of the school shooter, too," he said. "I've got my angers, but I don't express them. I don't think anyone wants to hear them. I feel like I'm under a lot of pressure, and I just want to explode sometimes. So does that mean I'm liable to do something like that? Or does it mean that other people think I'm going to even if I'm not?"

Was he worried about his own thoughts? "Sometimes," he said. "Usually I knew I was never going to do anything like that. But just the fact that I kept thinking about it bothered me." I asked him if he thought other kids might go through the same thing. "I know they do," he answered. "A lot of them. But nobody wants to hear about it. They'll be afraid that if a kid thinks about it, he'll do it. Or at least the kids are afraid that adults will think that, and they don't want to risk what might happen. So we just think about it more because we can't talk about it. And so do adults. Everybody goes crazy with it."

Fantasy and reality again: the reality of Columbine had touched such a chord in Dan that he'd had to fantasize about it again and again, but the fantasies disturbed him because they reminded him too much of reality. And he was afraid to articulate them because he knew they might remind adults too much of reality.

I asked him how it felt to put his fantasies out in such a public forum. "Good," he said. "What kind of good?" I asked. "A relief," he said. And how did he feel when I held the page up for the class and praised it? "Good," he said. "Can you give me something more specific?" I asked. He laughed, the most emotion I'd gotten out of him yet. "Okay," he said. "I felt like I was noticed. Accepted. I put these images out, I said these are mine, they're just my feelings. And I got the message that I was *okay*. So I could stop thinking about it, and just, you know, get on with my shit."

Dr. Ralph DiClementi of Emory University, a leading authority on adolescent risk-taking behavior, also sees a problem in our fear of violence at a national policy level. He believes there is too much violence among young people, but he has also pointed out that youth violence isn't nearly as pervasive as we often think it is and that most evidence suggests that it's declining. "In our anxiety we fall into a crisis mentality," he said. "A Columbine happens, and suddenly our entire discussion is about Columbine—which is of course an extremely unusual case. Then there will be another incident and everything will change. This prevents us from developing a sane, consistent, realistic policy, ways of helping young people to understand the realities of violence and take more control of their lives."

DiClementi is no fan of media violence. In his work with low-income teenagers, he's come to feel that media saturation, gangster rap, the bad values of commercial entertainment, all contribute something to the "complex web of causality" that leads to violence. "But you can't make it go away," he said. "Trying to legislate it away won't work, for one thing. But more importantly, even if you succeeded, you would lose more than you gain by taking something away from young people that they identify with so strongly and that so obviously speaks to them. What you need to do instead is find ways, through the family, schools, churches, service organizations to help them understand it better." I asked him if that involved accepting that they like it and trying to understand it better ourselves. "It would have to," he said. "But the crisis mentality gets in the way of that. We don't understand; we just react and restrict, which only makes matters worse."

It's the same story, in many different forms: adult fears about violence bring them into conflict with young people's thoughts and feelings, blurring the distinctions between reality and fantasy. Our fears are real and understandable, but they run away with us, too. The extent to which our fears cloud our thinking becomes evident when we compare the news coverage and public perception of adolescent crime to the reality of adolescent crime.

Mike A. Males of the Justice Policy Institute, author of *The Scapegoat Generation* and *Framing Youth,* reported on a remarkable focus group on violent crime that he conducted through the University of California at Irvine in 1997. The dozen attendees included men and women of diverse ethnicity, income, educational background, and age. He described them as mostly "affable," until he asked them this question: "How much of Orange County's violent crime is caused by youths under age eighteen?" He wrote, "These folks were rabid as no other topic had gotten them." The lowest estimate, made by a nineteen-year-old woman, was 40 percent. The highest, by an older man, was 80 percent. The group average was 65 percent. The truth, according to law enforcement reports, was 10 percent. People under eighteen years of age accounted for only 10 percent of the violent crimes in Orange County that year, six-and-a-half times less than those local adult citizens estimated.

Males wondered if their exaggeratedly negative impressions of young people were reactions to traumatic experiences. He asked the group if any of them had had any personal encounters with juvenile violence. Only one had: the nineteen-year-old who had overestimated youth violence by a relatively charitable factor of four. Her encounter consisted of a Latino teenager glaring at her boyfriend and saying, "You looking at me?" and then moving on. The group's perceptions came almost entirely from the news.

Studies in other parts of the country have borne similar results. Youth Vision in Chicago found that adults surveyed cited "a general feeling that youth are out of control" and that most of them attributed their perception to the press. Surveys of newspaper and TV news content show why. One media study found that two-thirds of TV news reports on violent crime in California concerned juveniles or young adults, age groups that actually accounted for less than one-third of the crimes. Another found that news reports on gang activity increased tenfold in the state of Hawaii from 1992 to 1996, while police reports showed that real gang activity remained about the same and that the number of young people arrested for serious crimes had steadily declined. A survey of *Los Angeles Times* articles in 1997 found that a murder committed by someone under eighteen was three times more likely to be reported than a murder by an adult.

We seem to want to believe that kids are more violent than they are. Some respected news outlets have even been caught distorting the facts in order to play on our anxieties about out-of-control kids. A flurry of stories from the major networks and wire services in 1996 reported, in the words of one AP entry, "Although crime rates in general are going down, rates of juvenile crime appear to be rising." Subsequent media studies found that the stories came from a cobbling together of two very different sets of data from the Justice Department showing that the opposite was true. The truth, in fact, was quite dramatically opposite: from 1980 to 1996, serious crime among American children seventeen and younger dropped by 15 percent; among young adults, eighteen to twenty-nine, it dropped by 11 percent. But among adults in their thirties, serious crime *increased* by a staggering 36 percent. Even among adults in their forties, serious crime increased by 20 percent.

As Mike Males pointed out, youth crime rates tend to reflect the state of the economy and availability of jobs. Those other numbers more closely parallel patterns of drug abuse among baby boomers, people born from about 1945 to 1965 who passed through adolescence in the drug culture and turbulence of the 1960s and 1970s. To view it another way, a teenage boy in the 1970s was about eleven times more likely than his forty-year-old father to be arrested for a felony. By the late 1990s, the forty-year-old was almost equally likely to be arrested. Kids today are not only behaving better than their parents did at the same age, but in many cases, they're behaving better than their parents do now.

Even youth advocates feed into the alarmism about youth violence. A recent plea for support for a youth-crime intervention program, appearing as an op-ed piece in a number of West Coast newspapers, stated, "Homicide is now the fourth-leading cause of death among juveniles in America. The tragic truth is that kids are killing kids." What gets lost between those sentences is that nearly 80 percent of slain children are victims of adults, not other kids. Fewer than

1 percent of those children are the victims of violence at school. School shootings dominate the headlines when they occur not because they are epidemic but because they are rare—and because we are haunted by our own frightened fantasies of what might become of our children.

By one calculation, about one teenager in 5,000 will commit an act of serious violence. The great majority of those are very poor, and their crimes are economic. The great majority also come from troubled households and have grown up surrounded by violence, intoxication, and abuse. The likelihood of a child from a decent home with decent economic prospects perpetrating any serious violence is infinitesimal. This is not to dismiss the reality or the terror of violence. It is to say, however, that our fears have become disproportionate to the reality, which prevents us from dealing with the problem realistically. And this, in turn, may be part of the reason there is still too much real violence in the world.

What are we afraid of?

"I think it's less that I actually thought Harrison might turn out to be violent," said Gina Weinberg, "than that I didn't want to be *reminded* of violence. I didn't want to be reminded of my own capacity for it, I didn't want to be reminded of the slightest possibility that he might be a victim of it, nothing. I wanted to make it go *away* by just willing it away in every form."

Even after she changed her mind about make-believe violence, Gina still caught herself making her sons' fantasies too real. Once she had Harrison and a couple of his friends in her car ("*female* friends, I should note"), and the kids started making guns with their hands and shooting passing cars. To Gina's ears, their shooting sounds were a little too realistic. She didn't stop them, but she cringed all the way home. Afterward, when she and Harrison were alone, she said, "You know when you were shooting in the car . . . ?" Harrison instantly said, "You didn't like that, did you?" And Gina said, "No, I didn't. But you know what? That's *me*. I know you were just pretending."

It was the perfect response. She told him her reaction *as* her reaction, but she still made it clear that his make-believe was safe. Had he sensed her anxiety and not heard what it was about, he might have taken that anxiety on himself. Her response gave him a clear picture of reality. Her *feelings* were real, and she expressed that reality. Harrison's gunshots were unreal, and she reinforced the distinction for him. Best of all, it was simply the truth. We can confuse kids when we try too hard to manage their feelings and experiences. They do better when we're simply honest. "It's all about fantasy and reality again," said Gina. "It's about focusing on the reality of who they are and what they need, not some fantasy of what we wish they were."

The reality is that we have been making great progress over the past few generations in teaching our children to be *less* violent, and their violent fantasies are helping them to accomplish that. At the same time, those fantasies put them at odds with ideas that we have been struggling with for more than a century.

8

The Courage to Change

For millennia, symbolic violence held a noble and accepted place in human culture. Rage, cataclysm, and irreconcilable conflict, both external and internal, were once taken for granted as elements of the human condition, and violence stood as a symbol of them in every kind of narrative. The keynote of Classical literature is sounded in the opening phrase of *The Iliad*: "*Menîn aide Thea*," "Of rage sing, Goddess," an invocation of poetic power to express the divine but destructive passion of Achilles. Every body of sacred lore is woven of conflicts and murders and bloody devourings. Even pacifist traditions are transmitted through metaphors of violence; Jesus brought not peace but a sword, and if we meet the Buddha in the road we are urged to kill him. Until the last few decades, all our civic myths, all our entreaties to collective action, were written in war and martyrdom. Generations of children were soothed to sleep with the witch-torturing, limb-severing, child-devouring horror of fairy tales. Across every social and philosophical stratum, children were expected to carry toy weapons and gleefully reenact the stories of murderous pirates, monsters, and heroes.

Now we tell kids to stop playing war. We've turned history class into a series of quaint reenactments of daily life. By the deftest bowdlerizations we've cut the images of slaughter from the background of the Christmas and Passover stories. The narratives we consider good for them are devoid not only of bloody violence but nearly all physical conflict. We leave the telling of violent stories to the commercial entertainment industry—and then spend considerable intellectual and political resources trying to demonstrate that they're harmful.

What changed?

The rise of science and rationality in the eighteenth century brought the belief that reason and planning had the power to change human behavior. During the nineteenth century, the strains of industrialization put a premium on the reduction of civil conflict and the promulgation of polite values. Then the development of modern weaponry steadily raised the stakes of war, until the threat of nuclear holocaust made thoughts of violence more horrifying than ever before. Those forces have brought us to a profound, unprecedented questioning of the role and rightness of violence in every form. Every society has condemned violence that threatened order. Many have cherished ideals of a lost age or a coming salvation marked by absolute peace. But even those accepted violence as inevitable in this world and celebrated it unquestioningly when it served the group. Some small, isolated groups may have eschewed violence, but no large society has ever attempted a thoroughgoing reconsideration of violence as such—until the modern, industrialized world.

Our renunciation of violence is still far from complete. Every nation continues to use it in law enforcement, and many use it in foreign policy. America, in particular, tolerates forms of violence—capital punishment, individual gun use—that have been rejected by most other nations in the industrialized world. But we are deep in the same process of reconsideration. Even our responses to the terrorism of 2001, both governmental and popular, were tempered by a remarkable restraint, compassion, and questioning of the value of force.

We have internalized our abhorrence of violence to such an extent that it often feels like second nature, and we forget how new these views are to human history. Until the twentieth century, no large cultural mainstream had ever called into question the basic rightness of capital punishment, corporeal punishment for children, the settling of disputes with fists, or warfare. No culture had ever fostered a popular belief that violence might be banished through education, child rearing, science, or other human efforts. We've entered new ground. We've set ourselves the heroic mission of creating a nonviolent world, but we don't know what one looks like. We're left with as many questions as answers, and among the most vexing is this: What is the place of imaginary violence in a world that denounces violence in reality?

The question isn't new. Plato, in imagining his ideal Republic, said he would ban entertainers because their stories would give the citizens improper ideas. His student Aristotle, less concerned with ideals than with comprehending the present reality, argued that drama was helpful to society because it provided a *katharsis*, a release of dangerous emotions. For a long time, that argument was mainly philosophical. But in the culture of antiviolence, it's become a very real matter of public policy and child rearing.

When imaginary violence was more widely accepted, so was real violence. Only a century ago, lynching was a common tool of social control in much of America. A president could chortle over a "splendid little war." Domestic violence was taken for granted in all but the most educated classes (and usually politely overlooked even there). The boyhood described in nineteenth-century popular fiction was an endless parade of beatings, bullyings, and rock-throwing battles. My grandfather used to chuckle over stories of growing up in the 1890s that chilled me. "Oh, there were some naughty boys, all right," he said of a group of friends who chopped off the tails of mice and laughed as they scurried in agony. Although crime rates weren't yet systematically calculated, the evidence of court records and social histories strongly suggests that murder, rape, and grievous assaults were considerably more common then than now. As Michael Lesy demonstrated in his harrowing *Wisconsin Death Trip,* an economic depression in the relatively placid agricultural heartland in the 1890s sparked a wave of homicides, suicides, arsons, and assaults that, had it happened today, would dominate the headlines. No one much noticed it then. That was life.

And no one doubted the connection between the imaginary and the real. During the buildup to the First World War, Kaiser Wilhelm berated a Berlin toyseller for not stocking toy submarines. The German people, he said, must be taught the importance of the submarine in their nation's future wars, and they must be taught in the nursery. A few years later, when that war was under way, a reviewer for the *Baltimore Sun* urged his readers to rush to a movie called *My Four Years in Germany* "if you want the loose ends of your hatred of German militarism gathered together and concentrated in a steady resolve for war until the beast is brought cowering and whining to earth—as beasts do when they find their masters—and if you want to enjoy thoroughly the process of concentration of hate." Societies have always used games and stories to teach people who to hate and how to fight.

It seemed obvious, then, that one step toward teaching future generations a new way to live was to change the games and stories on which they were raised. By the 1960s, teachers, pediatricians, psychologists, politicians, and millions of concerned parents joined together to sweep violence from the education and culture of children. Surely if children weren't indoctrinated with violence, they wouldn't learn it.

The problem was, they wanted it. And as we removed violence from their officially sanctioned culture—from the classroom, from bedtime stories, from adult-approved play—they were left with no source for it but the commercial entertainment industry. That industry can be contained by public sentiment and political pressure up to a point, but ultimately its purpose is to discover popular appetites and fill them for profit. The popular appetite for fantasy violence turned out to be bigger than ever. Violence with a heroic bent was selling fairly well in movies by the 1970s, even though filmmakers presented it with ugly realism and a nauseating ambivalence: *Billy Jack, Dirty Harry, Death Wish*. Then, in 1977, *Star Wars* announced that fantasy violence should be *fun*. This was fantasy joyfully removed from the glorified violence against real political and social groups that had made Westerns, war epics, and crime dramas unpalatable to most modern Americans; there were no Indians, Communists, or urban poor here, only aliens representing the simplest and most archetypal "other." Its mayhem was liberating and triumphant, but it was also huge and brutal. A planet is cruelly destroyed and Obi Wan Kenobi hears the psychic screams of dying billions. An alien's hand is sliced off in a bar fight. Justice is restored by the colossal explosion of the Death Star and its countless inhabitants. Instantly, *Star Wars* seized the youth audience as no movie ever had and became the most profitable entertainment product ever.

The more the adult world condemned violence, the more young people seemed to want it. The action movie became a juggernaut in the 1980s on the appetites of people raised in the 1970s heyday of antiviolent parenting. *Rambo, Indiana Jones, Lethal Weapon, Terminator, Jurassic Park*—violence of varying contexts and styles, but all intense, visceral, glorified, and utterly unapologetic—became the greatest commercial franchises in entertainment history. With them came the intensification of violence on television, the auditory violence of heavy metal, the explosion of video games, action figures, and a souped-up new generation of toy weapons. And it wasn't just the aggressive, unenlightened kids who wanted that make-believe violence, either. The best-raised, most peaceful, most socially aware of them were lining up for those movies, too.

Nor was it only American kids. We sometimes think that our popular culture is far more violent than that of Europe, because what we *produce* is so much more violent. In fact, Hollywood's action movies dominate the European market. The European movies we see are usually produced with government support as conscious alternatives to Hollywood products, and they often enjoy as much commercial success here as at home. Cable television now brings Europe as much small-screen violence as it brings us. Nintendo and Play Station and their often-violent software sell as well in the United Kingdom, Canada, and Australia as in the United States. In Japan, meanwhile, young people not only gobble up Hollywood action fantasies but support a huge domestic pop culture that is more intensely and explicitly violent than our own. Even in those nations with enviably low crime rates and seemingly more civilized citizenry, young people's appetite for fantasy violence is enormous.

The result has been an ideological war. And the first casualty of any war is truth. Medical and psychological establishments join with politicians in demonizing fantasy violence and accusing the soulless entertainment industry of knowingly wreaking havoc on children and society for the sake of a buck. The entertainment industry hides behind disingenuous evasions and stomps off muttering about censorship. As Christopher Perrius of the University of Chicago Cultural Policy Center put it, "The industry has to pretend that its products have no effect on society at all, and the psychological establishment has to pretend that violence can be completely removed without violence to the psyche."

The war has been going on for more than a century, but neither side has ever won a real victory. The critics prove their points to their own satisfaction, the entertainment industry retreats a little, then a few years later the industry surges back as violent as ever and the cycle begins again. The politicians get their votes, the researchers get their funding, the producers sell their tickets, and everyone is happy—except the parents, teachers, and children who are left with the fear and anger the war produces. As long as we're caught in the mentality of conflict (one must be wrong, one must be right), we'll never be able to break the cycle. One way out is to look back at past battles and see what it is that's really being fought over.

The first great modern conflict between the moral leaders of American society and mass entertainment was fought over the "dime novels" that exploded into popularity among young people in the wake of the Civil War. They were Westerns, crime stories, and romances, floridly written and filled with gunplay, danger, and mad passion, fantasies of violent conflict and individual power that thrilled the young people of an increasingly industrialized America who were spending more and more of their time in factories, offices, and schools. But to two very different groups these books looked dangerous. The religious reformer Anthony Comstock declared in 1884 that their editors were "willingly or unwillingly, Satan's efficient agents to advance his kingdom by destroying the young." Educators, librarians, and physicians, of a more progressive and scientific bent, accused them of overexciting youthful appetites, which they believed would contribute to a number of physical and behavioral maladies. Both the conservative religious critics and the progressive scientific critics blamed the dime novels for leading young men to crime and young women to immorality.

The terror inspired by dime novels is hard to comprehend from our distance. Their morality was simple: virtue was always triumphant, innocence was rewarded, and the unthinkable was averted. They lacked any explicit details that would offend Victorian society. But they posed two challenges to that society: they were a new medium, and they were in bad taste.

Books were an old medium, but they had always been expensive—a middle-class, adult preserve. With the spread of universal literacy and changes in methods of publication and distribution there was suddenly a body of literature that anyone could afford. Commercial storytellers were able, for the first time, to transmit stories directly to masses of young people, including less-educated young people of the working class. At the same time, the leaders of society were very anxious about the future. America was in a turmoil of change. Industrialization, urbanization, rapid expansion, Civil War and emancipation, vast dislocations of people, tidal waves of immigration were forming a world unlike any seen before. The durability of the new industrial society hadn't been proven yet, and the fear of utter social collapse underlay every discussion of society. Taming the young was of the utmost importance. Then, as now, adolescents were viewed by educators and physicians as being in a state of ongoing crisis. Every young male was viewed as a potential criminal, and stories of juvenile crime filled the newspapers far out of proportion to reality. That the minds of young people were being influenced by hack writers who thought of nothing but exploiting their appetites for cash was profoundly threatening.

The proof of the novels' danger, however, was their sensationalistic rejection of Victorian restraint. Their morality was conventional, but they described violence and villainy with a fervid, detailed, overwritten enthusiasm that flew in the face of every middle-class standard of good taste. Today we speak of "taste" as an individual idiosyncrasy or a marketing demographic, but in the nineteenth century it was a powerful concept. The spiritual and intellectual leaders of America were mostly of the educated middle class and believed deeply in the civilizing powers of middle-class values: restraint of emotions, constraint of expression, and educated taste. They saw around them a roiling, violent world driven by greed and split by class conflicts, striving for new heights of civilization but always threatening to plunge into barbarism. Even the most progressive advocates of the poor called them "the dangerous classes." Violations of middle-class propriety were perceived as real threats. When the *Atlantic Monthly* noted that dime novels were "almost exclusively for the use of the lower classes," it was enough to signal their danger. That a new medium of unpredictable influence was exciting young people with raw, working-class tastes raised fears of an impending social collapse.

Legal restrictions were placed on dime novels, and the furor died down. After a time of towing the line, of course, the publishing industry tested the boundaries again and was soon able to exceed them. By the early twentieth century, the new "pulp" magazines were far more lurid than the dime novels ever had been. By then, however, literary offenses to good taste were old hat, and no one paid them much mind. The motion picture had become the new nexus of conflict between those who wanted to improve society and those who wanted to entertain it.

This was a medium dramatically unlike any other, and it drew heat from the beginning. Some educators and clergymen warned that the medium itself, regardless of content, led to indolence, unrest, prostitution, and ignorance. The protests didn't really coalesce, however, until the 1920s. Things were changing: the World War, Prohibition, the automobile, the contraceptive diaphragm, and countless other factors had launched a cultural and moral revolution. Hollywood, meanwhile, brought the feature film to its pinnacle of visual power and popularity, added the potent medium of recorded sound, and used its power to exploit every aspect of the cultural revolution with risqué comedies, adulterous melodramas, glamorous criminals, short skirts, flimsy gowns, and blazing guns—spurred on by millions of eager ticket buyers.

As the film historian Jeanine Basinger pointed out in *A Woman's View: How Hollywood Spoke to Women, 1930–1960*, those movies offered very contained fantasies to an American public whose lives were mostly narrow and predictable. Women got to work at glamorous jobs, cheat on husbands, abandon children, shoot seducers, and wear fabulous clothes for an hour of fantasy, then were eased back to reality by endings in which the heroines suffered for their sins and rediscovered virtue. Gangster movies allowed men to strut, preen, fire machine guns, and slap their women around before they died in the final scene. But even as millions of Americans—especially the young—lined up for tickets, many others began to voice fears of what those glamorizations of passion and violence were doing to our children.

Organizations such as the Catholic Legion of Decency had been protesting movie immorality all through the 1920s to little effect. But in 1929 a group of sociologists, psychologists, and physicians formed the Motion Picture Research Council and, with funding from the progressive Payne Trust, launched the first wide-ranging studies of the impact of mass entertainment on children—studies that laid the groundwork for the media-effects research of the next seventy years. The Payne Trust studies asserted that movies inspired crime, aggression, sexual license, hysteria, and neurological damage in children. When the studies were released in 1933, they sparked a public furor. Soon senators, congressmen, and the Roosevelt administration were demanding new movie standards. Once again the combination of a new medium and assaults on conventional taste alarmed both conservative religious reformers and the science-minded liberals of the educated classes. Once again, their combined arguments that such entertainment harmed children focused parental anxieties. And once again, it occurred at a moment of high anxiety about the future, when the Depression and its resulting social and political turmoil had amplified the public's already high anxiety about social change.

Many of the claims of the Payne Trust studies look absurd in retrospect. That a young man from a bad neighborhood could be inspired to crime by *Little Caesar* is certainly plausible, but the idea that the thrills of *The Phantom of the Opera* affected children in the same way that shell shock affected soldiers, or that *Tarzan of the Apes* excited such morbidly violent feelings that even the healthiest child's neurological and physical health might be impaired, seems an almost lunatic overreaction. Yet such claims were made in a public document by respected physicians and professors at America's most august universities, and then treated with serious alarm by the press, the informed public, and the highest elected officials. Fear is a powerful distorter of thought.

"When you're going through a time like that, it feels like the end of the world," said Mick LaSalle, a movie reviewer for the *San Francisco Chronicle* through the 1980s and 1990s who later wrote *Complicated Women* and *Dangerous Men,* books about portrayals of power and morality in early 1930s Hollywood movies. "And the world *was* ending in some ways, at least the world that people had known before war, revolutions, Depression. Nobody knew what was coming—chaos, fascism, communism. It was easy to read the headlines and then go to the movies and feel like it was all part of the same crisis, that it wouldn't end unless somebody *did* something."

LaSalle said that he could understand the feeling. "As a reviewer, around 1993 and 1994 it felt like the end of the world to *me.* Everywhere you turned in the movies all you could see was mayhem. Not just summer blockbusters, but even supposedly serious projects like *Natural Born Killers.* The art houses were taken over by *Reservoir Dogs* and *Pulp Fiction.* And the news was full of crime. It seemed like there was no way out, like it was only going to get worse until the world fell apart."

Times of change are always terrifying. Times of change in which we also want profound improvement are even more terrifying, because we're not content just to survive and exploit the new situation as best we can. We see in every event a sign that we're making progress or sliding into disaster. The anxiety of not knowing which way we're heading makes us especially vigilant toward children. We try to see the future in them, and so we may see every change, fad, and statistical trend as evidence that something terrible is coming.

Entering unknown territory inspires contradictory emotions: anxiety and eagerness. Imagine stepping off a train into a teeming foreign city you know nothing about. Part of you wants to stay at the station, gather your bags close about you, watch carefully for thieves. Part of you wants to plunge down strange streets and see what this new world is. Our anxious vigilance is heightened, which makes us want to maintain tight control. But our enthusiasm for novelty and adventure is heightened, too. That's the conflict our society has been trying to negotiate for more than a century as we've hurtled through staggering changes but tried to make our world safer and more civilized at the same time.

Defenders of commercial entertainment often speak of the "unholy alliance" of liberal social reformers and religious conservatives arrayed against them, but they really aren't such strange bedfellows. They are all idealists who yearn to make something better of humankind. They believe in self-restraint and vigilance against one's own unhealthy emotions, they distrust untrained appetites and fantasies, and they feel that society needs some educated controls in order to progress in the right direction. Because they are idealists, they tend toward Plato's desire to keep dangerous stories out of the ideal Republic. Because they are teachers, they believe deeply in the *literal* power of stories, and they want entertainment to teach the lessons that will improve us.

One of the authors of the Payne Trust studies, Professor Edgar Dale of Ohio State University, vividly expressed the values that still underlie criticisms of the entertainment industry:

> It is apparent that children will rarely secure from the films goals of the type that have animated men like Jenner, Lister, Koch, Pasteur, Thomas Aquinas, Jesus Christ, Aristotle, Norman Thomas . . . and others. We ought to expect the cinema to show a better way of living than the average find outside the cinema. . . . We need to see the screen portraying more of the type of social goals which ought to be characteristic of a decent civilization. We need more often to catch a glimpse of the immortality of great characters who have sacrificed opportunities for personal aggrandizement in order that the larger community might have a fuller measure of life.

People who feel more invested in the established order and values—including teachers, social scientists, clergy, politicians, and a lot of parents—tend to respond to unpredictable change with a desire for more control. People who feel more invested in the future—including young people—respond with eagerness for novelty and adventure. The two groups' reactions feed on each other. Movies were alarming because they spoke directly and powerfully to masses of children, teenagers, poor people, and immigrants who hadn't been fully educated in society's loftier values. But the fear expressed by established cultural leaders made the movies even more exciting and adventurous to those young people and outsiders.

The more a medium threatens our control, the more we'll expect to see danger in it. Dime novels, movies, and the comic books accused of contributing to juvenile delinquency in the 1950s were threatening because they were readily available to everyone. Television was more threatening than any of them because it beamed its contents directly into our living rooms. A parent could prevent a child from going to a movie or newsstand, but with a TV in the house the only hope of control was constant supervision. So, even though its content was kept quite tame by a conservative FCC for decades, television from the beginning attracted unparalleled criticism.

New media anxiety sends us looking for negative effects. Young people, however, love new media, and they love media that bring entertainment to them easily and without adult screening. Making such media their own, separating it from our control, is part of how they plunge into the future and master it. And the more we fight to take control of it, the more powerful they know it must be.

Even now, our anxieties are triggered when a mass medium sells entertainment to the young and uneducated that challenges established taste. Those of us in the educated middle classes may have rejected the ideological underpinnings of the Victorian faith in taste, but it still shapes our preconceptions. Children from polite, educated homes still grow up hearing their parents speak agitatedly when some lowest-common-denominator, bad-taste entertainment achieves mass success. We still worry that the polite center of civilization will unravel if the impressionable and uneducated are encouraged to reject the rules, constraints, and standards we establish for public expression. The thought of children buying Ren and Stimpy dolls that make "authentic underleg noises" fills us not only with disgust but with a vague alarm. University researchers look for harmful effects in movies, comic books, professional wrestling, and video games, but never in books, plays, or even smart TV like *The Sopranos.* When mass entertainment assaults our taste with ghetto obscenities or raw gore, we see danger.

Media criticism of the past twenty years has been compounded by all these anxieties. There have been new media (computers and video games), developments of old media that made public vigilance over young people's entertainment more difficult (cable TV, VCRs, personal stereos), new entertainment forms (gangsta rap, special-effects blockbusters, mature-viewers TV), and unprecedented assaults on taste (obscene lyrics, mutilation, killing games, racism, misogyny, "Cop Killer," graphic sex, vomiting, farting, *South Park*). And although we haven't experienced turmoil comparable to that of the 1930s, we've been struggling through changes in work and family, crime waves, educational erosion—and now terrorism, war, and frightening economic news. It's no wonder that our anxieties about children, entertainment, and violence are high.

In 1982, Surgeon General C. Everett Koop said of a then-new medium, "Video games may be the leading cause of domestic violence in America today. It's reached the point where something's been done to one child and another child won't do a thing." Although the comment is only twenty years old, it now feels almost as peculiar as those from the Payne Trust studies. Certainly no evidence has emerged that domestic violence increased with the advent of video games, nor that it is more frequent in homes with video games. And it's difficult, in hindsight, to accept the idea that the video games of 1982—*Centipede, Pac Man, Space Invaders*—could have wreaked such havoc on American family life.

The Joint Statement on the Impact of Entertainment Violence on Children, of July 2000, stated, "Although less research has been done on the impact of violent interactive entertainment (video games and other interactive media) on young people, preliminary studies indicate that the negative impact may be significantly more severe than that wrought by television, movies, or music." That "may" is important. Some studies do suggest that possibility, but others, such as the 2000 University of Inverness study, suggest that video games may have much less of an impact than any of the other media. Our anxiety makes it easy to imagine, or expect, or even half hope that the new form will prove more dangerous than the old.

As those anxieties intensify, entertainers and their audience become more contentious. Kids—and the more puerile members of the entertainment industry—want to prove that they won't be beaten down by a humorless, meddlesome parental world. The market for defiant, intentionally provocative bad taste increases. In the 1990s, the willful pursuit of offensive violence hit a peak in the video game industry. *Mortal Kombat* allowed a player to rip the spine out of his opponent's body. *Duke Nukem* added a misogynistic twist, as it featured women only as bound captives and strippers, and when the player shot them they exploded into showers of blood and gold. At a panel at the 1997 Game Designers' Expo in Santa Clara, California, I heard a young video game producer respond angrily to criticism of that game with, "What kinds of games are we supposed to play? Duke *Huggem?* I don't need *my* fun to make these parent groups and teachers feel all squishy inside. I'm going to sit down at my game and say, what do you think of *this?*"

Offensive violence has many functions: it can express hostility, put scary thoughts in perspective, intensify a power fantasy, test machismo, and provide an exciting shock. In our permissive popular culture, it's also one of the few sources remaining to young people of truly, shockingly bad taste. And bad taste is a way to accelerate, test, and take some control of the process of social change. In blatantly presenting what was previously forbidden, offensive entertainment says that the old ways are breaking down. It sets kids apart from their parents' values and connects them with them peers, shows them that they're plunging into new territory. The more it appalls the adult world, the more exciting it is: this is their turf, the world they're making whether we like it or not. (And bloody violence is one thing that today's adult world is almost guaranteed not to like.) Then comes the relief: they break into the new territory and discover it's safe. The forbidden deed is done, adults are shocked, everyone gets used to it and moves on. Their parents are still there, and the world still works as well as it ever did. Periodic assaults on established taste help people play with change and be reassured that it'll be okay.

Entertainment relying on bad taste becomes boring quickly. *Duke Nukem* was dead in the marketplace before the arguments about it had died down. But every successful assault on taste changes standards. Longer-lived shooter games succeed on their complexity and suspense, but for many of them, overstated gore is now part of the package. What was once offensive becomes accepted. The cost of that is a coarsening of popular culture. Entertainment becomes less deft, less graceful, less subtle. Those of us who prefer more polite and suggestive aesthetics find less to like and more to steel ourselves against.

The gain, however, is that we are reminded what really matters. Our world isn't kept out of barbarism by concealing ugly realities or suppressing shocking images. The bonds that hold us together are empathy, acceptance, and a mutual desire to make the real world better, not a fragile web of constraints and controls.

Anxiety blocks empathy. When we view a new form that opposes the values that make us comfortable, we see only its outer shape—its apparent, literal meaning—and we can't feel what it *means* to the people who created it and the people who love it. In *The Uses of Enchantment,* the psychiatrist Bruno Bettelheim argued eloquently for the value of fairy tales for children's emotional development, even with—sometimes because of—their violence, gore, and terror. But he was unwilling to extend that value to any popular children's culture of his own time. All modern children's literature, he said, was vapid, lacking in imagination, and useless to children's development.

Once a group of parents and teachers asked Bettelheim about Maurice Sendak's *Where the Wild Things Are,* a children's book with a nightmarish quality reminiscent of fairy tales. He hadn't read it, but based on a plot description he denounced it as not only valueless but probably harmful: Max's mother is a bad parent for sending him to his room without supper, and children hearing that will be disturbed. That was precisely the sort of literalistic criticism that fairy tales had been subjected to for decades and that Bettelheim argued so passionately against. Bettelheim, however, was a product of the intellectual elite of prewar Austria, with an antipathy for the modern industrialized world forged by World War II and the Holocaust. America's mass, commercialized kid culture was alien and threatening to him; he couldn't empathize with it as fantasy and viewed it with anxious literalism. One mother asked him, "But if it's harmful, why do children love it so much?" Bettelheim had no reply.

Those parents and teachers understood what Sendak's young fans were experiencing. Even they, however, may not have understood all of American children's culture. Reviewing the parenting magazines and library journals from the same period, I found denunciation after denunciation of commercial children's television. It's true that *Where the Wild Things Are* is alive in a way that ratings-driven, formulaic kids'TV never is—and it's completely free of candy commercials. But the question that mother asked Bettelheim can be asked of cartoons, too: if it's harmful, why do children love it so much?

Angry, frightened public debate doesn't help us understand what our children are experiencing. It stands in our way by trapping us self-protectively within our own perceptions and preventing us from opening up to their perceptions. At the peak of the dime novel furor, in 1883, a young teacher and literary critic named Brander Matthews expressed the anger and fear of the moment: "The dreadful damage wrought to-day in every city, town, and village . . . by the horrible and hideous stuff set before the boys and girls of America by the villainous sheets which pander greedily and viciously to the natural taste of young readers for excitement, the irreparable wrong done by these vile publications, is hidden from no one."

Forty years later, that same Brander Matthews looked back from an America that hadn't gone completely to hell after all and remembered this: "The saffron-backed Dime Novels of the late Mr. Beadle, ill-famed among the ignorant who are unaware of their ultra-Puritan purity . . . began to appear in the early years of the Civil War; and when I was a boy in a dismal boarding school at Sing Sing . . . I reveled in their thrilling and innocuous record of innocent and imminent danger." Removed from the anxieties of the moment, he could remember who he had been as a child.

When we're struggling to control our children's world, commercial entertainment looks like an enemy. More quickly than we can educate the violence out of children's heads it comes pouring in more. But when we look at entertainment's greatest powers, it turns out that it may be doing just what it's supposed to. An old actors' legend holds that the Devil created the modern theater: when medieval churches couldn't find locals willing to play the role, they had to hire ne'er-do-wells from other villages, and so was born the professional actor. The Devil soon became the most popular character in the plays, because he allowed people to look at their baser desires and experience a forbidden defiance to propriety without risk. When the church banned the plays, the actors went off on their own—and ever since, the professional entertainer has played a necessary devil to society, always at odds with those who want to improve us, but always beloved because he affirms us as the flawed creatures we are.

We ask commercial entertainment to teach the lessons that we want the world to learn, and sometimes it does, but that's not its strength. It's a sloppy teacher, and it's likely to bore us or lose our trust when it tries to instruct. The real value of commercial entertainment, from the most demanding films to the most simple-minded arcade games, is that it provides fantasy. By telling passionate stories unfettered by our standards of who we should be, it allows us to feel the emotions and experience the imaginary lives that reality doesn't allow. It gives us a relief from the pressure of always having to be good. Indulging in unapproved passions helps us to accept our imperfections. Sharing those passions with millions of peers through mass entertainment reassures us that no one else is perfect either. And that makes reality a bit less onerous when we return to it, so that being good is just a little easier. The greatest power of commercial entertainment has always been to give people exactly what our better natures say we can't have. It fills the emotional gaps that open between our ideals and our reality.

Family therapist Diane Stern described her son Sam as a highly conscientious, rule-conscious boy who could be very hard on himself when he didn't meet the teacher's expectations or his own. He was also extremely sensitive to others' pain and kept his own emotions in check. Only once in his childhood did he ever come close to hitting his little brother in anger, and then he caught himself and was genuinely shaken: "Mom, I could have hurt *Gabe!*" But the entertainment he loved presented the exact opposite.

"I'll admit," said Stern, "that my husband and I had some serious doubts about letting him listen to Eminem or Limp Bizkit in fifth grade. But we could see in his face and his body what a pure, relaxed pleasure they brought him. It's like he was floating on a cloud. I thought about what it must be like to be such a responsible young boy, standing there patiently in the lunch line, nodding attentively to the teacher no matter how much he'd rather be elsewhere, doing homework instead of playing—and what a tremendous *relief* it must be just to feel that tremendous wave of lyrics—all that anger and confrontation and willingness just to tell the world to go to hell— obscenely, even—just wash over you."

That devil can be dangerous. The excitement of those unapproved passions may encourage some people to question the validity of the ideals they've been holding on to. A few people, those who feel very angry at or cut off from the larger society, may act out what they've seen. But for our progress in general, it plays a vital role.

The key is to notice that general progress and not only the alarming anomalies. One of the pitfalls of fear is that we see only danger signs. When we're afraid of the future we become afraid for our children. We also, however, become afraid *of* our children. During the early 1930s, the common opinion expressed in the popular press and the journals of educators and doctors was that the young generation was the most damaged and troubled of modern times. Children and teenagers were widely seen as "nervous, neurotic, chronically ill, alienated, and prone to delinquency." Those kids, of course, grew up to be Tom Brokaw's "Greatest Generation," the generation of "civics" who conquered the Depression, won World War II, built the orderly society of the 1950s, and raised the Baby Boom.

It was my father's generation. Born in 1921, fatherless and dirt poor before the New Deal, neglected by a profoundly depressed mother, raised by his peers on the streets of Oakland, California, his family kicked out of their house by the sheriff, growing up a strong and relentlessly law-abiding man, savior of several shipmates when his cruiser was sunk off Guadalcanal, putting himself through college on the GI Bill, a dedicated high school teacher, steadfast husband and father who rescued spiders from the bathtub and never raised his hand in violence, loyal caretaker to his dying wife even as his own eighty-year-old body and mind broke down—his is a story almost as common as it powerful.

Among the bonds I found with him as a child and find with him now in his old age is the violent popular culture of his youth. He can still vividly describe how the Shadow of the pulp magazines would blow villains off their feet with his twin .45s, how King Kong ripped open the Tyrannosaurus's jaw with a sickening noise and a stream of blood, how the body of Jimmy Cagney toppled forward horribly at the end of *The Public Enemy.* He can still remember cheering at *Tarzan* and shrieking at *The Phantom of the Opera,* just like the kids the Payne Trust studies warned about. His only criminal behavior as a child was sneaking into movies that he couldn't afford.

"Why did you love them so much?" I asked him once.

"Hell," he said, "they were my only way *out!*"

And they helped him to get out literally. The Flagg and Quirt military comedies made him want to be a Marine. *The Mask of Fu-Manchu* made him want to see other lands. A radio play of "The Most Dangerous Game" made him want to read fiction. A lot of his peers were lining up for jobs on the General Motors assembly line, but my father's dreams wouldn't let him: dreams that only action-packed entertainment could have made exciting to a frustrated kid with the whole world against him.

I believe the current generation of young people will be much like my father's. They'll be fretted over by nervous adults for their entire youth and then surprise us all with how well they turn out. I also believe that these young people are considerably less violent in their behavior and values than generations before them. There are still violent children, troubled children. Because we don't value them enough in our public policy, there are far too many of them. But most young people, whether we notice it or not, are making exactly the changes in the world that we hoped they would.

I see their progress toward nonviolence every day in myriad little ways. I remember going to a park in the Sierras as a kid where the lake was full of bullfrogs. Dozens of excited kids had discovered the frogs, and most had responded by slaughtering them. The shore of the lake was strewn with the carcasses of frogs that had been stomped on, slammed on rocks, flung into the air and let drop. I was sickened at the sight, but I didn't say anything. The bulk of my peers were against me. That's just what boys did with frogs in 1965.

Thirty-five years later, Nicky and I went to another lake in the same area. This one was also full of frogs, and dozens of excited kids were catching these, too. But nearly all of them were putting them in buckets, looking at them, and letting them go. When a few kids started throwing them into the water, other kids yelled: "Don't do that! You'll hurt them!" I didn't see a single dead frog in the days we were there, and I only saw one adult rebuke a kid for being rough. The kids themselves were enforcing the rules.

The strain of enforcing their own rules is hard, however. It requires a constant battle with their own impulses. Sometimes they need relief from their vigilance.

Right before our trip to the Sierras, Nicky and I had watched *Lost World: Jurassic Park 2* on tape, and Nicky was still chattering happily about it during the trip. One afternoon, not long after he'd been brought to tears by the intensity of his insistence that two older boys stop swinging their nets so hard at the frogs, I caught him smiling about something. "What is it?" I asked. "I was just thinking about that scene where the two Tyrannosaurs tear that guy in half," he said. "That was so *cool!*"

That devil of entertainment brings a compensatory power. Nicky has learned to be so empathetic and tender, to find a frog's injury so agonizing, that he finds a huge relief in being able to enjoy and endorse the brutality of his reptilian self. The teaching of nonviolence is going well and we need to continue it. We need to keep that ideal of nonviolence in front of us. Along the way, we also need to allow our children and ourselves the fantasies that permit us to be just the opposite. They'll help give us the courage we need to go on changing our world.

9

Vampire Slayers

When we look at entertainment violence through the years, it's easy to see only the most frightening changes: increasing explicitness, intensity, moral ambiguity. But some of the biggest changes are also the most encouraging. One was the separation of fantasy violence from celebrations of historical or politically loaded real violence through movies like *Star Wars*. A shift perhaps just as profound has occurred more recently, in the relationship of women to power, sex, and aggression.

Traditionally, women in action stories played either the victim to be rescued (thus an object of male power and a prize to be won) or the victim who *isn't* rescued (an object again, usually to make evil seem more horrific and its destruction more urgently needed). When women took power for themselves, the effect was usually destructive, and the women served as *femmes fatales*. There were exceptions, from Wonder Woman to Princess Leia, but they appealed overwhelmingly to very little girls. Others, like Emma Peel of *The Avengers*, won cult followings mainly among late adolescents and adults. In generations past, as boys and girls passed through the ages of intense sexual differentiation, they usually showed a great loss of interest in, even a discomfort with, fantasies of powerful women.

During the 1980s that tendency reached an offensive apex in commercial entertainment. Action movies from *Commando* to *Lethal*

Weapon to *48 Hours* to *Raw Deal* featured a gamut of female victims and hangers-on: whiny, limpid, petty, depressive, stupid, self-absorbed, infantile, cowardly, always sexy but never potent. Even the Indiana Jones series ditched the hero's strong female counterpoint after the first movie in favor of screeching airheads and treacherous ice maidens. Meanwhile, teenagers of both sexes revealed a sudden appetite for slasher movies about male psychopaths terrorizing teenage girls.

Those trends faded as the '80s became the '90s not because of any adult outcry but because of the tastes of the next generation. The movie *Alien* showed that millions of teenagers and young adults of both sexes could connect powerfully to the image of a beautiful heroine getting sweaty and bloody in brutal physical combat with a monster. Video game designers found that the voluptuous female fighters in *Mortal Kombat* and other games were becoming favorites of adolescent players—not only as *femme fatale* opponents but as surrogates for the players themselves. Movies and video games featuring violence against women were steadily marginalized to a tiny audience of young men; every once in a while one achieves some notoriety in the news, but none sell well. When horror movies returned, they made fun of earlier slasher clichés and featured heroines who were more proactive and potent. The *Tomb Raider* game became a huge hit on the strength of its underdressed, gun-packing female adventurer, Lara Croft, who, according to market studies, wielded an unprecedented "bimodal" appeal for both male and female gamers. The comic book industry was commercially revitalized partly by the fad for "bad girls"—angry, powerful heroines who wrapped their exaggeratedly female bodies in skimpy clothes and went head-to-head with the toughest males—who proved to be extremely popular with boys in their mid-teens but who also, at least when they were developed as characters, drew a remarkable number of pubescent female readers to the superhero genre. Young people wanted to see, as one female movie fan told me, "any chick in cool clothes who *kicks ass!*"

The change was signaled most clearly in 1992, when a low-budget action-comedy named *Buffy the Vampire Slayer* turned into a hit as big, surprising, and influential among teenagers as *Friday the 13th* had been a decade earlier. It was the story of a cute, popular, and fairly vapid high-school girl charged with the mission of killing vampires who threaten to take over her suburban community. It contained gore, suspense, bad-taste gags, and cool teen references in the slasher-movie tradition, but it wrapped them around a new kind of movie heroine; the sexy but naive girl who could have been one of the victims (or perhaps the terrified sole survivor) of a horror-movie monster was *herself* the ultimate dispenser of violence. She defeated her vampiric foes with the aid of a trait quite typical of young movie heroines—the vapid veneer that conceals an unexpected cleverness—but she combined it with something new: a complete shedding of the squeamishness and fear of violence that have always been part of the pop-culture image of the "good girl."

"She just plain drove the stakes right into their hearts," said Anne Sardik, an English professor who first saw *Buffy* as an undergraduate, "and then she'd check her nails. We howled and we clapped. No matter what she had to do, she somehow never lost her sexiness, her likability, or her ordinariness. For girls who had always seen physical power as either destroying women or masculinizing them, it was incredibly liberating."

Then, a few years later, the fantasy took on a new dimension: *Buffy the Vampire Slayer* was retooled as a television series. The humor and the violence were toned down in favor of plots emphasizing Buffy's cleverness at manipulating relationships and situations. The characters were made more complex and believable, and Buffy's on-again, off-again romance with a vampire named Angel became a running subplot. The role of Buffy was given to Sarah Michelle Gellar, a soap-opera veteran and Maybelline spokesmodel who brought more glamour and poise to the character than Valley Girl cuteness. It immediately became a huge craze among preteen and teenage girls, with enough boys joining them to make it a ratings hit. By the late '90s the Buffy-style heroine—cool, cute, sexy, young, fearless, and willing to use violence—had become a TV staple.

Adult reactions to the new female action heroes have been mixed. Educators and cultural commentators have been saying for decades that girls need more media role models of power and heroism, and those models have finally arrived. But, as usual, youth culture refuses to follow the patterns that adults wish it would.

"I have a tremendous ambivalence about shows like *Buffy*," said developmental psychologist Carla Seal-Wanner, "and even more problems with things like *Tomb Raider*. I love the fact that girls have these symbols of power now. But I'll sit down with Lindzay, my ten-year-old, to watch *Buffy*, and I keep asking, '*Why* is she wearing that *bustier?*' It's totally impractical for fighting vampires. Obviously it serves no purpose other than to make her sexier—by a standard, adolescent-male model of sexiness that means perky breasts and cleavage."

She and Lindzay were able to turn that into a running gag. Lindzay asked her once, when Buffy was doing some acrobatic stunt in a little halter top, "Wouldn't she just, you know, fly *out* of it?" "Which gave me," said Seal-Wanner, "a chance to give her some behind-the-scenes information about the magic of *tape*." She is concerned, however, about girls who don't have anyone to help them process these images, particularly the girls who can never expect to attain the physical ideal held up by heroines like Buffy. She wonders what that tells them about the need to be sexy in order to be powerful. Is it reinforcing the idea that girls can't be powerful, cool, admirable, unless they also look and dress like cover girls?

The linking of sexuality and power disturbs us; we don't want our young girls thinking that they have to make themselves into sexual objects in order to be powerful, nor girls thinking that they're less potent because they don't fit a physical ideal, nor boys objectifying girls sexually and dismissing their other strengths. The more I talk to the kids, however, the clearer it becomes that this very link is precisely what makes fantasies like *Buffy* so compelling—and, often, so useful.

Buffy has become a familiar figure to me through the stories of middle-school girls. In the early grades, boys are somewhat more likely than girls to cast their make-believe in the form of *Pokémon*, *Harry Potter*, or some other mass-media property. By middle school, however, the roles are completely reversed: boys will go to great lengths to avoid seeming "geeky" or juvenile by playing with pop-culture icons, whereas girls often wear their fannish passions as a kind of identity. Even a boy I know to be a fanatic Batman follower will make up parodic superheroes of his own ("Bluntman," "Man-Man," "Duh-Man") rather than be caught fantasizing about childhood heroes. But every class will produce a handful of Charlie's Angels, Darias, or Harry Potters from the girls. Of all the mass-media heroes, Buffy has been the most common and has also inspired some of the most interesting stories. She figured prominently, in fact, in one of the most revelatory workshops I've ever led.

It was an eighth-grade class in San Francisco, and of the possible themes I'd presented for stories, they had chosen, as middle schoolers often do, "power." The kids started by brainstorming types of power: political, physical, superhuman, economic, military. It was a fairly standard list. Then a girl named Eva raised her hand, waited until the class was quiet and she had my full attention, and said, "Sexual power."

The phrase jolted the room. I've never seen thirty people trying harder *not* to react to something in my life. I asked her what she meant, and she started talking about a girl being able to dominate a room with just an outfit or a look, about her ability to make boys act ridiculous, about retail clerks giving her special attention if she smiled and made eye contact; and about the undesirable side effects of the power, too, like making other girls resent her, getting whistled at on the street, and drawing too much attention from older men. She was remarkably poised as she talked. She'd obviously been mulling these things over for quite a while, and she was just as obviously speaking from her own experience. She was tall, pretty, genially flirtatious, dressed in the trendy mode of tight pants, bare midriff, and spaghetti straps. From talking to her mother and teacher over the ensuing days, I also gathered that she was a confident kid and a decent student, popular among her classmates and close to her parents. Her explorations of sexual power were self-conscious and overt but within sensible boundaries.

The teacher and I told her that we'd love to see what she could come up with, and she grabbed a pencil and dove in, announcing that she was going to pull anecdotes from her own life and "make it funny and serious at the same time." Meanwhile, the kids around her were dealing with this bomb she'd thrown into the classroom. Her best friend, Kaitlin, decided to draw a poster called "Woman Power," about "the ups and downs of puberty." A boy named Evan drew a gag cartoon about a politician being destroyed by a sex scandal. Zach, a louder and more macho kid who spent a fair amount of time trying lamely to get Eva's attention, reeled off a silly comic strip about battling martial artists, then suddenly switched the focus to a voluptuous "samurai mega-babe" who burst into the action and slaughtered them both. When I asked why she was able to kill his heroes so easily he said, "Because it's realistic! Chicks always *do* win!"

A few seats away, very quietly and privately, a girl named Sophie worked on a comic strip about Buffy and her endless romance with Angel. She was very different from the trendy, flirty Eva and Kaitlin: a good student and earnest athlete, pleasant but shy, her changing body well hidden under a Berkeley t-shirt and loose jeans. I read her rough draft and thought it was a cute but very restrained comment on the way TV soap operas never resolve their plots. But Sophie was frustrated. "I don't know how to end it!" she snapped. "It doesn't go anywhere!" I told her to put it aside, doodle on another piece of paper, and see what came up.

I went back to see what Eva had done. She'd done nothing. She grabbed her hair and said she couldn't figure out where to start. I spent ten minutes talking to her about the anecdotes she had in mind and how to focus her theme, and put her back to work. At the next seat, Kaitlin had filled her "Woman Power" page with a few gags about brassieres and makeup and then started floundering. I was trying to get her jump-started when I noticed that Eva was across the room, trying to get help from another student.

Over the next couple of days, Kaitlin finished her poster up half-heartedly and turned it in early. Zach lavished great care on his mega-babe samurai. Meanwhile, Eva had asked for help from half the class, crumpled several sheets of paper, grabbed her hair a lot, and produced absolutely nothing. "I just couldn't figure out how to say it!" she said. When I asked if she might have been embarrassed, she blushed and said in the smallest voice I'd heard out of her all week, "Yeah."

Sophie, I discovered, had completely changed her story. It began the same, but now, halfway through, her Buffy had become frustrated with her endlessly unresolved relationship, announced that she herself was a vampire, flashed a pair of fangs, and in a lurid but hilarious final panel ripped Angel's throat out. Sophie was pleased with herself. She would look at the huge, bloody Buffy in the final panel, exploding from the end of a sequence of smaller and more constrained figures, and she would positively glow. "What does it mean to you?" I asked. "I don't know," she said. "But it would be hilarious if they did it on the show!"

The mixed results of that workshop gave me a glimpse into the function of stories and entertainment in these kids' lives. For all her courage in wading directly and publicly into the swirling issues of "sexual power," Eva wasn't ready yet to make anything coherent of her concerns. Kaitlin had tried a slightly less blunt and less personal approach to the same topic but had also quickly struck the limits of what she was willing or able to express. Evan and Zach hadn't said a word about sexual power in class, and Zach, at least, had seemed overwhelmed by Eva's power; but they'd been able to play with the idea through media-based parodies. Sophie had done the most exciting work of all by funneling her titillation, anxiety, and frustration about the power of sex through a television fantasy. Entertainment provides the essential function of play for kids who feel too old to play openly: it enables them to manipulate and master the ideas and feelings that concern them until they feel ready to grapple with them in reality.

The issues surrounding body image and male attention are powerful and troublesome for girls. It's important that the adult world help girls like Eva to develop personal potency beyond their sexuality, and help girls like Sophie to understand that they can feel powerful without fitting some impossible physical ideal. But it's also important to understand that the sexiness of a character like Buffy isn't just a gratuitous media manipulation that kids would do better without; it is, in fact, essential to her value as a power fantasy.

These kids know about sexual power. They experience its positive and negative effects intensely and constantly. With increasingly extensive sex and AIDS education, and seemingly endless and unprecedentedly explicit media discussions of sex, the generation now entering adolescence is accustomed to speaking about it more frankly than any generation before. With the increased attention paid recently to the crises of self-confidence that confront girls in early adolescence, it's also a generation more accustomed to thinking about their own psyches in relation to gender, power, and puberty. In many ways, these kids are better prepared for adolescence than kids before them, but in other ways they have even more worrisome information to make sense of. Like younger kids, they seek stories to give predictable, controllable, and reassuring forms to the powerful new emotions and concepts they suddenly find themselves having to deal with. And since parents and schools so often fail to discuss issues like the emotions and psychology of sex, power, and gender roles in a way that kids find relevant, mass entertainment that deals with those issues becomes especially compelling.

The particular genius of Buffy in reassuring girls about their potential power is precisely that she is a vampire slayer and that she is so sexy. Vampires have been overtly sexual symbols since they became popular in the Victorian era. Dracula was a charming man who took power over women by kissing their necks and awakening their repressed sexual passions; the "vamps" of early Hollywood were seductresses who essentially did the same to upstanding young men. The characters who defeated the vampires were always symbols of societal repression: professors, doctors, virginal fiancées. Decades later, with the sexual revolution, came a new spin on vampires, as seen in the novels of Anne Rice: the sympathetic vampire who can liberate as well as destroy by awakening sexual power and who makes fools of the prudes who would destroy him. The new vampires still wielded the power, though. Sex was presented more positively, but it was still a power that would master us, not one that we would master.

Buffy is a whole new model. As a vampire slayer she might have been another symbol of repression, but she's the sexiest woman on the show. She's also in love with a seductive male vampire, but she is pointedly not under his power. She's the perfect symbol of a girl taking power over sexuality not by bottling it up (which, as even the traditional vampire stories showed us, never works for long) but by facing it, loving it, and then outsmarting it. It's important, then, that girls find Buffy impossibly cool and that they know boys drool over her. Buffy is an object, and her fans respond to her as such. But there is a power in being an object. An object elicits powerful feelings from others without having to expose any of her own vulnerability. To be able to be an object, or identify with an object, as long as one isn't trapped in objecthood, gives one a great symbolic power.

I asked that eighth-grade class what TV shows they liked. Eva and Kaitlin didn't watch anything regularly, but they did think Buffy was "cool." Zach leered and said, "I like *Buffy* . . . 'cause I like Sarah Michelle Gellar!" The leer was a way of taking a little bit of power back from the sex object: she was there for him to ogle, and that made her fleetingly *his*. But in order to enjoy her in her bustier, he also had to enjoy her beating up bad guys; as his comic strip showed, he understood and respected the power wielded by the "babe." If Buffy were a parent's dream and developed her intellect and strength while dressing sensibly and looking more like an average high school girl, she wouldn't be nearly as valuable a fantasy. This is the same dynamic I've seen in the Britney Spears fixation of little girls like Emily. In encouraging our girls to be strong and competent while also urging them not to worry so much about being attractive and fashionable, we can unintentionally reinforce the idea that real power is incompatible with sexuality and femaleness. In the conformist world of early adolescence, maintaining a stable social persona as "one of the girls" or "one of the boys" can be an important part of building confidence.

This is what I call the *optimism* of popular entertainment. It's the job of parents and teachers to make sure kids know the dangers brought by sexuality, but in our adult anxiety we can easily fail to acknowledge what the kids are discovering for themselves: that sexuality is joyful as well as scary, and the power that girls may suddenly find themselves wielding is exhilarating and fun and usually doesn't lead to bad outcomes. The movie version of *Charlie's Angels* was almost universally blasted by adult critics not only because it was a mess of a movie but because it paraded its female leads as sex objects even as it showed them fighting evil. But teenage girls and young women fell in love with its cute, fun-loving, potent, violent, and frankly objectified heroines. Shortly after, *Josie and the Pussycats* got more credit from the critics for its attempt to deliver a message about corporations manipulating the youth culture, but the kids stayed away. TV shows like *Buffy* and movies like *Charlie's Angels* give girls a chance to celebrate and play with their newfound powers without having to act on them. Where the adult world says, "Watch out," and presents reality as a procession of dangers, hard choices, and self-sacrifices, entertainment says, "Be everything you want to be." If kids are allowed their fantasy lives, but shown how to modulate them into a productive real life, those fantasies have the power to encourage and reassure them through some of life's most harrowing passages.

The arrival of sexuality is hard on boys, too, although our culture doesn't provide them with as many ways to view it or as many venues to talk about it. Girls are given images of the power of sexiness, but they're also given encouragement to remain innocent; they receive countless cautionary tales about the dangers of sex, and recently we've devoted great thought and resources to boosting their self-confidence. Boys enter puberty with less support, yearning to be as strong and confident as their adult male role models. If they're not— and hardly any of them are—they're likely to feel like geeks. If they try to compensate with excessive displays of fearlessness and power, they're liable to be labeled as troublemakers. I've heard from many young teenage boys who feel that adults fear, dislike, or ignore them, while lavishing all their attention on girls.

Boys begin to judge themselves by their relationships with girls in adolescence and want desperately to be cool, in control, and admired. But girls grow faster, know more about sexuality, and talk about things that boys are afraid to, leaving boys confused, desirous, envious of the apparent power and wisdom of girls—and afraid to let it show. Some adopt strategies to take power back from girls: physical intimidation or chasing much younger girls. Most just armor themselves with a macho bravado or pull back into boyish geek pursuits— video games, chess, comic books, sports fandom—where they can play at imaginary power among other nervous guys while putting off the coming struggle.

Puberty is a time when exaggerated images of maleness and femaleness become very powerful for both boys and girls. The over-muscled Hulk meant a lot to me when I was feeling like a nearly invisible wisp of a boy; at the same time, the Black Widow and other voluptuous women in the comics held my young libido transfixed. And, as many a culture critic has pointed out, when society at large is going through periods of anxiety about changing gender roles, the most common popular-culture images take on an adolescent bent. Movies of the 1930s and early 1940s feature many images of powerful women and complex men, reflecting an increase in women's independence and economic power. But postwar Hollywood brought a reaction in the forms of *femmes fatales* who had to be destroyed and impossibly voluptuous sexpots with tiny minds who wanted square-jawed he-men with sweaty chests. In the wake of the '60s and '70s, the '80s brought Schwarzenegger and Stallone movies, along with thousands of underdressed, dewy-lipped women who were suddenly everywhere from MTV to *Sports Illustrated*. By the '90s that had contributed to the intentionally offensive extreme of *Duke Nukem*.

However, as that exaggerated boyishness was still dominating teenage boys' entertainment, a new trend was rising. The pop-culture girls that boys began falling for were becoming tougher, more physically powerful, and (implicitly or explicitly) more violent than ever before. Confrontational girl rockers and rappers from Courtney Love to Li'l Kim not only won over angry girls but became poster girls for boys as well. Jennifer Lopez became a sex symbol with a powerful body, a forceful style, and a series of hard-hitting roles in action movies. Even the dancers in music videos were noticeably more muscular and aggressive than a decade earlier. Gillian Anderson became a pin-up girl for a while, even though she rarely appeared dressed in anything but boxy suits, thanks to an *X-Files* role that had her brandishing guns, wielding the authority of an FBI agent and a doctor, and plunging into gory autopsies of monsters and their mangled victims.

The most extreme representatives of the trend are the "bad girls." Zach's mega-samurai babe, like dozens of other killer babes I've seen teenage boys draw, is a manifestation of an icon that thrills millions of teenage boys but, like so many fantasy images that combine violence and sexuality, makes parents nervous. Like Buffy, these are sexy women who defeat mostly male opponents, but instead of Buffy's Maybelline-model cool, they sport exaggerated breasts, skimpy clothing, huge guns or blood-dripping swords, and nasty attitudes. And although market research shows that a lot of girls love them in every medium, their principal fan base is composed of boys.

When I ask boys why they like these fantasy women, they usually respond with a variant of Zach's leer. "Lara Croft is hot!" "Elektra's wicked!" "Jessica Alba is fine!" And, indeed, any excuse to look at and fantasize about a voluptuous female body is welcome to most teenage boys. These female bodies, however, would be no less "hot" if the women were damsels in distress or helpless victims. In fact, if objectification were the main point of the fantasy, they would serve a boy's needs much better if they were passive and nonthreatening. The current generation of adolescent boys love active, powerful, threatening female figures—often as protagonists and often, as in the case of video games in which the male player "becomes" *Tomb Raiders'* Lara Croft or one of the female warriors in *Mortal Kombat,* as a heroic surrogate for the boy himself. When Zach brings his mega-samurai babe into his comic strip, she immediately takes center stage in his fantasies. These kids may approach their bad girls as objects at first, and they may tell themselves and each other that that's why they like them, but as the game or the movie or the TV show begins to unfold, they are clearly *identifying* with them.

Zach's remark that "Chicks really *do* always win" was a meaningful gag. From looking at the stories boys are selecting for their fantasy lives, I think they're both excited and scared by girls' increasing desire to hold and express power, sexual and otherwise. They envy girl power, may resent it sometimes, but also want to partake in it and match it with their own. Since one of the functions of play is to help us take control over what frightens us, the teenage boys playing with sexy, destructive, exaggerated images of women are easing their fears of girls in much the way little boys playing with Darth Vader are easing their fears of death, destruction, and bad guys. At the same time, "becoming" mega-babes helps them contain some of their anxiety about girl power by enabling them to say to themselves in their imagination, "It's *my* power, too."

By objectifying those same babes sexually (or pretending to), they take even more control of that anxiety-provoking power and feel they're reinforcing their boyishness at the same time. Indirectly, these boys are accommodating to shifting gender roles, building confidence that they can find even strong, challenging women attractive and that they won't be overwhelmed by their own fears as they deal with real girls. We meet the power of being an *object* again. These girls are sexual objects to the boys, but the boys gain some power by becoming those objects themselves. Popular culture doesn't allow men to be such blatant objects; of action movie stars, only Schwarzenegger really qualifies, and his old-school he-man no longer speaks to many young men. Girls have long been known to identify with male fantasy figures. Now it looks as though boys are finally learning the same art.

I glimpsed the rewards of that cross-identification when I was writing comic books, including the early 90s incarnations of Wonder Woman and Power Girl. Although they were just as powerful and heroic as their male counterparts, they differed in subtle but profound ways. The writers and artists who had developed their characters hadn't made them quite like male heroes. The heroines were less stoic, though no less tough, in the face of adversity and were allowed a much broader spectrum of emotion. They could be loving, nurturing, and overtly protective of the weak in a way the grim Superman and Batman never were. They could be flirtatious, cute, embarrassed, silly, self-indulgent, and knowingly sexy. And if they flew into a savage rage against a villain, it was liable to be a much more personal, and more human, reaction. By combining the "frailties" normally allowed to women in commercial entertainment with the power and anger allowed to men, they became much more complete characters.

Talking to fans, I began to realize that they would perceive female heroes along those lines even if they weren't written so. Writers, artists, and readers alike saw more vulnerability and more tenderness in a fantasy character simply because she was female. Even when I asked about the meanest, baddest girls, the likes of Marvel's Elektra, who could scarcely be called vulnerable or tender, I heard descriptions that suggested a greater emotional freedom than their male equivalents: they were "sensuous," "passionate," "artistic," "in love with what she's doing," "could love an opponent even when she has to kill him." The image of *woman* automatically created room for a teenager's imagination to project emotions onto her that he (or she) couldn't project onto the classic stiff-necked male adventurer.

As parents and teachers have worked harder to help little girls and boys recognize and express their feelings, particularly the softer and less aggressive feelings, and as emotionality becomes more central to mass entertainment, from children's television to *Jerry Springer*, kids are given a new challenge: weaving vulnerability and emotional messiness into fantasy selves that still feel powerful, invulnerable, and competent. The usual models of manhood—both in the media and the reality of most dads and other adult males—don't show very well how that can be done. Male heroes may be stoic or angry or funny, but our expectations of them usually don't allow them volatility, tenderness, or vanity. Girls have long been able to identify with male characters to experience courage, calm, and mastery in fantasy. Now boys are showing themselves able to identify with female characters to experience other parts of the human spectrum, without feeling that they're sacrificing their power or boyishness.

Those fantasies become particularly heated when sexuality enters the mix. Teenage boys will always be overwhelmed by their own sudden desires. The amount of sexual stimulation kids experience today through advertising and entertainment only makes those more overwhelming. Add the dangers kids have grown up hearing about sex, add all the messages and realities around girls' physical and sexual power, add the ideals that boys think they are supposed to meet, and adolescence can be a time of intense anxiety for boys. Since one of the powers of imaginary violence, as we've seen, is to explode anxiety, no aspect of adolescence calls more urgently for violent fantasy than sexuality. That's also where male heroes are often most inadequate. A male hero might get the girl, might defeat a *femme fatale,* might establish dominance over sexual power in many ways, but he'll almost never be allowed to play with sexuality, or enjoy it, or make it a part of his personality. What Buffy does for girls, no Arnold Schwarzenegger character could possibly do for boys. But if a boy allows himself to identify secretly with her, Lara Croft can do it very well.

As adults, we find the linking of sexuality and violence disturbing, especially when those images are gory and intense. *Buffy the Vampire Slayer* and *Dark Angel* are mild in comparison to games like *Mortal Kombat, D.O.A.,* and *Tomb Raider.* Watching a teenage boy manipulating those sexualized figures as they hammer at bad guys and each other, grinning triumphantly as they make blood fly, is troubling. But we need to differentiate our reactions from what they're experiencing.

I watched a fourteen-year-old boy playing *D.O.A.* in the form of a female warrior for a while. He was a poor city kid, skinny, glasses, friends mostly gamers. He was into fighting with body English and exclamations of "Yeah!" when his female combat-self landed a blow. Between levels I asked him, "Why'd you pick her?" "She's the best fighter," he said. But I knew enough about these games to know that every player has his own idea of the best fighter. "The best fighter for *you,*" I said. "How come?" He thought a minute. "She's smooth," he said. "She doesn't do it with just strength, but she's fierce. She's *intense.*" No game arcade is sophisticated enough to give such personalities to its combat images. But the kid was smooth, and fierce, and intense when he was her.

Sexuality and violence are an explosive mix, and they can come together with serious, negative, real-world consequences. As parents, as teachers, and as a society, it's important to give kids constructive messages about body image, sexuality, gender roles, and the emotional turmoil of adolescence. It's also important that they have the stories they need to integrate those messages effectively with their own yearnings and fantasies. The stories that adolescents choose also give us glimpses into the issues they're struggling with and give us an arena for communicating with them, whether we're joking about

Buffy's bustier or just asking a kid to tell us why he picked a female warrior. Every adolescent is confronted by sudden physical, emotional, and social changes. The current generation of adolescents is also bearing the brunt of vast, frightening, and potentially liberating changes in our culture. Characters from Buffy to Lara Croft help them face all those changes with greater confidence.

Keeping the lines of communication open with young people who are playing with fantasies that trouble us is a challenge. None, however, may be more challenging, or erect higher walls between children and parents, than the video games known as "shooters."

10

Shooters

*M*ost of the experts I know see the value of superheroes, action figures, and slapstick cartoons. But the mere mention
of gory video games provokes a very different reaction. After a passionate defense of superheroes at a conference panel, one developmental psychologist paused and then said with special vehemence,
"But I don't think video games in which the player is induced to
shoot at other human beings are ever good for *anyone*." A psychiatrist
who helped me with my research cringed slightly at the mention of
Quake and said, "There has to be something wrong with a person
who'd want to look at that."

Once, on a cable news channel, I debated a New York state senator
who was pushing legislation to ban violent video games for children
under eighteen. I talked about the benefits many teenagers have
found in various sorts of games—not realizing that the producers
were running images from a gory first-person shooter game on the
screen as I spoke. When I watched the tape later and heard myself
saying, "I know of many kids who thrive in the gaming culture" as
bullets blew through skulls and blood went flying, I was appalled at
my own words.

Nothing sets off our revulsion like explicit gore. Nothing triggers
our worries about how our kids may turn out than watching them
gun down real-looking people on screen. It's understandable that hy-

potheses suggesting that video games are training our children to be killers have garnered tremendous publicity, even though the evidence doesn't support them. It's understandable that the Joint Statement on the Impact of Entertainment Violence on Children would expect "that they may be significantly more harmful" than other media. It's understandable that when we learned that the boys who attacked their classmates at Columbine High School were heavy players of shooter games, we assumed the games had helped make them killers.

But when concerned adults condemn entertainment that millions of well-adjusted young people love and insist is perfectly good for them, we owe it to the young people—and ourselves—to learn more about it. When I launched my exploration of bloody video games I felt as though I were taking a journey into one of the darkest recesses of contemporary youth culture. But the more I got to know those games and the people who played them, the less I saw to fear. Ultimately I've come to feel that video games are the least powerful and least dangerous of all forms of entertainment violence.

When we encounter something new, we try to understand it in terms of other things already known to us. In a powerful book, *On Killing,* U.S. Army psychologist Dave Grossman described operant conditioning methods used during the Vietnam War that resembled some of today's video games and revealed that some military units are now using those same video games to train soldiers. He argued well for the effectiveness of using animated but human-looking targets, the rapidity of a game, and instant rewards for quick shooting as tools to desensitize soldiers to the human dimension of what they were doing—and he asserted that video games are doing precisely the same thing to our kids.

There are problems with Grossman's argument, however. Effective conditioning requires structured application and a well-controlled environment, which is scarcely what gamers are experiencing when they're fiddling with a video game in their own rooms or messing around an arcade with hundreds of other kids. Grossman frequently quotes B. F. Skinner, who developed operant conditioning, but doesn't mention one of the essential human truths that Skinner himself acknowledged our reactions, unlike those of dogs or rats, are profoundly affected by the feelings, thoughts, and meanings that we assign to the stimuli in our environments. All the military training Grossman described takes place in an authoritarian environment in which the soldiers know full well that the purpose of the game is to make them better killers; they generally want to cooperate (especially in a volunteer army), and every message they hear is, "Kill for your country." What our kids are doing with their video games is playing, and they know it. Games have always been a part of military training, and nearly all competitive games have a warlike subtext. Wellington said that the Battle of Waterloo "was won on the playing fields of Eton," but cricket and rugby haven't turned subsequent generations of Etonians into killers. Just because shooter games remind us of real shooting and military training doesn't mean that kids experience them as such when they play, any more than they experience plastic army men or chess pieces as real warriors.

After a decade of these games being played by millions of kids, Grossman and other critics have provided no evidence of the effects they have predicted. Certainly video games haven't had any significant impact on real-world crime. "The research on video games and crime is compelling to read," said Helen Smith, forensic psychologist, youth violence specialist, and author of *The Scarred Heart*. "But it just doesn't hold up. Kids have been getting less violent since those games came out. That includes gun violence and every other sort of violence that might be inspired by a video game." The contemporary style of the first-person shooter game hit the market with *Castle Wolfenstein* in 1991; *Doom* and *Quake,* still by far the best-sellers of the genre, followed in 1992. The peak of shooter-game play by teenagers was from approximately 1992 to 1995, by which time the games' sales had dropped, and they'd gone from being the fad of the moment to one of many genres in the industry. Violent crime dropped during those years. We've now had time for those millions of game players to reach adulthood, and the generation of "killer kids" predicted by the games' critics never materialized.

"There's no connection between video gaming and violence in the profiles of the kids I see," noted Smith. "In fact, the lower-income kids who make up the great majority of violent kids usually don't have any interest in games—and they couldn't afford the hobby even if they did." Both her practice and her survey show that extremely angry and violent kids often show interest in violent music, Web sites, and movies, but rarely in video games. "I don't discount the influence some media may have on very hostile young people," she concluded. "But there just doesn't seem to be any connection with games."

A few studies of adolescents have found a correlation between heavy video game use and various sorts of delinquent behavior. Among teenagers, unemployed boys who aren't great academic achievers are more likely to amuse themselves with video games; unemployed boys who aren't great academic achievers are also more likely to misbehave. Kids who work for high grades, play sports, do community work, and have jobs often play *Quake*, too, but they don't have the time to show up as "heavy users" in a correlative study. Several laboratory studies have recorded increases in aggression in young people after playing video games. Those studies, however, have had the subjects play for limited times, usually fifteen minutes, and then stop abruptly—a situation guaranteed to frustrate anyone in a high-suspense, high-adrenaline game. And the readings have been taken immediately after the kids have finished, when their arousal is as heightened as it would have been at the end of any competitive or exciting experience. The research process itself may create the reactions it measures.

Then there's Columbine. The planned, systematic way in which Dylan Klebold and Eric Harris attacked and slaughtered their schoolmates made it the most horrific of all the teen rampage shootings. We needed an explanation for it, and the discovery that Klebold and Harris loved these as yet little-known shooter games provided one. The boys apparently reprogrammed their copy of *Doom* to simulate the slaughter they were planning and used the game to practice for it. Those hours upon hours spent shooting imaginary foes very likely made it easier for them to make their terrible fantasies real. But some perspective is needed.

Based on the data of Dr. James McGee, an authority on the "classroom avenger," there have been sixteen rampage shootings at schools by adolescents in recent years, involving eighteen boys. Only at

Columbine, the thirteenth of the rampages, did the perpetrators turn out to be heavy game players. A few other boys liked shooter video games to one extent or another, though less, in every case, than they liked target shooting with real guns. Most of the shooters showed no interest in games at all. Other elements were much more common to the eighteen boys: bullying by peers, hostility with or dissociation from parents, suicidal threats, and fascination with news coverage of earlier rampage shootings show up among all of them. Several shared a preoccupation with Adolf Hitler or other symbols of historical violence, certain angry rock songs and violent movies, and real weapons. Klebold and Harris's costumes and rhetoric were unlike any in the games they played, but they owed an obvious debt to earlier school shooters (especially the first nationally publicized shooter, Barry Loukaitis of Moses Lake, Washington) and to right-wing extremists. The news and history seem to have been far deadlier influences on them than the unreality of *Doom*.

Significantly, Loukaitis and other early school shooters were fascinated by the many earlier workplace rampages of adult men. In fact, school shooters resemble adult rampage shooters in nearly all important respects: demographics, personality types, the pattern of perceived slights and escalating grudges leading to the incidents, fascination with media notoriety, and even the sorts of comments made during and after the shootings. School shootings appear to be a case of teenagers imitating their elders. Those adult rampaging killers, who have erupted periodically since the late 1970s, have never been linked to video games.

Like the Beatles song that Charles Manson claimed inspired him to murder or the poetry that Timothy McVeigh quoted to justify his bombing of the Oklahoma City federal building, shooter video games have sometimes been plucked and twisted by troubled souls to give some shape to the rages within them. Sometimes they seem to help such people contain their rage. Sometimes they aren't powerful enough, and they may become part of a rehearsal for murder and suicide. But to condemn them because they lend themselves so easily to such terrible uses is to fail to understand their place in the lives of modern teenagers.

Helen Smith's principal objection to theorists who try to link video games to real-life crime is the same as mine: "They're not listening to the kids." Critic Dave Grossman asked in one chapter title, "What Are We Doing to Our Kids?" But not once did he ask the kids, "What are you doing?" He has viewed gamers not as imaginative people using a mechanical toy but as cyborgs whose reactions are determined by the machine. "In video arcades," he wrote, "children stand slackjawed but intent behind machine guns and shoot at electronic targets. . . ." I don't know what arcade Grossman went to, but it would take a Zen master to play a video game slack-jawed. What gamers describe to me as the "video game face" is quite the opposite: twisted by tooth-gnashing, jaw-jerking, and occasional open-mouthed suspense. More experienced gamers may be tense and stoic, but they are viscerally, emotionally engaged in competition, choosing to devote their leisure time, money, and a great deal of effort to becoming better at a game. Most contemporary gamers are also involved in social and intellectual processes far more complex than merely playing in an arcade.

In talking to gamers visiting the annual Game Designers' Expo in Silicon Valley, reading the research, and playing the games myself, I've been struck by how different the video game world is from my preconceptions. The games are becoming remarkably creative. All the successful first-person shooter games now allow users to design their own "maps" in which the battles will take place, to create new "levels" with customized backgrounds and challenges, and to choose their own "skins," the physical appearance of their game selves. One teenage gamer led me through a communal tournament fought in the land of Oz by two Nazis, a cowboy, a mercenary, a teddy bear, and a loaf of bread. Although the basic story line remains the same— the player has to find his way through labyrinthine structures and fight off ambushing opponents to reach a distant goal—gamers are essentially scripting their own adventures.

According to Dr. Mihaly Csikszentmihalyi, a leading authority on adolescent development and the originator of the concept of "flow states," any media experience that demands activity, interaction, control, and emotional stimulation is far more constructive than a passive experience like watching television. Traditional forms of entertainment, such as storytelling, puppet plays, and live musical performances, challenge children to more vital intellectual and emotional states by requiring that they bring more imagination and more of their own psychic contents to comprehending material than do the electronic media, which typically supply prepackaged information. Csikszentmihalyi noted that the simpler video games, "those that involve primarily piling up as many cadavers as possible," offer more than television, but not much more. "However, the newer, more complex video games," he said, "give players worlds to explore and decisions to make that can stir some of the emotions of discovery. They may prove to be very valuable forms."

I experienced those emotions of discovery when I had a young player lead me through a level of *Quake 3*. We picked our way through the claustrophobic corridors of an abandoned castle, vigilant every moment to the possibility of ambush—although the attacks were far from constant, leaving us more time to dread them than to relieve the suspense in action—when suddenly we came to a staircase. We shot our way through one more pair of zombies and raced upward to freedom. Stepping through a door to the battlements of the castle, where the black stone suddenly fell away to reveal a vast sunset, filled me with an elation of freedom and courage. I wanted nothing more than to plunge into the next level.

Gaming is also becoming an increasingly social activity. Gamers talk and e-mail incessantly about strategies and shortcuts they've discovered, plan communal tournaments, pass around copies of *PC Gamer* magazine, and invite friends over to see their new games. Although "heavy gamers" may stick to their own esoteric cliques, most gamers are part of adolescent society and use games as icebreakers and bonding mechanisms. Most gamers now prefer not to play alone against the computer but against other gamers by way of multiplayer consoles or Internet-based games that can include dozens of players at once. The video game, at this point, becomes an athletic competition for kids who may not be able to throw far or run fast. Its players aren't cyborgs being conditioned by a machine but competitors assessing their own and their opponents' skills: who's quicker, who knows the "map" better, who can strategize most intelligently? Afterward there's usually a lot of talking or e-mailing about how the tournament played out and why. Gaming isn't a complete social life, but it can be a vital piece of one, especially for kids who don't fit well into other juvenile cliques.

Not surprisingly, then, gaming is also becoming a steadily less male-dominated world. "Heavy gamers" are more likely to be male, but among preteens, nearly as many girls as boys own and play video games—even the more violent games. As Dr. Jeanne Funk's focus groups with children suggest, girls tend to like violent games less than boys, and they prefer to use the word "action" for what boys call "violence," but they commonly play even the gorier shooting and fighting games in social situations. Unlike some violent music and movies, video games generally don't appeal to the more aggressive teenagers. As one game-industry marketer put it, "Heavy gamers are nerds. There are some borderline tough kids who also game, but the real bad-asses look down at this as kid stuff. Gamers are reasonably bright but not big achievers, hang with other gamers and don't like to attract too much attention. They can be socially clueless, self-absorbed, and arrogant, but one of the main reasons they disappear into the gaming world is that they want to avoid real-life trouble."

Perhaps, then, it should have surprised me less than it did to learn that the extreme violence and realistic gore that disturbs us so much really doesn't matter much to the gamers. Studies show that if a gamer is given a choice between a gory game that doesn't challenge his skills and a non-gory one that does, he'll usually choose the challenge over the gore. Some of the best-selling first-person shooter games, such as *Goldeneye* with James Bond, feature bloodless violence in old-time Hollywood style. The ultraviolent games now account for less than 10 percent of the game market, and industry surveys show that few gamers specialize in them but typically play a wide variety of types. One fourteen-year-old gamer I talked to listed his five favorite games as *Quake 3*, *Half-Life*, *Starcraft* (science-fiction strategy), *The Legend of Zelda: Ocarina of Time* (humorous adventure), and *Tony Hawk Skateboarding*.

"Gore is at best a tertiary appeal of shooter games," said Dallas Middaugh, an editor of many books about gaming and a gamer himself. "Game play is by far the most important element—the difficulty, the strategy required, the complexity of variations, the suspense. Next comes the overall environment and appearance of the game world. Gore just adds a bit to the realism and visual impact."

Some game designers have tried to cash in on the negative, but lucrative, publicity that bad taste brings. One, *Soldier of Fortune,* successfully stirred up controversy with its sadistic portrayals of Americans attacking Vietnamese and Latin American villages, thus glorifying some of our most haunting atrocities. After a flurry of publicity, however, it faded in the marketplace. One adult gamer told me, "It wasn't challenging enough. Your opponents were too weak. It was all shock value, and gamers resent that." The shooter games that have remained successful are more fantastical and less vicious, and pit the player against more overwhelming odds. In *Half-Life,* the player is an innocent scientist who has to fight his way through hundreds of invading aliens and soldiers sent by a corrupt government. In *Quake 3,* he is a normal human battling a legion of zombies. These games are not about slaughtering victims but about killing monsters.

Video games are most threatening to adults who have seen images of them but never tried to play them. When I first saw the games, I saw animated people being blown away by the dozen. But in just a few minutes of play, I saw that the whole point of the game is suspense: "I" was in constant danger and had to battle through overwhelming odds to survive. The experience of shooting an opponent is one of relief, not cruelty. One teenager put it simply: "The purpose of the blood is just so you can see if you've hit your target. You need to be able to tell that to play the game."

I went into this research expecting to find that kids were processing rage through their games, and that's what the psychologists and psychiatrists I spoke with told me to look for. It made sense: if a kid wants to shoot holes in imaginary enemies, he must be blowing off anger about something. Certainly there *are* angry gamers. Several therapists have brought me cases of young people who have suffered abuse at home or at school and have, consciously or not, turned to video games as a safe arena in which to act out fantasies of retribution. Dr. Craig Anderson, who has testified before Congress and other governmental bodies as one of psychology's leading critics of media violence, has revealed that he has been the object of so many raging e-mails from gamers who resent his criticism of their hobby that he's begun to fear for his safety. In such cases, the games may not contribute to the anger, but they don't seem to dispel it either. As I got to know more gamers, however, I began to realize I wasn't seeing much rage. I was seeing a fair amount of tension, repression, and irritability—but never the fury or dissociation or seething depression of some of the kids I'd met who were into gangster rap, death rock, or real guns.

Even in crowded, low-budget downtown arcades gamers tend to be quiet, patient, and self-contained. I once watched a quartet of black high school kids in an arcade in a working-class California city. The two boys made a point of being absolutely cool and composed, whether they were shooting bad guys or choosing their next game. The girls were more playful. One, in a glitter-paint "Diva" t-shirt and cornrows, fought her way through a level, put her hand on her hip, drew her gun back effetely like James Bond, and chirped, "Damn I'm bad!" They were all politely intrigued when I introduced myself and told them what I was researching. I asked what they got out of gaming. "It's *fun!*" said the girls together. "It feels good to be good," said one of the boys. And did they ever get involved in real violence? The other boy smiled condescendingly. "We're not *stupid*," he said. When I ask gamers what they feel when they decide to play a first-person shooter, most have a hard time identifying an emotional state at all, but those who do never mention anger. They talk about tension and boredom beforehand, suspense and excitement during the battle.

An adult gamer, Oscar Munoz, finally made sense of it for me: "You *can't* be angry when you play a video game. You have to be *calm*, or you're going to get wasted. I've played against other gamers who get pissed, overreact on the controls, and it's over. It's like softball. You're seething with rage at the pitcher and you think, I'm gonna *cream* that ball, and what happens, you overswing. It's all about being alert, focused, but loose, having fun. Staying *cool*, even when guys are coming at you with guns."

Munoz is a progressive political activist, an advocate for increasing the legal and political access of poor and nonwhite Americans, and a self-described "closet gamer." "My buddies and I played a lot of *Wolfenstein* and *Doom* in high school," he said. "We were inner-city kids, not great athletes, we wanted to have something that was ours. We didn't want to get in trouble but we didn't want to be geeks. The games were our thing. They were hard, and they were bloody, and a lot of the jocks and tough guys got into them, too. But we played *better* than them. That gave us something." In college Munoz thought he should be more serious, so he put his games away. Pretty soon, though, he discovered that they were his best avenue to relieve stress. When he chose politics as a career, he started using them regularly to wind down, especially after difficult wranglings with city governments and community programs. He discovered that some of his fellow activists felt the same, and they brought a game console into their offices. "Our work is very intense, high-stakes, detail-driven. We need to blow off steam at the end of the day. We bond over them, too—shared suspense, shared laughs. Our work piles up a lot of annoyances between us, and we need those out of there to keep going."

A screenwriter named Sam Hamm, writer of Tim Burton's *Batman* and Henry Selick's *Monkeybone*, was one of the few adult game players I knew in the early 1990s, when the first wave of sophisticated shooter games was coming out. "*Doom* is the only game I've seen," he said, "that has the real quality of a dream." He described the feeling of immersion in its unreal world, the almost unbearable tension of waiting for unseen attackers, the release of attack, counterattack, and moving on—or of "dying" and coming back to face the suspense again. The realism of the violence, he made clear, was essential to surrendering himself to the dream state.

Shauna is a high school junior and a gamer. She uses multiplayer consoles to play against friends in her room, and she goes on-line with her computer to play anonymous gamers on the Internet. She likes car-racing games and *Gex*, but she said that when she's especially tense, as when she comes home from her part-time retail job, she prefers what she calls "realistic fantasy games." Some of those are shooters, some are adventures like *Oni Musha*, in which a samurai battles monsters, demons, and evil warriors in medieval Japan. When the samurai swords hit their marks, blood flies and limbs roll. "It's a world I can go into," she said. "With movie-quality graphics and realistic gore, everything looks real enough for me to feel like I'm there. It's spooky, things I'd never want to see in reality. But that's why it's such a good fantasy. I am that warrior, I'm in that world, but I can handle anything."

Then there's that function of gore that has attracted teens and preteens as long as commercial entertainment has existed: to make them feel tough and grown up. I know a boy named Jake who announced when he was twelve that he wanted *Half-Life*. He'd read a review in a gaming magazine that said it was the most sophisticated shooter game yet, with great game play, significant replay value—and luridly rendered bloodshed. His favorite video game until then was *Starcraft*, and his favorite part of it was designing the "game maps" with a friend, hours of collaborative world-building to which the climactic spaceship battle was only a punctuation mark. Otherwise his tastes ran to Disneyland, Weird Al Yankovic, *Mystery Science Theater*, and his pet cat. He was a strong-willed kid, and he had regular conflicts with his mom, his bossy older sister, and occasionally even his mellow dad, but his anger was appropriate and well expressed. The family was close, and he got along well in school. Suddenly, though, he wanted to shoot animated soldiers and watch the blood fly.

"What do you like about that?" I asked him. "*Gore!*" he said. "Why?" I asked. "It's *cool!*" he cackled. Jake would tell whoever listened that he loved gore. It made his mother squirm. It bugged his sister, who found everything about the culture of young boys annoying. It drew expressions of bemusement from his father, who liked to read Jane Austen, listen to Bill Evans, and avoid roller coasters, hard rock, and anything else too viscerally disturbing. Until then, Jake had been the little kid in the family who was squeamish about spiders and afraid of the skeletons in the Indiana Jones ride. Suddenly, as he found himself heading for the disquieting new world of adolescence, he wanted to be the tough guy. His parents understood that and had faith in him. They told him that if he still wanted *Half-Life* when he turned thirteen, they'd get it for him. They were true to their word, and for a month or so he virtually lived to play *Half-Life*.

When I talked to him six months later, however, he said his favorite game was again *Starcraft*. He still liked *Half-Life*, but only enough to play it about once a week. I asked him if he was losing interest in the gore. He snorted, as only a thirteen-year-old can snort. "I'm not into the *gore*," he said. "You were," I said. "I was not," he said. He insisted that he was into the game play, the difficulty of the levels, the strategy, the suspense. The more adult-oriented games are the most challenging to play, and they also happen to have the most gore. The "gore level" of most games can be adjusted, he explained, and he always set them to "normal." "I tried 'low,'" he said, echoing other gamers I've talked to, "but then you can hardly see the blood. You can't tell if you hit your target or not."

I asked him why he doesn't set them to "high," and he answered, "It's distracting. And just kind of . . . weird." He told me that he only knows one other kid who sets the gore to "high," because he thinks it's funny. But Jake finds him "weird," too. I asked, "You're telling me you find the gore disturbing?" "A little bit," he said quietly. He added that he knows other kids who feel the same. When I asked why he thinks the gore is there, he rallied with a bit of adolescent bravado: "It's part of violence, right? It would be a lie not to have it. And violence has been afflicting our society for thousands of years. It's what's on people's minds." I asked him if it's on his mind. Quieter again: "Well. Yeah. I mean, people commit violence all the time. It's on the news *constantly.*"

When I asked him about Columbine Jake gave me a response that could have come from an editorial in a gaming magazine: "Those games have been played by millions of people, and only two of them did that. Only *two* out of *millions*. I'd say the problem was with those two people, not the games." Then I asked him if he ever thought about school shootings when he played. "*Welllllll*," he said, and I heard that same impishness in him that I heard months ago when he first told me that gore was cool. "One of my friends and I spent a long time trying to create an *Unreal Tournament* level based on our school!" As much as I trusted Jake, that raised the little hairs on the back of my neck. I asked him why, and he said, "The architecture at my school is really strange. The walls are orange and blank, and the bars in the gates look like they were built to withstand a nuclear war. It looks like a *prison*." I asked him if he felt confined there. "Not much," he said. "We just thought it would be exciting to have the whole place torn inside-out by this ultimate death battle!"

The daily tension of school can be intense for a sensitive kid, and few experiences would be as liberating as turning that school "inside out." In the consequence-free fantasy of a game, kids can make themselves grown-up, powerful, and free to blow the walls off their daily prison. After a game like that, the real school might be much more likable. This is a very different use of pretend violence than the calming of anxieties through repetition—but an equally helpful one. The same child may use games to contain his feelings at some times, and to act them out at others.

Gore, as we've seen, has many functions. It can express hostility. "*Duke Nukem* was obviously a game designed by a guy who couldn't get girls to go out with him when he was thirteen," said Dallas Middaugh, "and this was his way of saying, 'Take that!'" It can provide a powerful compensation for young people who feel especially frustrated by a culture of restraint; kids who don't feel free to act up in real life can feel a great release when they blow an enemy apart. It can release tension around subjects that polite conversation doesn't allow us to explore; a bloody video game can seem honest, fearless, and refreshing for confronting what adults are squeamish about. It can help young people set themselves apart from parental society and bond with their peers.

It can also add a quality of "realism" to play that helps older children and teenagers immerse themselves in it. The fantasy states these gamers describe remind me of playing "war" in the front yard with my friends when I was eight or nine. Although all I saw in reality were my friends groaning and falling down, what I saw in my mind was as bloody as anything in today's video games. I knew that people bled and died in real wars. I knew my father had fought in the war. I remember asking him once if he'd really killed anyone—and hoping that the answer would be no. When I was young I could play through my mingled excitement, curiosity, and discomfort. By the age of ten, though, it was no longer possible to lose myself in the game. Suddenly I didn't see bullets and blood in my mind's eye; I saw myself as a goofy-looking kid running around yelling on the lawn. Video games allow people to go on playing past the age of self-consciousness.

The danger of these games is that by enabling people to immerse themselves so completely in play, they may make it hard to climb back out. The typical video-gamer plays only five or six hours a week, and the activity most often sacrificed in favor of gaming is television watching. But there are gamers who play five or six hours a day, who sacrifice their social lives and school performance and every other constructive activity. This seems to be most true of fantasy role-playing games, in which players become unique characters on the Internet and participate in long adventures and relationships with other gamers. But among standard video games, the first-person shooter games seem more likely than most to take the place of some gamers' real lives. They create such a viscerally compelling but controllable reality that the quiet tensions and messy ambivalence of reality can become increasingly unbearable by contrast. Gamers tell me about going into a "tournament" with the intention of passing a few minutes and finding that two hours have suddenly gone by. Some take that as a reminder to manage their time more consciously. Others go back in at the first opportunity.

"Some of my adolescent patients speak of being 'addicted' to video games," said Lynn Ponton. "I don't like to use the word addiction, but it is habitual behavior. They use video games to contain their anxiety. And the games will do that for them for quite a while. But with time they can also desensitize them. The players need more and more stimulation to contain their anxieties, which not only keeps them from dealing with the causes of their anxiety but can actually increase their anxieties."

Psychiatrist Nancy Marks has also seen patients who seem to play video games instead of living. "For many people it's a way of avoiding the real existential issues, the angst, of life," she said. "They may try to deal with their pain and anxiety through the surrogate selves of

these games, but there's really no way to work through significant issues in a game, not unless someone is sitting there talking to you
about what you're doing in the game and what that might mean
about your real life. These games can be constructive as long as the
players know they're playing and come back to real life. But some
people forget that this is just play."

Too often we just dismiss gamers, let them retreat into isolation, or
chase them away by worrying too much about their gaming. Doctors
Ponton and Marks both have stressed the power of communication.
Ponton has advocated trying to play the games occasionally with the
kids, which she does with both her daughters and her patients. "I
don't usually last long at the games," she confessed. "But beating
mom or Dr. Ponton makes them feel good in its own way and can
ease some of the barriers between us." If a parent can't stand to play
the game, just being available can help young people resurface. If a
teenager disappears into his room for too many hours at the expense
of the rest of life, consider moving the game console into the family
room. "Sometimes," Ponton said, "it can be helpful to young people
just to have a parent nearby, reading or balancing the checkbook."

When parents aren't available, teachers, friends, or any interested
party can help habitual gamers integrate their fantasies with real life
just by communicating with them about the games. Simply talking
about the games calmly and respecting young people's passion for
them, whether that means discussing them in schools or putting
them in public places, will help open the door for gamers to connect
more meaningfully with society at large. I contrast Jimmy, the boy
from Pennsylvania who felt so ostracized by his teachers' reactions to
his games, with Richard, the Quaker youth worker playing *Quake 3*
at a public conference. Fear and hostility can make any entertainment
problematic communication and empathy can help make any entertainment constructive.

We are frightened by the images we see in the games, and so we
become frightened of the people who love them, which makes us
shove those people further from us and induces them to play the
games more often and in greater isolation. Because the hobby looks
bizarre to us, we seek evidence of its effects in bizarre events. "It's

true that crime rates in general have gone down," said New York State Senator Michael Balboni in the course of his campaign for video-game regulation. "But according to a detective on the New York City Police Force I was speaking to, certain types of crimes are up. Beheadings are up. Burnings are up. These are the types of violence portrayed in these games. Is this a coincidence?" The question is a misdirection. Horrific, sadistic crimes have been with us for centuries, many of them perpetrated by adolescents. The 1924 Leopold and Loeb case, in which two wealthy young men murdered a younger boy mostly just to prove they could get away with it, sparked debates about the new generation of soulless youth and the pernicious influence of movies, jazz, and liberal education. But from the distance of time, it's clear that the cruelty of those two boys did not reflect any trend or pattern. There is no evidence to support the fear that video games have increased the amount or changed the nature of crime anywhere.

We are troubled by the idea of repetition. We fear that if kids do something over and over again in play they're more likely to replicate it in life. But the evidence suggests that repeated play is usually a good tool to diminish the power of their thoughts and feelings, not to strengthen them. We're also troubled by the thought of kids playing actively with disturbing images. But the example of video games suggests that kids' ability to write their own "scripts" and build their own "maps" gives them more control over those images. This is why I feel that the Joint Statement may have had it exactly backward when it suggested that video games "may be even more harmful" than other media. There do seem to be cases of movies and songs exacerbating young people's aggression or providing them scripts for acting out, but not games. Because games are so obviously artificial, so completely the player's tool, they are the medium least capable of inspiring any powerful emotion beyond the thrills of the playing itself. If they condition children to do anything, it's only to play more—which may be their one real pitfall.

Even if video games have inspired some acts of real violence, trying to prevent such incidents by restricting access to the games is an absurd and potentially dangerous idea. As the examples of alcohol, tobacco, and drugs have shown us trying to restrict access usually means that the young people most fascinated with them will still get them, but they'll have to be covert in their use. They won't be able to work them into an open social life, won't discuss them with their parents, and will be even more likely to disappear into their rooms with them. They'll see themselves as outlaws just by playing the game. Already branding themselves "bad kids" because they play a forbidden game, they'll have been pushed one step closer to allowing themselves to do something really bad. What's true of the older forms of entertainment violence is true of this unsettling new one. All of us—parents, teachers, policymakers, children—will benefit not from more control but from more understanding.

When one of my articles was published, a reader responded: "My husband and I were at the Cliff House in San Francisco and I saw an Asian teenager playing that video game in which the player is supposed to destroy a peaceful Southeast Asian village. I wanted to jerk the controls out of his hands and ask him if he had any idea what he was doing! Didn't he know what messages this was sending him about his own history, about his own culture, about the cost of violence in the world?"

I answered that I understood; I came of age politically abhorring the Vietnam War, and I find glorification and trivialization of it appalling. But I pointed out that there's an arrogance, too, in thinking that a middle-aged white person's noblest response is to jerk the controls out of the boy's hands. That kid knows more about being a teenager and an Asian-American in contemporary America than we ever will. The only message jerking the controls from him will send is that adults don't care what he likes or why. Instead, we should ask the kid why he wants to play that game. I don't know what he would say, but we should ask. And I believe something good will come from the asking alone.

11

Model, Mirror, and Mentor

There's an old adage that holds that as soon a man's become especially good at something he immediately begins to overestimate its importance. Baseball players speak of being witnesses to a great moment in history whenever the home-run record is challenged, forgetting that the event in question is all about hitting a ball with a stick.

The same is true of those of us who study the media. Whether we love it or hate it, whether we work in it, critique it, run scientific studies on it, or just pay special attention to it as parents, the more time we spend with it, the more important we think it is in our children's lives. In fact, it becomes far more important to us than to the children, who are blissfully unaware of it as anything but entertainment.

The opposite may be true of parenting. Because none of us ever feel like we *really* know what we're doing, it's easy for us to fear that we're insignificant and powerless—especially in the face of a huge, arrogant, intrusive entertainment industry that's criticized by so many experts. Senator Joe Lieberman recently said that the purpose of congressional hearings on entertainment isn't so much to open the door to legislation as to educate parents and reassure them that someone's on their side. Parents, he said, "feel they are competing with the entertainment industry to teach their kids values."

I've talked to many parents who do believe just that. But the more research I do, the more I see the belief as just a perception—and a self-defeating perception at that. Most of the trouble adults and children have around entertainment, including some young people's tendency to be overly influenced by it, derives from adults falling into that competitive relationship. Children's entertainment can be a very constructive aspect of life when adults break out of the belief that they have to compete with it and instead start using it as a partner and a tool. There are many techniques that adults can employ to help children use entertainment well. I group them into three categories: modeling, mirroring, and mentoring.

MODELING

Be what you want them to be

Every bit of research on the relationship between children's behavior and entertainment, even those that find substantial correlations, shows that entertainment is a far less significant influence than peers, school, socioeconomic environment, and, especially, family. The Leonard Eron studies, the bedrock of all psychological criticism of violent television, found a correlation of about 10 percent between aggression and viewing habits, but the correlation it found between aggression and family patterns ran as high as 50 percent. Parents who were aggressive were far more likely to have kids who were aggressive, no matter what they watched on TV. Similar patterns hold true whatever kind of behavior is being studied. Teenagers who smoke, drink, commit suicide, take too many risks, have eating disorders, and are sexually promiscuous usually have parents or other adult role models with similar self-destructive habits. The power of parents is so much greater than the power of the media that any reasonably good parenting renders any media influence insignificant.

The greatest power we have is *modeling*. What we tell them matters, the limits and consequences we impose on them matter, the experiences we expose them to matter—but far more important is simply who we *are* when they're watching. And they're watching from the beginning. When we feed a baby, and he gazes up at us with those huge, all-absorbing eyes, he is gobbling up not just milk but every piece of information he can comprehend on what a human being is. From the moment a child understands that he will someday grow up into an adult, the adults he sees every day become his vision of what an adult is supposed to be. Even if a teenager wants to be radically different from his parents, they remain the source of his most basic, unquestioned picture of adulthood.

The way to teach empathy is to be empathetic with your child. The way to teach nonviolence is to be nonviolent. And the way to teach a healthy perspective toward entertainment is to model a healthy perspective. Whatever power the entertainment industry has in a child's life is usually given to it by his or her parents.

Model responses to entertainment

Cynthia, whose daughter Emily was so interested in guns and then Britney Spears, told me that she once caught herself in the middle of complaining about the power of the media to pull her daughter's values away from her own. "I could suddenly hear my mother saying the same thing about *me!*" When she was little she liked *Mad* magazine and other humor that her mother thought was in bad taste. In her teens it was rock music. Cynthia was always looking for something that would push her mother's buttons and assert her independence. She still has that anti-authoritarian streak, and she will often opt for confrontation rather than playing the game. But so did her mother. And so does Emily, a trait that Cynthia values in her. "It suddenly hit me that with the guns and Britney, Emily was doing exactly what *I'd* done. If she was going to be independent it *had* to be about things I didn't like. She was objecting to my *tastes*, but as far as the fundamental values went, they were completely mine."

Young people will always play with fantasy selves startlingly different from their parents in order to broaden their personalities and build their own lives. No matter how much a child may want to be like a media figure in fantasy, however, no matter how precisely she may dress and talk like a TV character, at bottom she knows that she isn't going to grow up to be a flashing image on a glass screen. TV shows, movies, and music may speak to her emotions and fantasies in many ways, but they don't teach her how to get from moment to moment through the whole day or how to respond to every little incident of real life. We parents become so accustomed just to *being there* that we forget that we are our children's points of reference, every day and in every way. Even if a child's attention is mostly focused on a TV show, it won't be the show that will make the deepest impression on her idea of how she is supposed to behave—it will be the way mom or dad behaves while the show is on. Expressing anger or anxiety about a child's entertainment won't make her like the entertainment less—but it *will* model anger and anxiety for her. She's not likely to shape her real behavior around what she sees characters do on the glass screen. But if she sees parents allowing entertainment violence but treating others lovingly, she will get the message, "An adult is supposed to be okay with make-believe violence but not make it real."

Effective modeling can certainly involve telling children what we don't like. We can get so caught up in the debate about whether entertainment is "harmful" that we forget our right to an opinion. Saying, "I don't like that show," or "I don't want that hateful song to be played in my house," models decisiveness and moral courage. It's far more useful for a child to see a parent calmly stating an opinion than dithering in worry. The kids, of course, will learn from their parents' example and start declaring their own tastes with equal strength. But mutually respectful arguments are good ways for families to explore problems, bond, and broaden their limits.

MIRRORING

Affirm who they are

Mirroring is one of the basic tools that parents use to help children develop, usually without even thinking about it. The baby smiles and we smile back. He runs around laughing and we run and laugh with him, and punctuate it with a squealed, "You're running!" Students of language development see it as one of the building blocks of speech. "Ball!" "That's a ball! Where is the ball?" "Nicky hand!" "Yes, the ball is in Nicky's hand!" Developmental experts now see mirroring (under one name or another) as a vital process in healthy emotional maturation as well. Only a few decades ago, parents would say, "He's only crying because he wants attention." They feared that giving in to a child's desires would make him more needy or less able to control his desires. We've come to understand that meeting a child's need for attention early in his development has the opposite effect. Children need to be *seen*. They need to know they exist, that adults are aware of them and what they're doing. Simply repeating back to a young child what she says strengthens her self-confidence. If she says, "The doggie scares me," the response she probably needs most of all is just, "Yeah, the doggie scares you." From there she'll be better able to respond to "The doggie's safe," or "Why does it scare you?"

The need for mirroring becomes more subtle as childhood progresses, but it remains strong. In my workshops I see how kids brighten up when I do little more than acknowledge their work and their fantasies. It's most overt in the early grades, when kids beam at me the whole time I'm looking at their pictures or listening to their stories. But even an eighth-grader at the nadir of self-consciousness and pretended indifference will usually puff up a little or make brief eye contact when I say, "You're into Goth, huh?" As parents, one of the simplest and best things we can do is just acknowledge what they like. Look at them and smile as they shoot you, listen to their retellings of *Jurassic Park*, ask them what shooter video games they think are coolest.

Sometimes, of course, kids will resist discussing their tastes with us, especially as they're passing through their early teens. They need to set themselves apart from their parents and may push for confrontations or small-scale rejections to achieve it. They may also consider their own desire for adult attention immature and go to great lengths to conceal it. They may not respond cheerfully to a mother asking, "Did you beat that level on *Half-Life* today, dear?" And they do need their privacy. Watching television or playing video games in isolation is usually a productive way to shut out real stresses and regroup for real life. The music-formed fantasyland of a Walkman can be a very soothing retreat.

Psychiatrist Lynn Ponton has stressed, however, that parents often think that separation and privacy are all teenagers really need, when in fact their need for attention, guidance, and approval is even greater in early adolescence than in the preteen years. They're in a frightening transition; like a toddler who darts away from his mother and then stops anxiously and demands to be picked up, adolescents want to push adults away but still know that someone is watching over them.

The key, she said, is maintaining an open relationship in which communication flows easily back and forth about every subject of concern to both the parent and the child. Because it is important to keep fantasy in a realistic perspective, entertainment should neither be a closed topic nor one that becomes overemphasized by rules, cautions, or anxious parental lectures. Even when parents find their children's entertainment offensive or troubling, the best way for them to keep it in perspective is just to let it be "what the kids are into." Ponton often begins her relationships with teenage patients by asking them to bring in the CDs, movies, video games, or books they like. She'll often spend several sessions with a new patient just listening to Pearl Jam together or playing *D.O.A.* against each other. Conversations about their deeper concerns—conversations they've resisted with adults until then—often open up from that shared immersion in fantasy. Respecting teenagers' privacy and separate lives is crucial to maintaining an open relationship with them, but merely letting them know that someone is aware of them and supports them in the painful struggle of growing up is very reassuring to them. Encourage them to play their music on the family stereo sometimes instead of always on a Walkman—and if you hate it, tell them so. Roll your eyes in mock disgust and say, "Where did I go wrong?" Give them room to disagree or dismiss you with, "It's just a *song!*"

Trust the child's desires

Our culture leads us to be leery of a child's most fervent appetites—especially when those appetites are excited by a profiteering industry. Children's desires, however, usually reflect their needs. Children love sugar and force adults to make decisions several times a day about whether to say yes or no. We feel in competition with sugar's power, resent the candy and cereal industries for pushing it, and are quick to believe that it's harmful. In the 1970s, some spotty research linking sugar to hyperactivity, attention deficit disorder, and other maladies touched the nerves of millions of parents; the studies were soon debunked, but fear of its effects still lingers. Sugar does present challenges—it kills kids' appetites, too much of it causes an energy rush followed by a sharp decline, it's conducive to tooth decay—but it's also a useful part of a complete diet. An increasing number of teachers and coaches encourage their students to load up on sugar and carbohydrates for energy right before a big test, arts performance, or game. And the human craving for sugar is fundamental; it induces newborns to take milk and, later on, draws kids to fruit and other foods. We may need to set limits, but children crave it for very good reasons.

Action entertainment is similarly appealing to kids and just as ruthlessly marketed to them. We feel a similar threat from it and look for danger signs in research. But children also crave it for very healthy and legitimate reasons. Obviously people don't always crave things that are good for them, as drugs and cigarettes show. But young children almost never crave anything harmful, and even most adolescents handle their experimentations well, unless depression or anger makes them self-destructive. "Young people generally make sensible choices," said Lynn Ponton. "It's important to take action if they are clearly making a mistake, but it's just as important that they learn to trust themselves and make their own decisions."

It can be hard to trust those choices, especially when they're choosing just what the adult world deplores: gross humor, bloody video games, misogynistic rappers, professional wrestling. It's tempting to mirror only the behavior we like and ignore the others, hoping they'll fade away. It's the behavior we refuse to acknowledge, however, that will trouble them most. They'll need to have those sides of themselves seen, and if parents won't do it, they'll find someone who will. One of the great appeals of the entertainment industry is its ability to make its audience feel acknowledged. An angry kid who feels ignored by his parents and school is thrilled to hear a rocker or rapper reflect his anger back to him. A kid who feels powerless knows that the video game industry is noticing his desire for power, if only by creating fantasies to sell to him. His desire to feel more powerful is healthy, and so is his desire to have it seen and ac-knowledged. The adults in his life can help him become more com-plete and self-aware simply by affirming that.

Pay attention to how they're using their fantasies

My son always used power fantasies to help himself through anxiety-provoking transitions. At the beginning of every school year from preschool through first grade, he became a dinosaur—no docile plant eater either, but the biggest and most savage carnivore he could think of. He'd want to play dinosaur fights with his friends and family, and if no one wanted to play he'd go off by himself and fight invisible en-emies. I was happy to play along because I could see how stressful he found social challenges, and I could see the calm the fantasies brought him. After the jitters of the first few weeks, the dinosaurs would yield to fish, frogs, and the other creatures of his imagination.

When Nicky was in the first grade, however, his mother and I sep-arated. I expected him to turn to violent games with greater intensity than ever, but he went to the opposite extreme; he transformed into cute little animals that spoke baby-talk, acted silly, loved to be cud-dled, and needed to be rescued. I realized that he was so frightened by this huge shift in his world that he didn't feel safe in the combat-ive fantasies that he'd used to feel strong and self-reliant before. He didn't want to be self-reliant. He wanted to be little again, like he'd been before we split up, and be taken care of.

Jennie and I responded in two ways: we gave him as much reassur-ance as we could that he would always be taken care of, even if his parents weren't living together, and we paid special attention to en-couraging any glimmer of the power fantasies that we saw. We con-tinued to recognize and affirm his cuddly fantasies, because he clearly needed them, but we felt that it was at least as important that he re-cover his "Tyrannosaurus self." Whenever he'd mention sharks or *Digimon* or any other symbol of savagery or courage, I'd show special interest. When he started to show interest again in playing our "war game," I made sure I had the time and energy to oblige.

Then something interesting happened; some silly stories he'd be-gun telling about his hedgehog Beanie Baby began to take an adventurous turn. He and I took turns telling "chapters" at bedtime, and pretty soon the "Hedge Fighter" stories, about a silly but intrepid (and often violent) band of animal action heroes, were running through all his "Daddy days." He started asking Jennie to contribute characters, too, a way of linking us together. With time, as he became more secure in the new status quo, those fantasies settled back among his others. When Jennie and I started the marriage over again, at the beginning of Nicky's third grade, the whole gamut of his power fantasies exploded in celebration: Hedge Fighters jockeying with dinosaurs, Ultraman, and other imaginary combatants of days past.

Encourage them to tell their stories

As part of our unconscious policy of ignoring scary feelings and hoping they'll go away, we fall into the trap of thinking that a child's violent fantasies are safest when they're passive and most threatening when they're active. In fact, as my own work with storytelling has shown me, kids integrate their thoughts and feelings more effectively the more actively they work through those fantasies.

Heather Adamson is a journalist, the mother of three boys, and an officer with the parents' association at their school. She deals frequently with the message from teachers, school administrators, and other parents that violent entertainment is a bad influence, and she has tried to minimize her sons' exposure to it. For the most part, they didn't show much interest in it until her oldest son Noel entered the fourth grade. He was the mildest of her boys, a shy kid who was overwhelmed by his more aggressive peers. Suddenly, he threw himself into a Japanese cartoon called *Tenchi* with a consuming passion that he'd never shown for anything before—such a consuming passion that Heather began to worry about it.

"One evening he came to me in tears," she remembered. "I asked him what was wrong and he blurted out, 'I wish reincarnation were true!' I was thrown by that and all I could do was ask him what had brought it on." Noel started talking about a character in *Tenchi* who was reincarnated, and then said he wished he could live in the world of *Tenchi,* where no one had to die. Heather had already gathered that much of *Tenchi's* appeal was that it was very complex but predictable, that nothing bad ever really happened, at least permanently, to the characters he cared about. At the time, Noel's father was often taken away by work, Heather was trying to take care of the two younger boys, run the household, and keep her career afloat, and neither of them was as available to Noel as they would have liked. The cartoon world was his refuge.

"But as he talked about it, he told me something that really startled me," she said. "He was worried about how much he loved *Tenchi*. He was troubled by the fact that he thought about it so much, and he thought if other people knew what was going on inside his mind they'd think he was *crazy*."

Heather reassured him that his interest in *Tenchi* was sane and safe. Only then did Noel reveal what had kicked off the whole process: he'd had a *Tenchi*-inspired dream. The fourth-graders and fifth-graders were having a war, one grade with ice powers and the other with fire. Noel had the power to act like a connection between them, so he stepped into the middle of the war and brought them together. "Then they were all just like warm water," he said, "and everyone was peaceful."

Heather told him that not only was there nothing wrong with him but that she would help him write down the dream as soon as she could. He didn't wait until she was free; he wrote it down by himself, the first time he'd ever sat down for an hour and written something that he didn't have to. "He brought it to me at the dinner table," Heather said, "and as I was reading it, the kid was literally dancing around the room. He was so proud of himself for having done this. He was even proud of himself for having such a crazy imagination!" Noel started writing down other dreams and fantasies, and Heather could see his spirits lift. "He told me later that school was a lot better because he didn't feel like he had to stop himself from thinking about *Tenchi* anymore."

Noel used a superheroic cartoon universe to give form to his terrors about life changes, big kids, and his own powerlessness. While he dwelt in that universe in isolation, it worried him. All his mother had to do was suggest a way to open that universe to others, and he took it from there.

MENTORING

Give them the tools to take control

One worry parents mention often is their inability to supervise their kids when they watch TV or play video games. Even when they control media use tightly in the home, the kids will always have opportunities for unsupervised watching and playing at friends' homes. These parents trust that their presence can mitigate the media's effects, but they fear what may happen in their absence.

The reality is that the power of parents is so much greater than that of entertainment that one good conversation is worth countless hours of media time. Ray Portillo, a retired educator and public policy consultant, told me about an incident he still remembered vividly from his childhood, nearly seventy years earlier. He loved radio serials when he was little, but sometimes he found the suspense almost unbearable. Once his father was passing through the room as the Shadow was caught in a deathtrap, and Ray asked him nervously, "Do you think he'll survive?" His father said, "Son, if he doesn't survive, that'll be the end of the show." Then he left the room. "That one little remark changed the way I looked at entertainment forever," Portillo said. "I still loved it, but I always knew that someone was behind it, selling it to me."

After years studying the link between media use and behavior, Dr. Stuart Fischoff of the California State University at Los Angeles Media Psychology Laboratory has concluded: "Kids want to know what's real. They *want* to make sense of what they see. They only run into trouble if they don't know how to fit it into a real context. If you take even just a little time to talk to a child about what he or she is watching, then you have to worry not at all about the effects of the media."

Help them distinguish fantasy from reality

We often underestimate children's ability to grasp what's real and what's not. "Children have no trouble recognizing cartoon violence as unreal at a very early age, generally as early as two years," reported Lenore Terr, author of *Beyond Love and Work*. Although children typically haven't completely mastered the difference between their own fantasies and reality until the age of seven or eight, video images are much easier for them. They look nothing like reality, after all: flat images contained in a box that change instantaneously—a face suddenly replaced by a whole body, another face, a building—that often resemble nothing a child ever sees in life. In fact, they are more likely not to recognize cartoon characters or strange figures like Power Rangers as even being human at first, instead seeing them as something humanlike but unique to TV. The TV-watching child's first task isn't usually distinguishing video from reality but learning that the strange images on TV are supposed to relate to reality in some way.

The danger isn't so much that a child of any age would ever imagine that a make-believe show represents a condition that really exists, but that children might invest too much importance in their own emotional reactions to it. They need to understand that what they experience during a fight scene is a fun *feeling* of power but not an emotion that's dangerously powerful itself. Some people fear that kids will develop a "false sense of power" by fantasizing or playing a video game, but in fact the feeling of make-believe power, if enjoyed openly, eases some of their need to pretend to themselves that they're really more powerful than they are. What matters is what children *do* with their entertainment in real-world behavior, not what it reminds us of. If we can make that distinction clear through our reactions, we'll pass it on to them.

Many critics have argued that entertainment teaches children that violence is a good way to settle problems. Reality, however, is a good corrective to that. The first time a child imitates a Power Ranger by kicking a playmate and is rewarded with a crying friend, angry parents, an abrupt end to the game, and a sore foot, he learns that make-believe and the real world operate on fundamentally different laws. One of the great charms of a make-believe world is that the very behaviors that we know *won't* solve problems in the complex, constraining real world will work there.

The limits of the media's instructive powers become obvious when we look at advertising. Both the practitioners and the critics of advertising have shown that no sales campaign can make people buy what they fundamentally don't want. The most expensive and artful campaigns fail when consumers are disposed against the product. This is why marketers hire "cool hunters" to discover what kids want and develop ways to package it—first comes the buyer's desire, then the product to exploit it. As one TV marketer told me, "If a kid wants a new toy to play with, or wants to be as cool as his friends, then a commercial can excite his appetite and focus it on one product. The slickest commercials ever made, inundating every kids' show, wouldn't make him want to eat brussels sprouts or clean his room." Children want to have exciting fantasies, but they usually don't want to suffer injuries, get in serious trouble, or alienate the rest of the world. Consequently, the media can inspire them to play violent games—but not even a constant diet of the most exciting media violence will induce them to be violent in reality.

Of course, if a child's real world teaches him that violence is rewarded—as some brutal social and family realities do—then entertainment may reinforce the lesson. And positive associations with violence can be problematic for young people who are angry enough to behave irrationally or self-destructively. According to Stanford's Donald Roberts, "A child will store up templates of media violence as sources of excitement, victory, or the relief of tension. If real life makes him angry, those templates can key in to his anger." Roberts argued that our culture in general would benefit from more realistic presentations of the consequences of violence, citing anecdotal reports from emergency rooms of young men wounded in gunfights and knife fights who say, "I didn't know it would *hurt* so much!" "A lot of people think media violence is fine when it's cartoony and fun," Roberts said, "that it shouldn't be messy or disturbing. But it *should* be messy, at least some of the time. And when it isn't, young people need to know that the *reality* is messy."

Roberts also believes, however, in respecting the joy and emotional legitimacy of the fantasy. "My kids have always loved Looney Tunes—and so do *I*. But those cartoons do link pain and injury to fun. So every once in a while I'll ask them, what do you think would *really* happen if a coyote fell off a cliff? Not right at the moment—I don't want to be a killjoy. But later, when we're all in the mood to think more about reality."

Jib Fowles of the University of Houston, on the other hand, has cautioned against imposing adult viewpoints on children's fantasies. "If they want to talk about what they see, that's great. But sitting them down and making them talk about it can interfere with the workings of their imaginations." According to Fowles, parents need to discuss only two aspects of TV content with their children: commercials and the news, because they both claim to represent reality but often distort it. Children learn quickly that fiction is a world apart, and they need to feel safe about entering that world. "Children are constantly being impacted by reality, often quite stressfully. Entertainment is the *antidote* to reality. Fantasy is therapeutic if it's allowed to work incrementally over time, but that requires that it be allowed to remain fantasy. A parent-led discussion may be only another anxiety-provoking intrusion of reality."

Dr. Fowles may have more faith in television than I do—and I think Dr. Roberts may worry a little more than necessary. But I believe they're both right: respect children's fantasies but encourage talking. The degree of each doesn't matter much. We can't go wrong if we approach them with love and acceptance.

It's worth noting, too, that a bit of mentoring can be a good way for parents to relieve their own anxieties. Once I was visiting some friends whose twelve-year-old son was listening to "Stan," Eminem's song about a deranged rap fan who ends up killing himself and his girlfriend. My friend Susan grew more noticeably agitated as the song went on. She kept asking her son, "Do you like that song? Don't you think that's kind of dark? What do you like about it?" Jeff blew off every question with an increasingly annoyed, "Just let me *listen!*" When it was finally over, Susan said, "Okay. One thing. You do know it's not okay to lock your girlfriend in the trunk of your car, right?" Jeff answered, "Duh!" And everyone was happy.

Allow them their own reactions

Donald Roberts has stressed that the point of talking to kids is to inspire them to think, not to change their minds. Family communication breaks down not only when parents won't listen or talk to their kids but when they can't accept that their kids simply feel, and will go on feeling, fundamentally different about some issues. Whenever he discussed violence with his son Roberts was careful not to make it judgmental or confrontational. "I'd ask, what was it about, what did you think of this or that. I'd say, this movie shows violence as a good way to solve problems—what do you think of that? When I invite them to think and respond, they don't have to resist what I'm saying in order to protect their turf." After his son had children of his own, he disagreed with Roberts's concerns about the grandkids playing with realistic toy guns. "But in disagreeing with me he quoted chapter and verse everything I'd told him when *he* was young. That was the important thing—that every talk we'd ever had was still in there, a part of his personal template of violence."

Sometimes kids can lead us to interesting places when we trust their reactions rather than trying to shape or anticipate them. When Nicky was four years old, many of his friends started playing on a tree outside a children's museum where they used to take classes. It was a perfect climbing tree—thick branches, low and almost level with the ground—and its deeply grooved trunk was home to countless bugs. I expected Nicky to love both the climbing and the bugs, but he was afraid. While his friends played around the tree, he'd drift away and play by himself. He wouldn't say why he was afraid ("I just don't *want* to play on the tree!" he'd say tearily), but Jennie and I were certain that he was afraid of falling, and it was costing him a joyful experience.

I decided to apply my ideas about power fantasies and read him some comics about the heroic lord of the trees, Tarzan. I brought him the most exciting version I knew, reprints of *Tarzan* newspaper strips from the 1930s, full of flashing knives and battles to the death. For a while he loved them. I began to imagine him racing to that tree and scaling its branches, pretending to be Tarzan. Then we came to a story in which the hero was poisoned by a witch doctor's dart and collapsed to the ground. Suddenly Nicky said, "I don't want to read Tarzan anymore!" I asked, "Don't you want to see if he gets better?" He stuck his lower lip out, pushed the book away, and started to cry. "I don't *want* to read Tarzan anymore!"

I wanted to throw the book away and never read him another violent story. At the same time I wanted to say what disappointed dads have been saying for generations: "Oh, come on! It's just a story! What are you so afraid of?"

So I shut up for a minute. I let us both calm down, and then I looked at the book again and said, "It's kind of scary, huh?" "Yeah." "I'm sure glad Tarzan comes out okay." "How do you know he's okay?" "I read it before. He gets better and stops the bad guy." "How does he get better from the poison?" "Do you want to see?" "How does he get better?" "It's more fun to read it and see. But I promise he gets better." I had to reassure him twice more before he'd let me read it, and then, just as Tarzan swallowed an antidote, he interrupted me agitatedly, "But poison makes you die!" "Where did you hear that?" I asked. "Peter told me!" he cried. "He told me the centipedes in the tree trunk were poison and poison makes you *die!*"

Suddenly everything made sense. It wasn't falling he was afraid of. It was the deadly centipedes that a seven-year-old classmate had invented to make the crevices in the trunk more exciting. Nicky had never been afraid of a bug before; in fact, he'd always prided himself on being the boldest of his friends at catching and holding them. But this talk of poison and death by an older boy who acted like he knew everything was too much for him. The pain and confusion of finding his own fears suddenly keeping him away from a tree full of wonderful bugs must only have amplified his shame and anxiety and made it harder to look at those fears.

He hadn't reacted at all as I'd expected, but I was glad I'd brought the stories to him and that I hadn't just put the book down when he first became upset. Now he had a chance for a reality check. I assured him that the kinds of centipedes we had around here were safe and that nothing would happen to him if he played on the tree. He still wasn't ready to go back to the tree, but he loved looking at that scene in the book. For the next two weeks, he wanted to hear Tarzan every night. Then, suddenly, he said he wanted to read a fish book instead. We never went back to the ape man. But he did climb the tree.

Intervene when necessary—but with care

When young people have problems with entertainment violence, parents may need to make a change in the way they use it. But an overreaction won't help. As psychiatrist Edwin Cook said, "If my son watches an action show and hits his sister, then, definitely, it's, guess what you don't get to watch for two weeks. But the most aggressive kid in our neighborhood is the one who doesn't get to watch TV at all, because he has no outlet."

One family therapist with two sons told me, "Our older boy was usually mild and self-controlled no matter what he watched. But when his little brother watched cartoons he'd become too aggressive—squeezing the dog too hard and that sort of thing. We didn't want to tell him that he couldn't watch cartoons, because that would send the message that he wasn't strong enough to handle his own feelings or reactions. So we told him that he could watch cartoons only if he could play without being too rough. We made it something to accomplish and told him we believed he could do it." She encouraged her son to yell, beat on the couch, wrestle with his brother—but within limits. He had a lot of lapses, long stretches when action shows were off-limits, but he kept asking for new chances, and after several months he was handling himself well. "He felt good about that. It wasn't an easy process for any of us, but in the end we were glad he'd done it."

Sometimes children need us to help them break a cycle. A teenager disappearing from the rest of his life to play video games might need time limits or need the game console moved out of the bedroom. It's important, however, to make clear to him that the problem isn't him, or the entertainment that reflects his self-image and needs, but rather a behavior that you believe is making life harder for him. Let him know that you're changing the rules of the household in order to help him bring himself, complete with tastes and fantasies, into the world as a happier and more effective person.

Help them make it into more

There's far more to helping young people use their entertainment than simply minimizing its negative influences. Psychologist Mihaly Csikszentmihalyi has stressed that the social and creative experiences a child has around entertainment can contribute to his development into a more complex and effective person.

Csikszentmihalyi developed the concept of "flow," a confluence of emotion, cognitive function, social affect, and self-perception. In "high flow" states, people feel happy and learn quickly, present themselves appealingly to the world, and think well of themselves. In "low flow," they feel depressed, have trouble processing information, chase the world away with their affect, and criticize themselves harshly. Csikszentmihalyi has found that teenagers' highest flow states occur when they are deeply immersed in a demanding activity or socializing. Their lowest states occur during classroom lectures, when they feel bored, disaffected, passive, and trapped. Almost as low are the flow states they experience during solitary, passive entertainment, especially watching TV. The research indicates that teenagers who engage in less passive entertainment and more activities, whether individual or social, tend to do better in later life. "Activities that encourage high flow states make demands of us," Csikszentmihalyi said, "force us to expand our personalities and learn new dimensions of ourselves. The difficulty is that the low flow state is so much easier to settle into and remain trapped in. The danger of television is that it is such a seductive medium. We may turn it on because there is something we truly want to learn from it, but once it's on it is so easy just to sit there. Our mood lowers and lowers, and still we sit."

He has pointed out, however, that the situation is more complex than TV-is-bad, activities-are-good. Research suggests that through the age of about twelve, children considered "talented" tend to watch *more* television than "less talented" children. From the age of about fourteen, that reverses; more talented teenagers watch less TV. "I believe this is because younger children use television as a source of ideas and fantasies," he said. "They watch, they discover, and then they think about what they've discovered, play games with it, and draw pictures of it. Then, at a certain point, the medium becomes redundant. They've seen just about everything it has to offer, or they've discovered more fertile sources of ideas. The young people who continue to watch large amounts of television through adolescence tend to be using it as a relaxant or time killer, and so keep themselves in a low mood."

The critical difference is in the viewer's relationship with the material. Csikszentmihalyi has found that flow states can be quite high when a child is watching TV with a friend or family member and talking about what he sees. Even solitary watching can be active: "If a person watches a historical documentary because he wants to understand the topic, and he looks at it very closely, perhaps saying, 'Wait, that isn't true. Who produced this? What are they trying to put across?' Or if he watches a basketball game and is wondering, why isn't Kobe Bryant playing his best game? Or if he watches an action movie and tries to understand how the effects were achieved, or what's going to happen next, or why the screenwriter made that decision. These are very active states, and they can be very valuable. Another activity, even a lecture or the opera, will be far less useful if we're only going through the motions."

In my work in the comic book business, I encountered a lot of young people caught spinning in fantasy: gobbling up superhero stories to ease their anxieties but never resolving their conflicts or taking authority over their real lives, so that they just spun to the next comic book or video game without ever moving on to more complex or demanding interests. Many of them spin right through adolescence and into adulthood, using the fantasy to resist lifting themselves up to a higher developmental level. One of the joys of the comics business, however, was the vast range of opportunities it gave fans to participate in organized fandom, interact socially with the creators of the comics, and get their own stories and art into print. I saw many young readers seize those opportunities to make more complex use of their adolescent fantasies and begin developing into happier and more interesting people.

Adults can encourage young people to build their fantasies into their social and creative lives—as long as we allow them to find their own ways of doing so. I've seen the downside of trying to push their creativity into channels that are more gratifying to us.

A boy named Adam in one of my seventh-grade workshops wore his pop-culture tastes as an obvious armor. This was two months after Columbine, and he was wearing a long black trench coat just like the killers wore, a fashion decision guaranteed to provoke adult reaction. He wasn't a disruptive kid; he did his schoolwork, followed instructions, but gave no more to school than it asked of him. As his teacher said of him, "Adam just gave up on school."

The page he drew for my Art and Story Workshop was a tribute to a rap group called the Insane Clown Posse, a group known for violent lyrics. That his enthusiasm for ICP was real, but the execution was perfunctory: angry, bad taste, quick and thoughtless. It bothered me. The kid obviously had brains and passion, could probably say something powerful if he tried, and I wanted him to see that. I told him that I thought what he'd done had some impact, and I could sense him opening up a little bit. Then I kept going. I told myself I was encouraging him to open up about what was bothering him, but what came out of my mouth was a critical, "I can tell you've got some very angry feelings—why don't you do a story that has *your* feelings in it instead of just some tribute to a rap group?"

My tension was a reaction to his armor. The Columbine-style trench coat unnerved and annoyed me, as he had intended it to. Encouraging him to keep telling the stories he wanted might have opened him up, but I wanted to force a change in him instead of hearing what he wanted to say. I could see him closing up. I'd lost the kid.

Lynn Ponton told a story that played out differently. Joe was a teenage suburban boy who felt abandoned by his parents when they became overwhelmed by their own marital and professional issues. He spent his afternoons and evenings watching TV, sometimes alone, sometimes with a buddy or two. He became fascinated with old westerns, with their images of potent, self-contained maleness. Wanting to emulate his cowboy heroes, to be as tough and as free of loneliness as Lee Marvin or Jack Palance, he started drinking. His parents' attempts to control his behavior came to nothing, until a frightening car accident left no doubt that something had to change.

Dr. Ponton encouraged Joe's parents to make changes that would open up communication in the family and encouraged Joe to deal directly with his drinking—but she also encouraged him to talk about the westerns he loved. Rather than viewing them as a problem to be controlled, she helped him go deeper into an understanding of the movies and what they gave him that his real life didn't. He quit drinking and started thinking about what he wanted his life to be. Joe still watched his westerns, but he watched them increasingly with an eye to how they were made, what they meant, how he could use them creatively, socially, and intellectually. He decided to take a film class. The more he learned about filmmaking, the more he opened up to the world and the less he needed to play out the self-destructive fantasy he'd taken from the movies.

Entertainment has its greatest influence when it's speaking to something that isn't otherwise being addressed in a child's life. It's crucial to bring in a parent's adult knowledge of the world without discounting the child's very real perspective. It's teaching first by modeling, then by mirroring, and then by communicating. We can model nonaggression, empathy, respect, a clear distinction between fantasy and reality, and the integration of aggression and other scary feelings. We can help young people learn to trust and take care of themselves by affirming their feelings and fantasies. We can mentor them in the subtexts and implications of their entertainment and encourage them to channel their fantasies productively.

Unfortunately, not all young people are lucky enough to have adults looking after them. Some of them have to work out their relationships with the media in the absence of adult guidance and in the face of adult hostility.

12

Not So Alone

*M*y concern about media's influence isn't so much for children in supportive families," said developmental psychologist Carla Seal-Wanner, "but for those who lack other mediating influences. For them, media can have a more powerful, even dominant socializing role."

There's a lot to inspire concern in the media that young people love, especially to those of us raised on less harsh, less confrontational styles. On top of the quantity and intensity of violence, a trend in some ways even more distressing is the rage that has been increasingly shaping youth entertainment over the past two decades. It's in the rappers, the rockers, the games, the movies, even the cartoons and comic books kids love. Action heroes don't step up stoically to fight the bad guy but snarl, "This time it's *personal!*" Video game martial artists stomp on their fallen foes and turn to the player with a sadistic sneer. Eminem acts as though he's conciliating his critics for his anti-gay slurs by performing at the Grammies with Elton John, and then concludes by giving the world the finger. A gay teenager in one of my workshops loved Eminem for blasting the hypocritical adult world with his anger, even when the anger seemed directed at young men like himself. Then he flung himself back into his funny but angry story about a prostitute setting up a hypocritical cop for a fall. When I asked another kid, a smart, academically successful kid who never got in trouble, why he adopted the gangster-imitating "whigga" style of clothing, he said, "because it scares people."

Even in the mild, dorky world of comic books, the 1980s and 1990s were marked by the rise of the snarling hero. The blithely grinning Superman, the hyperrational Batman, the tormented but mild Spider-Man, were nudged aside by the bestial Wolverine with his slashing metal claws. To keep the old heroes popular, writers and artists had to keep pace with their audience's growing taste for rampant passion. Stories and dialogue got meaner. The art grew more jagged, more "in your face," heavier with black ink. Superman, the first and corniest of superheroes, was killed and brought back as a snarling, sweating, fist-clenching, eye-blazing embodiment of righteous rage. Even the kids who want the simplest dramas of good and evil also want their heroes to express a baseline of anger.

It's natural to respond to anger with a defensive anger of our own or a fear of where it will lead. We respond more effectively, however, when we first ask, why are kids so angry?

In her nationwide surveys of violent youth, Dr. Helen Smith said she found "a tremendous number of young people who compare school to *prison*." She read me quote after quote from kids who feel they're being held captive, controlled, not cared about, not protected from the bullying of other kids. Many feel that home is just a different cell in the prison, especially if they have performance-driven parents who keep them under constant scrutiny. They look ahead to adult society and the work world and can only imagine more of the same, and they conclude, "I don't see how real prison could be any worse than this."

Most of them feel that they can't change their circumstances because adults won't acknowledge that there's a problem. "They feel anger and alienation from what they perceive as the *hypocrisy* of the adult world," Smith said. Parents and teachers are preoccupied with violence but don't like to acknowledge young people's rage. Kids feel that complaining in school only gets *them* viewed as the problem, while their parents either don't care or side with the school in clamping down tighter on them. They feel that no one knows they're there, no one understands their feelings, no one cares. "Attacks on the school or the world as a whole," said Smith, "from vandalism to threats to actually bringing weapons are often presaged by specific complaints about being dismissed. Sometimes they just keep escalating their negative actions until they think they've finally been *noticed*."

Forensic psychologist James McGee, an authority on classroom violence, studied all the videotaped rants and Web postings left by the Columbine shooters and said one thread ran through nearly every minute and page of them: the demand to be seen. They drew attention to themselves with Gothic makeup and costumes, made offensively violent movies for class, posted to hate-mongering Web sites under their own names. They not only played the violent video game *Doom* but—much more importantly, in McGee's view—they proclaimed their love of the game and its violence loudly at a time when such games were drawing fire from parents, psychologists, and legislators for contributing to teen violence. When their parents and the authorities didn't respond as strongly as they wanted, their frustration increased. Their parents seemed unable or unwilling to notice even that they were filling their homes with guns and bombs. Finally, wanting attention more than life itself, the boys created a horrific scenario that would leave the world no choice but to notice them.

The late Dr. Rachel Lauer, chief psychologist of the New York City Schools, spoke of the adult world's inability, or unwillingness, to see the problem:"Doesn't the adult population cherish its young—do everything possible to turn kids into well behaved, attractive, skillful, productive citizens responsible for each other, for the fate of the world? Indeed we do. We cherish our young so much that when our determined ministrations are resisted we exercise a long repertoire of 'remedies.' We 'attack' the problem and 'handle' it by rewarding, punishing, requiring, mandating, directing, expecting, teasing, threatening, ridiculing, failing, jailing, beating, restricting, insulting, advising, ministering, assessing. Our young are our favorite objects for our manipulative skills—all for their own good, of course. As parents and educators we measure our own power and worth according to our success in producing youths who have learned what they're supposed to and how willing they are to learn it quickly, well, now, and better than someone else's kids."

Some fight back or drop out, but even kids who try to live by the rules may feel they're in a coercive society. "Like all hostages or slaves who comply with their oppressors, they build a rage inside," said Lauer. "Some identify with their oppressors and learn to act the same domineering way toward others. Sometimes they rage against themselves and become depressed. They constantly focus attention upon 'doing what you're supposed to do.' It means constantly attuning to external signals of what to do every moment of the day. Externally oriented, they live virtually in a state of, 'O.K. now I've done that, what do I have to do next?' By giving up so much authorship of their own lives, they lose the feeling of being alive or real."

They may feel that their lives are meaningless. Dr. William Damon of the Stanford Center on Adolescence has argued that everyone needs something to believe in, some greater cause to belong to in order to make our lives feel worthwhile, and that modern American society provides little of that for young people. We fear kids, we try to control them, we nervously track their scores on statistical tests, or we bring ourselves down to their level and try to win their favor, but we don't demand that they meet higher moral, social, and civic expectations. Damon has described the frustration and lonely anxiety of young people who aren't given a purpose—much like the feelings described by the "prisoners" of Helen Smith's survey, who feel that they are confined in adult institutions but never given a good reason to be there.

"If kids don't feel that society has anything meaningful to give them," Damon said, "then they'll find meaning wherever they can. That's likely to be the media. If they are particularly angry with society, they may come to identify with the media's most antisocial models. That's when they can be influenced by hate sites on the Web or a movie like *Natural Born Killers.*"

There have been young people like Barry Loukaitis of Moses Lake, Washington, rejected by his parents, picked on in high school, never very good at anything, who became obsessed with *Natural Born Killers* and a Pearl Jam video showing a teenager shooting classmates. Those quick-cut, Technicolor, grunge-rock revenge fantasies gave him the feeling of meaning he'd lacked. He started making pronouncements like, "Murder is pure—people make it impure." Then he took a gun to school and became America's first widely publicized school shooter.

There have been a lot of young people like Ruben Diaz, too. "I was the stereotype of the kid you're supposed to be afraid of," he said. He grew up in a public housing project in the South Bronx during the 1980s with no father and a working mother who couldn't be around much. Afraid at school and on the street, he spent his teen years in his apartment watching TV, listening to rap music, and reading comic books. He wasn't shown much by a negligent government, a decimated educational establishment, or a crime-obsessed news media to make him think that society had much use for a non-white, low-income teenager. He found his most meaningful models in gangster rappers and superheroes. In their very different ways, both demonstrated how individual anger could be channeled into the power to confront corruption and change the world. And both, Diaz realized, were created by commercial storytellers in not-quite-respectable fields who were willing to say what kids were really thinking and fantasizing.

Diaz discovered comic book fandom, a social group that helped channel his interests into a life direction. He got a job as an editorial assistant at DC Comics, then worked his way up to full editorship. I worked with him on a few projects—we'd come from very different worlds to the same place through a form of entertainment that had been able to speak powerfully to both of us in adolescence. He believed in comics like *X-Men* that excited young readers with combat, rage, and melodrama but also made them think about the way the world worked. He enjoyed contact with his young readers, and he discovered that he had something to say to them. After a few years, he left the business, went back to college for a teaching credential, and took a job as an English teacher at a high school in his old neighborhood in the Bronx.

"It was entertainment media that told me there were stories in me worth telling," Diaz said, "and that the world could be different from what we'd been handed. So I don't have a lot of patience for people from sheltered backgrounds saying that poor kids and kids without parental supervision need to be protected from the media."

When young people feel that the official world is hostile, indifferent, or irrelevant, the feelings of recognition and belonging that entertainment brings them can be transformative. Music historian Ricky Vincent has argued that gangster rap helped inner-city youths during the gang wars of the 1980s make sense of a fragmented society and take more control of their lives. This is the power of mirroring again. We speak of rap "glamorizing" gang violence, but more importantly it tells its audience that their reality has been seen, and so it helps them feel important enough to make more of themselves. The quieting of the gang wars in the 1990s was no doubt due in part to intervention programs, new school policies, and other official remedies. But it owed at least as much to the efforts of the gang leaders who finally said, "enough," and to those of the rappers who used their positions as trusted spokesmen for the community to spread the message.

Ice-T recorded a rap in 1993 called "Gotta Lotta Love," in which he described as "the most beautiful thing I'd seen in years," two guys settling their differences in a public park with "just a straight-up fistfight, one on one, nobody jumping in, nobody pulling a gun." It wasn't a sentiment that any school district could fit into its conflict-resolution program, but to an angry kid in a violent world, that punched-out, sentimental valorization of keeping rage within conscious bounds was a meaningful affirmation of personal power.

Ice-T's words had power because he'd proven that he could speak for the most alienated young people. On the same album with "Gotta Lotta Love" was "That's How I'm Livin'," Ice-T's story of how he became a street criminal in his teens and how creating raps lifted him out of crime by giving him purpose and perspective. Both of those raps would have been fairly easy for a parent or teacher to endorse—but the title track of the same album was "Home Invasion." That track opened with the sounds of a gang of armed thugs smashing their way into a house, threatening to kill the owners, screaming, "All we want are the motherfuckin' kids!" Ice-T then boasted to parents about his power to steal the minds of their children: "I might get 'em up under my fuckin' spell, they might start givin' you fuckin' hell . . . might start callin' you a fool, tellin' you why they hate school . . . ." It wasn't an easy rap for even the hippest adult to embrace as an ally in the work of socializing young people. But for many kids, who had been given so few symbols and so few outlets to express their rage at a controlling but uncomprehending adult world, it was powerfully liberating and emboldening—and not only for kids of Ice-T's social background.

I know a woman named Sarah who was fifteen when *Home Invasion* came out. Her parents were attorneys, she grew up in a luxury condo far from the ghetto, and she attended a top-ranked private school where she excelled academically. She was also alone a great deal while her parents worked, and when they were home they were often preoccupied with their own stresses and marital conflicts. Sarah felt they didn't spend much time trying to understand what she was going through, but they swooped down on her with anger and restrictions when she misbehaved. Ice-T, she said, "came through the door like my personal savior. From the first twenty seconds of 'Home Invasion' I felt like here was somebody who was going to fight for *me*, who wasn't afraid of parents and teachers, and wasn't going to tell the polite lies that we were always supposed to uphold." She clung to confrontational rap and rock music through a turbulent adolescence and bonded with other angry kids who shared her passions. She has credited the music with helping her channel her rage into politics and writing instead of the pointless, self-destructive rebellions that some of her peers fell into. In graduate school, she decided to become a schoolteacher and children's rights advocate.

Mary Cotter, whom I quoted earlier about the role of slasher movies in her adolescence, has stressed the power of entertainment to inspire the building of social groups and provide a feeling of belonging for young people who feel cast off or misunderstood by the world. She grew up feeling constricted by the limited options presented by her conservative, Catholic, working-class community. She was a bookish girl who didn't fit into the three or four cliques available to her in school, and her peers made her suffer for it. When she discovered the punk rock community, she found it "full of kids who wore pissed-off attitudes and bonded around revenge-fantasy songs like 'Under My Wheels' and 'Debaser' but who were in fact a very accepting community—much more accepting than the mainstream I knew."

After the death of her father during her fifteenth year, Mary turned angry and self-destructive. "My mother tried to send me to priests, psychiatrists, and so on, but they all felt very oppressive and untruthful to me. They didn't recognize the intensity and the value of my negative feelings. But extreme entertainment *did* recognize them. The kids who were into it with me came from a whole range of backgrounds, income levels, races, sexual orientations, everything, but nearly all of them had suffered some kind of trauma or mistreatment that the music or movies or underground comics spoke to. Because of that we were able to develop a real empathy for each other's pain and anger. We were able to make differences in each other's lives in a way that the rest of the world couldn't." That was part of the process that led Cotter to her work with the Soros Foundation, researching the criminal justice system, studying the uses of higher education in prison, helping convicts reconnect to society.

"I cannot say strongly enough how important violent entertainment was to making me who I am," she has said. "Or what a valuable role I've seen it play in the lives of many, many young people in difficult situations. It lets them go to scary places in imagination that help them understand what's happening to them and see the kinds of pain that other people have gone through. It helps them connect with someone, no matter how severe their pain or rage is. Ultimately, it's about not being so alone."

Such inward-turned peer cultures have their dangers, however. There was a sixteen-year-old named Scott in one of my workshops who also called himself Raven—his identity in the Gothic scene. I always like working with "Goth" kids. Their symbolism is disturbing, the icons of death and fetishism, the corpse-white facial makeup, the black clothes, the numbing music with its funereal lyrics, the pervading depressiveness. And yet, in its cultivation of introspective melancholy, the Gothic culture encourages aesthetic sensibilities and a reverence for storytelling, peaceful social selves, and a sweet vulnerability. There is a superficiality and an affectedness to Goth kids, but I've seen them display great empathy, tolerance, and mutual support. In talking to them, it becomes clear that the Goth community plucked many of them from the brink of suicidal despair and gave them an identity to make sense of their obsessive thoughts of death and desires to hurt themselves. Goth is an articulation of anger turned inward, of the violence of profound depression. For many kids who feel not only powerless but incapable of seizing power, even undeserving of power, it's a way to take control of themselves, to subdue their pains and fears into a poetically pleasing whole. As one of the characters in Scott's story said, "I tried to kill myself once, but now I live with death, so why should I have to?"

But through Scott I saw the power of a subculture to pull kids in deep and away from others. He loved the workshop, drew extravagantly detailed pictures of red roses and reposed faces, made artfully disturbing comments about death when I tried to draw him out, but otherwise would not engage with the world around him. When the classroom discussion swept every other student up in its contentious energy, Scott floated off into a calm pool of his own. That he was shy and depressed I could see, but the social energy lifted other shy and depressed kids up with it. Scott's artful Gothic pose kept him remote from it. One of the other kids, a sort of den mother to the class, looked at his work later and said to me, "Scott's so talented. I always used to look forward to whatever he did, until he became a Goth. Now everything is about being the most Gothic Goth of all his Goth friends. It's like Scott's gone."

I've known many kids who maintained a Gothic style in the context of friendships with other sorts of kids, many who cycled through an intensely Gothic phase and came out more sure of themselves and more at peace with their scariest emotions. But I've also known of a few who made themselves disappear utterly, who followed the Gothic glamorization of death to its literal extreme and committed suicide. One difference between the two outcomes seems to be the intensity of the individual's pain and depression. Another seems to be the presence of any sort of support group, any sort of recognition or approval, from outside the subculture. Scott, I gathered from his friends, had depressed and indifferent parents and drifted through his adolescent depression with little notice from teachers or other adults. When the Goth world empathized with him and gave him the feeling of being seen, he identified powerfully, he overidentified, with it.

When we try to make children banish or ignore their rage, they often respond by identifying themselves completely with it. When violent storytelling isn't allowed to serve its function, or is connected in young people's minds with transgression and self-destruction, it can begin to churn obsessively inside without catharsis or resolution. When children feel unsafe sharing their fantasies with us, or feel that the most powerful parts of themselves are not seen or acknowledged, then the hidden realm of violent stories can begin to feel like a reality in itself—a reality standing in irreconcilable opposition to the world of adults. Like the child of fundamentalists who labels himself "bad" when he cannot repress his desire for sex or alcohol or other tools of the Devil, the child of a controlling, violence-fearing society may feel ashamed and afraid of the visceral kick he gets from *Natural Born Killers* or the gunshots in a Wu-Tang song or the blood-lipped vampiress in a Goth comic book. Like the "fallen" fundamentalist, he may be unable to visualize any personal scripts other than dissociation from a powerful component of his own psyche—or overidentification with it.

"The question, then, isn't, 'Is violent media good or bad?'" said Dr. Roben Torosyan, who teaches critical thinking and leadership at New School University. "But rather, how can an educator empower a youth to neither dissociate from a powerful component of his own psyche, nor overidentify with it? How can youth benefit from rage and its enactment, and what kind of education can help youth to engage their rage in a constructive manner?"

Torosyan believes that children should be taught basic skills for managing conflict from their early school years: to get in touch with their emotions, learn to delay reactions, use the delay to choose responses more consciously, listen to and acknowledge each other. But in the process of teaching those skills, he says, we must avoid giving them the message that their feelings don't have power and legitimacy—that they shouldn't have rage or enjoy it in any way. "I believe that for youth to overcome powerlessness and hopelessness in the face of their own rageful stories," he said, "they need to make a whole developmental shift in meaning making. This entails a shift from the either-or dualism of 'rage is bad,' to a highly transcendent capacity to hold the tension of paradoxes and think 'I have rage, and I have empathy—how can I engage and yet "disidentify" from both these realities?'"

Torosyan sees adults' greatest tool for helping young people through that developmental shift as *empathy*. Young people who have suffered and perpetrated violence often respond remarkably well to adult empathy with their pains and struggles. Such empathy requires looking hard at what children's lives today are truly like and imagining what it must feel like to be them. "There are times when rage must be reveled in without reflection," he says. If the young are able to experience their rage fully, knowing that there's someone with whom they can talk about it, they can learn that although they may not be able to control their feelings, they *can* control their responses. Torosyan said that we can help them with our empathy, "especially for feelings that are not typically countenanced as prosocial. Play the bloody video game with the young person. See what it feels like for the young person to succeed at the game, or to fail at it. Acknowledge without judgment what is said—empathize with the youth's rage and its source."

Mary Cotter reported that criminal justice annals are full of the transformative powers of simple empathy. "Sometimes just letting people know that you understand what they've been going through can open the door to communication and self-examination that helps them turn their lives around." And she stressed that adults can use that power to help angry kids use popular culture more effectively. Sometimes it takes time, repetition, or a change of underlying conditions to make it effective. "But," said Cotter, "there were many times I would have benefited hugely by an adult relative or a teacher just saying, 'Are you as pissed off as that singer?' Or 'You really love that movie, don't you? What do you love about it?' And then just listening."

Anger, however, is a difficult emotion with which to empathize—especially when it seems to be directed at *us*. This is where stories become so powerful. Listening to the angry stories helps to tear down the walls of defensiveness and allows empathy in. Psychotherapist Diane Stern told me about a young female client from a broken home and a chaotic home life. She had had to deal with violent male rage several times in her life and, with Stern, was working on strengthening her own sense of worth and potency. Once Stern made a comment about the climate of rage in our culture as embodied by people like Eminem, and her client snapped back, "Now, wait a minute. Eminem is the first person who's ever gotten up there and told people what it was really like to be *us*—so-called 'white trash.' We put up with so much crap from our own lives, from what drugs and alcohol have done to our families, from having no money and nobody who'll do anything to help us—and then people come down on *us* like we're dirt, like we're the one group of poor people it's okay to hate and make fun of. And finally this rapper gets up and says *this* is what we're angry about. People don't want to hear it, but they *have* to hear it. And he *makes* them hear it."

Stern said, "That brought home to me that all these songs, movies, and video games are stories. Made up or real, they're the stories someone wants to tell and other people want to hear." As a therapist she spends her life listening to stories, seeing how the telling of them strengthens her clients and how the hearing of them deepens and enriches her. Stories like her client's, and like Eminem's story as viewed through her client's eyes, are reminders of the importance of letting people of all ages tell their stories and hear the stories they need.

We've been taught to fear stories. Popular articles, teacher training programs, handouts from pediatricians often list "an interest in violent stories or entertainment" as one of the warning signs that a child has the potential for violent behavior. And violent kids *are* interested in such things. But so are many of the kids who are trying mightily to take control of their feelings of anger and powerlessness *without* violence. If kids bully other kids, hit or verbally abuse their girlfriends or boyfriends, or explode over small slights; if they show cruelty to animals or boast of cruel deeds or plans; if they nurse long grudges, destroy property, or talk or write about specific revenge fantasies against real people; if they cut themselves or talk about suicide, then their fascination for violent stories may be part of a pattern that will escalate to real violence or self-violence. But the stories themselves are more likely to be the ways they speak their feelings and hope for us to listen.

Young people often haven't learned how to see their anger from the outside even as they experience it. Powerful stories can lead them into their feelings but leave them spinning there. That's where the adult ability to put emotions and fantasy in perspective can serve them well. The simplest displays of adult empathy can open the door for kids to engage with us, and the simplest applications of adult perspective can open doors within ourselves. In my workshops, I see kids' relief at being able to talk to an adult stranger about their games, movies, songs, or comics. I get e-mails from kids who are being told by their schools and their parents and every other adult in their lives that the video games or rap music they love are turning them into monsters. "The games make me feel stronger," wrote one. "I think me feeling stronger is what they don't want." I tell them that adults are afraid—of change and the future, and so of young people and new entertainment. And I tell them not to be afraid of themselves. Sometimes I point them toward Web sites or resources where intelligent people talk about these things in moderated forums, where they might get some modeling and mentoring. Mostly I just try to acknowledge what they're saying. It's like clutching your chest and falling down when you're shot, or just looking at a child and smiling.

13

Growing Up

$\mathcal{A}$ boy named Ash leaves home at ten. His mission is to capture and train monsters called Pokémon. His only weapon is Pikachu, an impulsive little rodent that turns its electrical powers against him when he tries to confine it in its Poké ball—just like the impulses that threaten to sabotage every boy on his life's journey. Ash must learn to understand its feelings and direct them toward winning the battles ahead. His companions are eleven-year-old Misty, who is beginning her own journey into the volatility of adolescence and turns her infatuation for Ash into wildly alternating hostility and nurturance, and thirteen-year-old Brock, who is vain, girl-crazy, and food-obsessed, a funny but annoying reminder of the appetites that Ash knows will awaken soon in himself and make his journey still more difficult. Together, they lead each other into endless trouble but ultimately compensate for one another's weaknesses and come out of every challenge triumphant.

Subduing the 150 kinds of Pokémon requires comprehending the widest possible range of attributes and personalities. There is Arcanine, a noble dog-like beast, and Meowth, a conniving, condescending cat. There is Gyarados, a raging, all-destroying sea dragon, and Squirtle, a turtle that acts like a juvenile delinquent. Snorlax does nothing but inhale food and fall asleep. Jigglypuff is a narcissistic ball of fuzz that makes everyone listen to its boring song and becomes furious when they fall asleep. Mewtwo is a tragic creation of evil science. Togepi is a baby in an eggshell diaper that requires its trainer's constant vigilance. To train them all to use their powers for the common good, Ash must learn to master all the emotions, all the personal twists, all the strengths and weaknesses life can present. He must also guide each in gaining enough life experience to evolve to its next form. After enough victories in battle, delinquent little Squirtle becomes the pugnacious Blastoise, which becomes the powerful but sober Wartortle. Along the way, Ash evolves, too. He bonds with fuzzy little Caterpie, and when it takes glorious flight as Butterfree he must learn to overcome his attachment and let it go.

Ash aspires to train all the varieties of Pokémon, win the ultimate tournament, and earn the title of Pokémon Master. Along the way, he has to battle villains like Team Rocket, formidable in raw power but constantly defeating themselves with selfish squabbles and blinding vanity, who teach him how not to grow up. His teacher and model is Professor Oak, a master who no longer needs to carry Pokémon clipped to his belt as the young trainers do. His Pokémon are inside him, in a sense, for his power is the wisdom of one who has won the battles of his life. To be a master, in short, is to be an adult. The story of *Pokémon,* whether told directly in the cartoons, turned into interactive variables in the video games, or made individually manipulable in the cards and toys, is the story of growing up.

Pokémon is an especially vivid metaphor of the journey to adulthood, an especially popular one at a global scale, but nearly every popular story of combat and victory is the same at heart. Nearly every one gives us a protagonist who is at first too small, too inexperienced, too lacking in power, too alone to conquer the massive challenge facing him, until by learning something about the opponent or himself, or by gaining a new power or ally, he overcomes. And in doing so, he enters a new role in life or makes the world somehow new and better. The gamer dies countless times as he tries to learn the game map, discover each new opponent's weaknesses, experiment with combination attacks, until he's finally able to beat even the once invincible "boss" foe and move on to the next level. The action movie plot turns on the uncovering of the enemy's weaknesses, or the hero's confrontation with his own weaknesses, to turn the "low point" into the sudden triumph (I can still hear development executives in every story conference demanding, "What's your third-act *reveal?*"). The rapper may strut as though he's the master of his world, but every rapper's body of songs sketches out the harsh childhood, the seemingly unbeatable forces of a hostile society, the rapper's own taking charge through the discovery of his own rage or the cynical rules of the game. All those stories are about confronting an intimidating challenge beyond anything encountered before and growing or learning enough to be able to master it.

When we look for stories that might help children grow up, we often think only of educational media or the stories like those in *The Book of Virtues,* with clear messages, lessons, and morals. But every story has its lessons, as does every emotional experience. Even if the child comes out with no lesson that he can articulate, the experience itself teaches him something about life and himself. And those are the lessons that stick—not even the most impressionable child will fully internalize a story calculated to carry a didactic message, which most of us know even as we optimistically plunk them in front of *Barney* or read from a *Berenstain Bears* book. He may enjoy the characters and stories, but if he notices the moral at all he'll usually just tolerate it as part of the package. *Barney*, apart from its contrived little messages, conveys powerful evidence of the value of being big and colorful and loud and full of movement, earning the attention of other people through unrestrained goofy good will. That's its most useful story. The stories that live inside us and shape us as we grow are those that engage our passions and turn us into someone else for a little while.

Nearly all the violent stories that kids love enact powerful lessons about courage, resiliency, and development. It doesn't matter who the good guys and bad guys are, who wins or loses, or what values are espoused by the characters in the course of the action. The action itself—the process of identifying emotionally with a character who is faced with a physical threat and fights back with every resource he can find—transmits some basic life lessons:

Achievement feels good.
Goals are achieved through complete commitment.
Clear choices must be made.
Sometimes conflict is useful.
Sometimes shattering old ways is necessary.
Loss and defeat are survivable.
Risk has its rewards.
We can feel fear—but do it anyway.
Monsters can be destroyed.
Self-assertion is powerful.
Simply being me is heroic.

Mass entertainment can portray these lessons with a special power and universality. Precisely because its purpose is to maximize sales worldwide, it emphasizes the simplest, most emotionally compelling fantasies, consciously removed from any educational agenda or individual artistic visions that might narrow its appeal. That's a weakness, but also a strength.

When I was asked to write Superman material, I set out to try to understand how this one simple character could be so compelling to people from toddlers in Superman pajamas to adults who loved the Christopher Reeves movies. I found that for preschoolers his one great power was simply being *above pain*. Pain is a central issue for young children—wondering how bad it will be, how to avoid it, how to be brave when it's inevitable—and Superman being attacked and defeating his foes is a comforting demonstration that one can pass through it and come out happy on the other side. As kids get older, they're more likely to value Superman just because he's *strong*. He can knock down buildings, throw jet planes around the sky, tear through the heart of a mountain; whatever seems unsurmountable to a child he can do. By the preteen years, fans become more interested in Superman's *secret identity*. Going through more complex social stresses, becoming aware of the need to maintain different personae among their buddies in the classroom and at home, trying to retain their fantasy lives without being "nerds," they respond deeply to a nearly omnipotent hero who can be endangered by no more than the revelation of his "real self" to the world. Many fans in their early teens see in the same hero the nexus and protector of a *community* of widely differing individuals: Lois Lane, Jimmy Olsen, Supergirl, assorted superheroes and aliens. Others love learning his decades-long fictional biography and real *history*. Adults respond to Superman most powerfully because he is, in one twenty-something fan's words, "an innocent individual who goes through the worst that a corrupt world can throw at him and comes through clean and pristine—while everybody else grabs hold of him and is lifted out of the swamp themselves."

Just as a battered action figure in a preschool sandbox and the same figure in mint condition on a teenager's shelf are the same toy, popular fantasies may be manufactured as one object but transformed into completely different symbols by each of their users. The changing uses of a simple, generic idea like Superman as young people pass through different developmental challenges show some of the ways in which we grow. Our fantasies and ideals blossom from the most self-interested and subjective to become ever more complex, more inclusive, more abstract, and more social.

Every successful children's action fantasy, like Pokémon, like Superman, is also an *organizing* fantasy. Mastering a world, finding the hero's proper place in that world, learning rules and limitations, integrating various powers and functions, completing collections, understanding the connections among the good, the bad, and the in-between can be more important to young fans than the simple excitement of the action. As the real world that our children have to master becomes more complicated, so do the fantasy worlds they're attracted to. *Pokémon* is a mind-boggling labyrinth of information and connections. At the peak of the fad, it was also an astonishingly consistent and all-encompassing imaginary world, one in which cartoons, collectible cards, Game Boys, computer games, comic books, toys, and every other kind of merchandise interlocked with perfect visual and thematic unity. Even fans of the World Wrestling Federation tend to talk less about the fighting itself than about the wrestlers and their exaggerated characters, about who's in a rivalry with whom, who breaks what rules, who looks coolest as an action figure, whose special attacks are the "undertaker pile-driver" and the "atomic drop." It's a more simplistic fantasy world than *Pokémon* but one with an equally precise organization. As in *Pokémon*, the battles test the way the organization works. Those fantasy worlds, like growing up, are all about building passion into the whole: integrating wild, selfish emotion into a complete, confident self that can function in a complex reality.

The danger of such gratifying fantasy worlds is that we won't want to leave them. I see them at every comic book convention, game designers' conference, children's film festival: the ten-year-old who can't stop talking about his Pokémon, the sixteen-year-old who lives in *Half-Life*, the forty-year-old who still yearns for the original Green Lantern to come back. Sometimes I can tell that they're frustrated or exhausted by spinning in fantasy, but they can't let it go. Even many of the professionals I worked with in the comic book industry were stuck spinning, and it seemed to trap them in developmental stages they should already have left in their early teens. Many of them were far happier than they had been before they entered the comic book world, but they were also afraid to move beyond it. I fell prey to some of the same problems during my years of writing nothing but action fantasies, finding myself caught in adolescent feuds, frustrated by silly power struggles, losing my adult perspective on my professional and social life. What lifted me out was integrating the fantasy world with the real world through parenthood, studying the powers of stories, and working with kids.

For a lot of young people, unfortunately, the wall between the fantasies they crave and the world they're asked to participate in has been raised too high. One of the forces that's built that wall has been our efforts to banish aggression and violence. We draw such a sharp ideological and social line between what's "good for us" and what's "junk" dealing with make-believe power and violence that some kids feel that they're in an either–or conflict. They don't have cues to show them how to build from their power fantasies and become more powerful in reality, and they feel that the world of fantasy entertainment is the only place that is safe and welcoming.

That line is reinforced within the media itself, where "educational" and "commercial" producers have drawn into two warring camps. Anna Home, OBE, the head of children's television for the BBC during its most adventurous years, has described the art of programming as "walking a tightrope between what children want to see and what adults think they should see. If one errs, it's far better to err on the side of what the children want. Unfortunately, the powers that be rarely let one do so." Attempts to integrate the two can produce good results, but they tend to founder when physical conflict enters the picture. The Fox network once tried to fill the "educational" portion of its programming with an intelligent action cartoon, *Sherlock Holmes in the 21st Century*. It was a smart show, produced by very conscientious creators at Dic Entertainment. Two children's media authorities, Drs. Donald Roberts and Donna Mitroff, made sure that every action scene demonstrated the superiority of brains to brawn, showed the hero turning his opponents' force back at them, and never depicted serious injury or death. But when the episodes were reviewed by the Annenberg Foundation, which advises producers and the FCC on educational content, every pratfall by a villain, every exploding evil machine, every deft judo throw, was blasted in the report as "violence." The show did reach the air, in a somewhat different form and with different people attached, but an opportunity for a major research foundation to reconsider what "violence" might be, an opportunity to bring the "official" version of what's good for kids together with what kids really like, was lost.

To help our children grow up more effectively as individuals, we need to grow up more as a society. Our two sides—the idealistic and the accepting, the official and the commercial—need to come together. Instead of reacting to make-believe violence like the nervous kindergartner who yells, "The boys are fighting again!" we need to accept it as a valuable part of children's emotional makeup and discuss with optimism and acceptance how it can best be used and how we can help children use it. That doesn't mean pressing action entertainment into the usual morals, lessons, or restrictions. Its strength is its unquestioning responsiveness to the public's desires, and curtailing that won't make it a more effective educator but only a less effective source of fantasy. It does mean making the industry itself more open to kids as individuals, creating more venues for young audience members to get their opinions heard, supporting programs for kids to tell their own stories and create their own entertainment, reaching out to parents and teachers to discuss what kids love and why.

A weakness of mass entertainment is its impersonality, its lack of a single guiding artistic vision or a personal statement. Maurice Sendak alone made *Where the Wild Things Are*, and any child who loves the book is engaging with Sendak's unique personality. *Superman* began as a collaboration of two young men in the 1930s, but over the next six decades it became an industry to which dozens of writers, artists, editors, filmmakers, toy makers, and game designers of different nationalities and generations have contributed in every entertainment medium. But that weakness is also a strength. Much of the power of mass entertainment derives from its communality. Every consumer feels invested in it, part of it, free to make it his own. The child playing with the action figure cares nothing about any meaning assigned to the figure by its manufacturer but only what it means to *him*. Even the older fan who studies every nuance of his favorite *X-Men* artists cares little about what the artist is trying to tell him but only how well he approximates the fan's own heroic fantasies.

The people who create the entertainment are usually former fans themselves. It was important to them in their childhoods, and now they want to immerse themselves in it again, to change it to fit their own visions and have a new generation of fans accept their visions as a legitimate part of the make-believe world. (Even the most commercial entertainers crave popular acceptance most of all. Money is a welcome by-product of that, but no one gets into the entertainment industry just to get rich—the market is too undependable and the odds are too long.) Their stories are shaped by the original material they knew, by their own needs and fantasies, and what they perceive to be the demands of their young audience. The audience responds to what they do, accepts, rejects, reinterprets, and contributes some new young talents to change the material yet again. Thus the whole process becomes a sort of giant conversation, to which participants of all generations and positions bring their fears, yearnings, aches, tastes, developmental challenges, and knowledge, bargaining and swapping for mutual gratification. That's a metaphor for growing up too: learning what we need and what we have to give and how to be a part of the world in a way that makes us and others happy.

When I worked in comics I met the men who created the Hulk, the monstrous hero who had been so significant in my own growing up. They were an artist and a writer of radically different temperaments and intents, Jack Kirby and Stan Lee, who came together for a few years in the 1960s to change American popular culture.

Kirby was a short, pugnacious kid from the ghettoes of Manhattan's Lower East Side who came of age on gangster movies and adventure comic strips in the Depression and put his rage into the most powerful action art anyone had ever seen. When we picture "superhero art" today, we picture some variant of Kirby's angry, rippling-muscled heroes, his brutal punches and hurtling bodies. The first time I talked to him, Kirby said, "You ever been punched in the jaw, kid?" I thought I'd offended him somehow. "I used to box at the Y when I was a kid," he continued. "When you take a really good shot in the jaw, that's when you know you've felt *reality*. I think every writer and artist ought to be punched in the jaw at least once." I was grateful that he didn't offer to do me the favor.

Stan Lee told me he'd never been punched in the jaw. The child of a successful publishing family, he grew up wanting to write the great American novel. In his teens he took a job in a relative's magazine firm (just until he could get his literary career going, he thought), where he'd climb impishly onto file cabinets and play the ocarina for the amusement of the pulp writers and comic book artists who'd pass through. Jack Kirby thought he was some kind of pansy. The years went by, and Lee never did get out of his cousin's company. He wrote vapid, trend-following comic book stories through decades of quiet desperation. He acted up to cover his shyness, but he was painfully sensitive, desperate for approval, and easily swayed by others. A liberal in the city, he moved to the suburbs and became a conservative, then let the youth movement swing him back to the left.

Meanwhile, Jack Kirby was battling his way through the business, constantly creating new genres and pissing off publishers. Eventually Lee was about the only editor who'd hire him, and Kirby was almost the only good artist Lee could afford. They came together at midlife, in the nadirs of their careers, and they decided to play around and see what happened. Their strengths merged in a chemical combustion. Kirby's angry, violent, monumental power met Lee's vulnerability, self-mocking charm and poignant sensitivity to human frailty. They created Marvel Comics: the Hulk, the Fantastic Four, the Silver Surfer, the X-Men, and dozens of others. They made comics a vital part of '60s pop culture, which opened the door to underground comics and changed visual storytelling forever. A whole generation of kids grew up on Lee and Kirby's shared fantasies and—beginning with George Lucas and his Kirbyesque *Star Wars*—went on to rewrite the way heroism and violence are portrayed in commercial entertainment.

X-Men was one of Kirby and Lee's less successful creations at first, but it resonated with a loyal cult of teenage fans. Some of those grew up to take it over themselves and rework it into one of the most vital symbols in kid culture of the last twenty-five years. That metaphor of alienation invented by a couple of Jewish New Yorkers who grew up in the 1920s and 1930s has been brought back to life by baby boomers from the suburbs, Generation Xers from California beach towns, Midwestern WASPs, Englishmen, Canadians, and a Korean-American artist, Jim Lee, who became a comic-book superstar in the early 1990s. Its bigger-than-life expressions of love and loyalty in a world of chaos and violence spoke to sensitive, alienated kids—teenage comics geeks, female fans, young gays—and eventually to that part of even the most mainstream preteen that feels persecuted by adult society.

Among the kids who loved *X-Men* in the late 1970s was Michael Chabon. Comic books helped lead him to science fiction and fantasy novels, which led him in turn to literature. All along the way he liked to make up stories inspired by what he read, and in time he became well regarded as a writer of fiction: *The Mysteries of Pittsburgh, A Model World, Wonder Boys*. And all along the way comics remained on his mind. He wrote a treatment for a planned *X-Men* movie. Then he wrote a novel, *The Amazing Adventures of Kavalier and Clay*, set in the early days of the comic-book business and drawing on the experiences of Jack Kirby, Stan Lee, and their colleagues. It also includes some passionate arguments for the necessity of escapism and violent fantasy of the kind that comics brought to American children.

After that novel won the Pulitzer Prize in 2001, Chabon addressed the San Diego Comics Convention on the confluence of comics and literature. He spoke of the "invitation to create a world" that any imaginative storytelling offers. "These writers and artists invited me to enter their worlds and play, and in so doing they invited me to create my own. Now I feel that I'm passing that same invitation on to new readers." Afterward, he said, "The problem for young people today is the way their lives are so totally mediated, so coopted, by adults, from scheduled playdates in corporate-run 'play zones' to the entire capitalistic pay-per-view worldmaking industry. But we have to remember that children are quite adept at taking the crappy materials of the world-retailers and cobbling them together, syncretizing them into something authentic and good." To Chabon, it's important that parents know what their kids are consuming, "but the most important thing is that they stay *out* of their kids' playworlds."

I saw another sort of world creation at the Cinemagic conference on youth and media in Belfast. I'd talked with young people from both sides of Northern Ireland's violent, centuries-old cultural and political war, watched them play video games, seen their amateur movies, and listened to the rap CDs they'd made, heard them voice their mingled rage at the "other side" and desire to make peace. Later, at a dinner table in a small hotel dining room in Belfast, one of my fellow conference attendees gave me a new perspective on it all. He was a Catholic Irishman, a producer with a local BBC station, and the topic he was discussing at the conference was the influence of American mass media on local culture. He asked me to explain a paradox he'd encountered when viewing our culture through Irish eyes: "We're always saying over here that Americans are too literal. That you don't understand irony, you can't take a joke, and you don't understand the value of the imagination. We see it in your educational philosophies, your political correctness, and so much of what your leaders say. But then you turn around and produce something as brilliant as *The Simpsons*, where the irony, the humanity, and the fantasy is almost on a level with Shakespeare!"

Struggling to pull myself together from the shock of hearing a BBC producer compare *The Simpsons* to Shakespeare, I babbled something about Calvinism, idealism, the fear of change, young people's need to have their emotions mirrored. He suggested a different way to express the philosophical divide: *lyricism*, which formed the central thread of Celtic and Catholic civilization, seeking truth through art and emotion more than through externalities; and *literalism*, a more Protestant thread, which seeks a single, objective reality to the world. Shakespeare and cartoons are lyrical. Barney is literal. Psychiatrists who explore dreams and understand the value of hidden fantasy are lyrical. Psychologists who quantify media effects are literal.

Then he began to describe his own experiences as a lyrical Irishman within a BBC dominated by English Protestants. "The Protestants can't help being frustrated with us sentimental, irrational Celts," he said. "And they drive me crazy with their uptight, control-freaky perfectionism in everything. But the more I'm with them, the more I can see the damned *nobility* in them wanting the world to be just so bloody . . . *good*. And then they'll start to admit what they gain from the passion and humor and *lunacy* I can bring to things." There are moments, he said, when the two unite, creatively and mentally, and provide a glimpse of the rich future Northern Ireland might have.

Empathy creates a union of all these opposing viewpoints: reform and acceptance, literalism and lyricism, idealism and sensualism, reason and imagination, virtue and devilishness, whatever we call them. Empathy for the emotions that make children love violent stories, empathy for the forces that make artists want to tell them, empathy for the ideals that make others want to banish them. I see parents achieving this union of opposites every day through empathy with their children. My mother would drive me to comic book stores to find old *Hulks*, even though they ran counter to all her ideals of the perfect child and the perfect world. Because she could feel that a part of me was being strengthened by them, she increased my trust in her and her ideals, while allowing me to increase my trust in myself through dramatically different fantasies. When thirteen-year-old Jake's father reads his Jane Austen and listens to his Bill Evans but opens the door to let Jake gush about his latest bloody triumph in *Half-Life*, he's doing the same.

As with so much else in my work, I come back in the end to my son. When he was five years old and feeling nervous about the coming of kindergarten, I watched Nicky become a Power Ranger to feel stronger, and a Teletubby to feel protected, and a "Tubby Ranger" to feel both at once. Then he discovered the Power Ranger toy line: the Zords, transforming robot-vehicles that could be snapped together to become one huge Mega-Zord, and a collection of weapons—ray-guns, shields, crossbows, one for each Ranger—that could be clicked together into a single Mega-Blaster. The pieces could be played with separately, as cool cars and weapons, or together, as the biggest battle toys he'd ever seen. He would play with them for hours. They were perfect challenges for his patterning and fine-motor skills, and a great focus for daddy-time when he needed my help. But as we played together, I realized that he took more than that out of them. He'd pretend to be a Mega-Zord coming together. He'd wait eagerly for the Zords to combine at the end of a TV episode to defeat the biggest of the bad guys. He returned again and again to the fantasy of diverse pieces combining into one more powerful form.

Then one day he was talking about "Tubby-Zords," Teletubbies hooking together to become more powerful than any Ranger alone or ordinary Zord, and it made perfect sense to me. Life is in so many pieces. So many people, so many messages, so many realities to pull together. Even he was in pieces. Angry Nicky, happy Nicky, scared Nicky, sad Nicky, loving Nicky behaved so differently and saw the world in such different ways. The very simple message of those plastic toys was the essence of growing up: getting all the pieces to fit just right makes us more powerful than any piece could be alone.

Notes

CHAPTER 1. BEING STRONG.

page

2 "The demon clutched a sleeping thane . . . ." From the edition my mother used to read to me, which I found years later on her shelf: Charles W. Kennedy, trans., *Beowulf*, in *The Literature of England,* ed. George B. Woods, Homer A. Watt, and George K. Anderson (Chicago: Scott, Foresman, 1953), p. 34.

6 Bruno Bettelheim, *The Uses of Enchantment: The Meaning and Importance of Fairy Tales* (New York: Random House, 1976).

7 "In March 2000, the American Academy of Pediatrics . . . ." Advice included in "The Role of the Pediatrician in Youth Violence Prevention in Clinical Practice and at the Community Level," a policy statement published in *Pediatrics* (January 1999); it was reiterated in an AAP press release (March 7, 2000) that received considerably more media attention.

10 "My words are like a dagger . . . ." Lyrics by Eminem, *The Marshall Mathers LP* (2000), Uni/Interscope Records.

11 "Anthropologists and psychologists who study play . . . ." The richest and most insightful of the resources on this topic are the works of Brian Sutton-Smith, the most recent and comprehensive being *The Ambiguity of Play* (Cambridge: Harvard University Press, 1997). See also his *The Psychology of Play* (North Stratford, N.H.: Ayer, 1976) and *Play and Learning* (New York: John Wiley, 1979).

233

11 "Soon after the terrorist attacks . . . ." Anne D'Innocenzio, "Toy Firms Downplay Violence," *San Francisco Chronicle,* September 28, 2001.

12 "Many of us worried . . . ." This was supported by a Rand study that found that during the week after the attacks, 90 percent of people over eighteen years old suffered stress reactions while only 35 percent of those five through seventeen years old did so. Mark A. Schuster et al., "A National Survey of Stress Reactions after the September 11, 2001, Terrorist Attacks," *New England Journal of Medicine* (November 2001).

19 "Many forces have been shown to . . . ." Russell G. Geen, *Human Aggression* (Pacific Grove, Calif.: McGraw-Hill, 1990); David H. Crowell, Ian M. Evans, and Clifford R. O'Donnell, eds., *Childhood Aggression and Violence* (New York: Plenum, 1987); and Leonard Berkowitz, *Aggression: Its Causes, Consequences, and Control* (New York: McGraw-Hill, 1993). See also Craig A. Anderson et al., "Hot Temperatures, Hostile Affect, Hostile Cognition, and Arousal: Tests of a General Model of Affective Aggression," *Personality and Social Psychology Bulletin* 21 (1995).

19 "'Narrative deals with the vicissitudes . . . .'" Jerome Bruner, *Actual Minds, Possible Worlds* (Cambridge: Harvard University Press, 1986), p. 16.

CHAPTER 2. SEEING WHAT WE'RE PREPARED TO SEE.

23 Stanford study described in Thomas N. Robinson, Marta L. Wilde, Lisa C. Navracruz, K. Farish Haydel, and Ann Varady, "Effects of Reducing Children's Television and Video Game Use on Aggressive Behavior," *Archives of Pediatrics and Adolescent Medicine* (January 2001).

23 "The *San Francisco Chronicle* . . . ." "Kids Less Violent after Watching Less TV," *San Francisco Chronicle,* January 15, 2001. I should note that the full Associated Press article, which many newspapers trimmed, "Less TV Time May Cut Aggression in Children," acknowledged the absence of correlation with media content and quoted Dr. Katherine Kaufer Christoffel of Northwestern University on the possibility of too much media time limiting children's opportunities to develop their social skills.

24 "In fact, in 1999, Dr. Robinson . . . ." Thomas N. Robinson, "Reducing Children's Television Viewing to Prevent Obesity," *Journal of the American Medical Association* (October 1999).

25 Regarding changing medical views of sexuality and psychopathology, see, among many other works, Lawrence Birken, *Sexual Science and the Emergence of a Culture of Abundance, 1871–1914* (Ithaca: Cornell University

Press, 1988); John D'Emilio and Estelle Friedman, *Intimate Matters: A History of Sexuality in America* (Chicago: University of Chicago Press, 1997); and Frank Mort, *Dangerous Sexualities* (London: Routledge, 2000).

26   Regarding changing views of autism and other developmental problems, see Uta Frith, ed., *Autism and Asperger Syndrome* (Cambridge: Cambridge University Press, 1991).

26   "People only see what they are prepared . . . ." Merton Sealts, ed., *Journals and Miscellaneous Notebooks of Ralph Waldo Emerson* (Cambridge: Harvard University Press, 1973), p. 138.

26   "On July 26, 2000 . . . ." *Joint Statement on the Effects of Entertainment Violence on Children*, Congressional Public Health Summit, July 26, 2000.

28   Stuart Fischoff, "Psychology's Quixotic Quest for the Media-Violence Connection," invited address to American Psychological Association Convention, Boston, 1999.

28   For more on Helen Smith's data, see her *The Scarred Heart: Understanding and Identifying Kids Who Kill* (Knoxville, Tenn.: Callisto, 2000).

28   The quotes from Drs. Edwin Cook and Lynn Ponton, like all unannotated quotes henceforth, are from interviews conducted by the author. For more on the views of Lynn Ponton, see *The Romance of Risk: Why Teenagers Do the Things They Do* (New York: Basic Books, 1997); and *The Sex Lives of Teenagers* (New York: Dutton, 2000).

29   "Even the Surgeon General's . . . ." *Youth Violence: A Report of the Surgeon General*, Department of Health and Human Services, January 2001.

29   "According to Dr. Jonathan Freedman . . . ." Quoted by Jonathan Storm, "Foes of TV Violence Turn Up Volume," *Philadelphia Inquirer*, December 28, 1994.

29   "According to every meta-analysis of the research . . . ." Jonathan L. Freedman, *Media Violence and Its Effect on Aggression: Assessing the Scientific Evidence* (Toronto: University of Toronto Press, in press). See also Haejung Paik and George Comstock, "The Effects of Television Violence on Anti-Social Behavior: A Meta-Analysis," *Communication Research* 28 (1994); and Russell G. Geen and Edward Donnerstein, eds., *Human Aggression: Theories, Research, and Implications for Social Policy* (New York: Academic Press, 1998).

The degree to which preconception has eclipsed research in the debate is shown by the continuing inflation of the imagined number of studies. A little more than a year after the American Academy of Pediatrics coauthored the Joint Statement, the same body issued a policy statement asserting that its conclusions were based on "over 3,500 studies" ("Media Aggression," *Pediatrics,* November 2001). This prompted an open letter from a group of psychologists, culture critics, and criminologists asking the AAP to reconsider the statement's "many misstatements . . . overall distortions and failure to acknowledge many serious questions about the interpretation of media violence studies." National Coalition Against Censorship Web site (http://www.ncac.org), December 5, 2001.

29   "AMA spokesman Edward Hill . . . ." Bruce Rolston, "The Skeptic," *Adrenaline Vault,* December 22, 2000.

30   "Since that time . . . ." For views on new methodologies, see, among many others, David Gauntlett, *Moving Experiences: Understanding Television's Influences and Effects* (London: J. Libbey, 1995); and Dolf Zillmann and Jennings Bryant, *Media Effects: Advances in Theory and Research* (Hillsdale, N.J.: Lawrence Erlbaum, 1994).

31   "Aggressive kids may be more drawn to . . . ." See Allan Fenigstein, "Does Aggression Cause a Preference for Viewing Media Violence?" *Journal of Personality and Social Psychology* 37 (1979); and Barrie Gunter, "Do Aggressive People Prefer Violent Television?" *Bulletin of the British Psychological Society* 36 (1983).

31   William A. Belson, *Television Violence and the Adolescent Boy* (London: Saxon House, 1978). Similar findings are discussed in Ann Hagell and Tim Newburn, *Young Offenders and the Media: Viewing Habits and Preferences* (London: Policy Studies Institute, 1994).

31   "The one correlative study that has . . . ." Leonard D. Eron, L. Rowell Huesmann, Monroe M. Lefkowitz, and Leopold O. Walder, "Does Television Violence Cause Aggression?" *American Psychologist* 27 (1972); L. Rowell Huesmann and Leonard D. Eron, *Television and the Aggressive Child: A Cross-National Comparison* (Hillsdale, N.J.: Lawrence Erlbaum, 1986).

32   "However, in the thirty years . . . ." Counterpoints to the Eron studies include Jonathan L. Freedman, "Violence in the Mass Media and Violence in Society: The Link Is Unproven," *Harvard Mental Health Letter* (May 1996); Jib Fowles, *The Case for Television Violence* (Thousand Oaks, Calif.: Sage, 1999); and Guy Cumberhatch and Dennis Howitt, *A Measure of Uncertainty: The Effects of the Mass Media* (London: J. Libbey, 1989).

33   "'It's in the laboratory . . . .'" Quoted by Storm, "Foes of TV Violence Turn Up Volume."

33   "Selected as a subject . . . ." Fowles, *The Case for Television Violence,* pp. 26–27.

34 "A child choosing to watch *Dragonball Z* . . . ." See, for example, David Buckingham, *Children Talking Television: The Making of Television Literacy* (London: Falmer, 1993).

35 "That may explain the results . . . ." Brian Coates, H. Ellison Pusser, and Irene Goodman, "The Influence of *Sesame Street* and *Mister Rogers' Neighborhood* on Children's Social Behavior in the Preschool," *Child Development* 47 (1976).

35 Paik and Comstock, "The Effects of Television Violence on Anti-Social Behavior: A Meta-Analysis." See also Fowles, *The Case for Television Violence.*

35 "Some have supported . . . ." Seymour Feshback and Robert D. Singer, *Television and Aggression: An Experimental Field Study* (San Francisco: Jossey-Bass, 1971).

36 "All of this research . . . ." The cigarette-smoking analogy is laid out in Sissela Bok, *Mayhem: Violence as Public Entertainment* (Reading, Mass.: Addison-Wesley, 1998). For views that I find more humanistic, see Henry Jenkins, "Lessons from Littleton: What Congress Doesn't Want to Hear about Youth and Media," *Independent School* (Winter 2000); and David Gauntlett, "Ten Things Wrong with the 'Effects Model,'" in *Approaches to Audiences: A Reader,* ed. Roger Dickinson et al. (London: Arnold, 1998), revised for the Web at http://www.newmediastudies.com (Institute of Communications Studies, University of Leeds, 1999).

36 "If we believed that kissing . . ." Morton Hunt, *The Story of Psychology* (New York: Anchor, 1994).

37 "It may be that John McCain . . . ." A fuller picture can be found in John McCain, *Faith of My Fathers* (New York: Random House, 1999).

37 "The cornerstone of all . . . ." Albert Bandura, Dorothea Ross, and Shiela A. Ross, "Imitation of Film-Mediated Aggressive Models," *Journal of Abnormal Social Psychology* 3 (1963).

39 Richard J. Borden, "Witnessed Aggression: Influence of an Observer's Sex and Values on Aggressive Responding," *Journal of Personality and Social Psychology* 31 (1975).

39 "Still others have attempted a physiological . . . ." See Craig A. Anderson and Brad J. Bushman, "Effects of Violent Video Games on Aggressive Behavior, Aggressive Cognition, Aggressive Affect, Physiological Arousal, and Prosocial Behavior: A Meta-Analytic Review of Scientific Literature," *Psychological Science* 12 (2001); and Freedman, *Media Violence and Its Effect on Aggression.*

39   "All emotions are intensified . . . ." For more on media and general arousal, see Dolf Zillmann and Jennings Bryant, eds., *Responding to the Screen: Reception and Reaction Processes* (Hillsdale, N.J.: Lawrence Erlbaum, 1991).

40   Penny Holland, "War Play in the Nursery: Zero Tolerance May Harm Both Boys and Girls," *New Therapist* (Winter 2000), London: European Therapy Studies Institute.

41   "By failing to consider the *meaning* of . . . ." A good overview of the preconceptions and misinterpretations through which viewer reactions are commonly described is Martin Barker and Julian Petley, eds., *Ill Effects: The Media/Violence Debate* (London: Routledge, 1997).

41   "In the late 1960s, ..." See Geoffrey Cowan, *See No Evil: The Backstage War over Sex and Violence on Television* (New York: Simon and Schuster, 1979).

43   *Joint Statement on the Effects of Entertainment Violence on Children.*

CHAPTER 3. THE MAGIC WAND.

48   "Childhood gun play is . . . ." See, for example, Laurence R. Goldman, *Child's Play: Myth, Mimesis, and Make-Believe* (Oxford: Berg, 1997); and N. Blurton Jones, ed., *Ethological Studies of Child Behaviour* (Cambridge: Cambridge University Press, 1972).

49   J. K. Rowling, *Harry Potter and the Sorcerer's Stone* (New York: Scholastic, 1997) and its sequels.

49   "The 'gun' of the young child's imagination . . . ." See also Brian Sutton-Smith, *The Ambiguity of Play* (Cambridge: Harvard University Press, 1997).

51   The Donald Roberts quotes are from an interview by the author, but more on his ideas can be found in Donald F. Roberts, "Media Templates," *Journal of Broadcasting and Electronic Media* 42 (1999). See also Dolf Zillmann, Jennings Bryant, and Aletha C. Houston, eds., *Media, Children, and the Family: Social Scientific, Psychodynamic, and Clinical Perspectives* (Hillsdale, N.J.: Lawrence Erlbaum, 1994).

54   "A 1998 UCLA study . . . ." Jeffery Cole, *The UCLA Television Violence Monitoring Report* (Los Angeles: University of California at Los Angeles, 1996).

54   "When children's viewing habits . . . ." This subject has not been systematically analyzed, but see data in Donald F. Roberts et al., *Kids and Media at the New Millennium* (Menlo Park, Calif.: Henry J. Kaiser Family

Foundation, 1999); *National Television Violence Study*, 3 vols. (Thousand Oaks, Calif.: Sage, 1996, 1997, 1998); and demographic data supplied by the various TV networks and cable channels.

55   "Similarly, a 2001 Harvard study . . . ." Kimberley M. Thompson and Kevin Haninger, "Violence in E-Rated Video Games," *Journal of the American Medical Association* (August 2001).

55   "Studies reveal that the vast majority . . . ." See, for example, *Youth Violence: A Report of the Surgeon General*, Department of Health and Human Services, January 2001; and David Bender and Bruno Leone, eds., *Juvenile Crime* (San Diego: Greenhaven Press, 1997).

55   "When the story of the first-grader . . . ." *Detroit Free Press*, March 1, 2, 3, and 9, 2000.

56–57   "That's why Isaac Bashevis Singer . . . ." This quote is from a source I've lost. I copied it down from an interview with him on the release of *Stories for Children* (1991). I would appreciate any reader's help in tracking it down.

57   "Every toy marketer knows . . . ." This comment springs from my own experiences with entertainment and toy marketers, but the ideas are explored in Daniel S. Acuff and Robert H. Reiher, *What Kids Buy and Why: The Psychology of Marketing to Kids* (New York: Free Press, 1997).

58   "Decades ago . . . ." Anna Freud, *Research at the Hampstead Child-Therapy Clinic and Other Papers, 1956–1965* (Madison, Conn.: International Universities Press, 1969).

59   "The philosopher . . . ." Ernest Becker, *The Denial of Death* (New York: Free Press, 1973).

59   Mary Pipher, *Reviving Ophelia: Saving the Selves of Adolescent Girls* (New York: Ballantine, 1994).

60   "This is why . . . ." Bruno Bettelheim, *The Uses of Enchantment: The Meaning and Importance of Fairy Tales* (New York: Random House, 1976). A more thorough argument, which appears to have been Bettelheim's primary source, was Julius Heuscher, *A Psychiatric Study of Fairy Tales: Their Origin, Meaning, and Usefulness* (Springfield, Ill.: Charles C. Thomas, 1963).

61   Vivian Gussin Paley, *Boys and Girls: Superheroes in the Doll Corner* (Chicago: University of Chicago Press, 1984), pp. 73–74, 80.

CHAPTER 4. THE GOOD FIGHT.

66   Lenore Terr, *Beyond Love and Work: Why Adults Need to Play* (New York: Scribner, 1999), pp. 206–208. For more on the functions of play, see Brian Sutton-Smith, *The Ambiguity of Play* (Cambridge: Harvard University Press, 1997); Brian Sutton-Smith, ed., *Play and Learning* (New York: John Wiley, 1979); and Iona Opie, *The People in the Playground* (Oxford: Oxford University Press, 1994).

67   "Wrestling, roughhousing, ..." See A. D. Pelligrini, "Boys' Rough and Tumble Play and Social Competence," in *The Future of Play Theory*, ed. A. D. Pelligrini (Albany: State University of New York Press, 1995).

70   "TV shows, movies, video games, and toys . . . ." For a more elaborate look at the play/media relationship, see Marsha Kinder, *Playing with Power in Movies, Television, and Video Games: From Muppet Babies to Teenage Mutant Ninja Turtles* (Berkeley: University of California Press, 1993).

71   Vivian Gussin Paley, *Boys and Girls: Superheroes in the Doll Corner* (Chicago: University of Chicago Press, 1984), pp. 70–71, 108.

72   "There are dangers to . . . ." Kinder, *Playing with Power.*

74   "Far too early we tell children to . . . ." Terr, *Beyond Love and Work*; and R. E. Herron and Brian Sutton-Smith, eds., *Child's Play* (New York: John Wiley, 1971).

75   "Interestingly, wrestling has had . . . ." See Sharon Mazer, *Professional Wrestling: Sport and Spectacle* (Jackson, Miss.: University Press of Mississippi, 1998).

CHAPTER 5. GIRL POWER.

77   Vivian Gussin Paley, *Boys and Girls: Superheroes in the Doll Corner* (Chicago: University of Chicago Press, 1984), p. ix.

77   "Even the girls of the San . . . ." Melvin Konner, "Aspects of the Developmental Ethology of a Foraging People," in *Ethological Studies of Child Behaviour*, ed. N. Blurton Jones (Cambridge: Cambridge University Press, 1972).

77–78   "Authorities offer various possible . . . ." Peter J. Smith and Kevin J. Connolly, *The Ecology of Preschool Behavior* (Cambridge: Cambridge University Press, 1972); and Lenore Terr, *Beyond Love and Work: Why Adults Need to Play* (New York: Scribner, 1999).

78   "In one study, the great play researcher . . . ." K. Conner, "Aggression: Is It in the Eye of the Beholder?" *Play and Culture* 2 (1989).

78 "From the end of preschool onward . . . ." See Barrie Thorne, *Gender Play: Boys and Girls in School* (New Brunswick, N.J.: Rutgers University Press, 1994); and Brian Sutton-Smith, "The Play of Girls," in *On Becoming Female,* ed. C. B. Knopp and M. Kirkpatrick (New York: Plenum, 1979).

80 "The popular culture of girls . . . ." See Sharon R. Mazzarella and Norma Odom Pecora, eds., *Growing Up Girls: Popular Culture and the Construction of Identity* (Bern: Peter Lang, 1999); and Mary F. Rogers, *Barbie Culture* (Thousand Oaks, Calif.: Sage, 2000).

82 "Girls have long shown . . . ." See Mazzarella and Pecora, *Growing Up Girls*; and Sherrie Inness, *Tough Girls: Women Warriors and Wonder Women in Popular Culture* (Philadelphia: University of Pennsylvania Press, 1998).

84 "Girls show a greater flexibility and complexity . . . ." See Justine Cassell and Henry Jenkins, eds., *From Barbie to Mortal Kombat: Gender and Computer Games* (Cambridge: MIT Press, 1998).

88 "An old saw of . . . ." For a fuller look at Hollywood preconceptions and the female audience's complex relationship with them, see Jeanine Basinger, *A Woman's View: How Hollywood Spoke to Women* (Middlefield, Conn.: Wesleyan University Press, 1995).

89 "Japanese culture stresses traditional . . . ." For more thoughts on Japanese popular culture, see Frederick L. Schodt, *Inside the Robot Kingdom* (Tokyo: Kodansha, 1998); and Frederick L. Schodt, *Manga! Manga! The World of Japanese Comics* (Tokyo: Kodansha, 1983). Also see (or listen to) Joseph Campbell, *The Eastern Way*, recorded lectures on audio tape (St. Paul: HighBridge, 1997).

94 "The woman who invented the Barbie doll . . . ." Ruth Handler and Jacqueline Shannon, *Dream Doll: The Ruth Handler Story* (Ann Arbor: Borders Press, 1994).

96 "As girlhood changes . . . ." See Cassell and Jenkins, *From Barbie to Mortal Kombat;* and Valerie Walkerdine, Helen Lucey, and June Melody, *Growing Up Girl: Psychosocial Explorations of Gender and Class* (New York: New York University Press, 2001).

CHAPTER 6. CALMING THE STORM.

97 "The late 1920s saw a rise in crime . . . ." See David E. Ruth, *Inventing the Public Enemy: The Gangster in American History, 1918–1934* (Chicago: University of Chicago Press, 1996).

99   "Shooter video games like . . . ." Data from the International Digital Software Association (http://www.idsa.org).

101   "Those are some of the essential . . . ." See Brian Sutton-Smith, *The Ambiguity of Play* (Cambridge: Harvard University Press, 1997); Brian Sutton-Smith, ed., *Play and Learning* (New York: John Wiley, 1979); and Lenore Terr, *Beyond Love and Work: Why Adults Need to Play* (New York: Scribner, 1999).

102   "In addition to asserting . . . ." *Joint Statement on the Effects of Entertainment Violence on Children*, Congressional Public Health Summit, July 26, 2000.

102   "Those words are taken almost verbatim . . . ." See George Gerbner, "Desensitization Toward Violence in Our Society as a Result of Violence in the Media," paper presented at the International Conference on Violence in the Media, New York, 1994; and George Gerbner, Michael Morgan, and Nancy Signorelli, "Violence on Television: The Cultural Indicators Project," *Journal of Broadcasting and Electronic Media* 39 (1995).

102   "Subsequent studies have . . . ." Paul Hirsch, "A Reanalysis of Gerbner et al.'s Findings on Cultivation Research," *Communication Research* (1980 and 1981); Jib Fowles, *The Case for Television Violence* (Thousand Oaks, Calif.: Sage, 1999); and Marilyn Jackson-Beeck and Jeff Sobal, "The Social World of Heavy Television Viewers," *Journal of Broadcasting* 24 (1980). See also Robert Kubey and Mihaly Csikszentmihaly, *Television and the Quality of Life* (Hillsdale, N.J.: Lawrence Erlbaum, 1990).

103   "The evidence shows, however, that . . . ." Fowles, *The Case for Television Violence.*

105   *Joint Statement on the Effects of Entertainment Violence on Children.*

105   "In 1964, in a placid . . . ." A. M. Rosenthal, *Thirty-Eight Witnesses: The Kitty Genovese Case,* rev. ed. (Berkeley: University of California Press, 1999).

106   "Later studies of the Genovese case . . . ." Bibb Latané and John M. Darley, *The Unresponsive Bystander: Why Doesn't He Help?* (New York: Appleton-Century Crofts, 1970); and Rosenthal, *Thirty-Eight Witnesses.*

106   "In the most recent of these . . . ." Fred Molitor and Kenneth William Hirsch, "Children's Toleration of Real-Life Aggression after Exposure to Media Violence: A Replication of the Drabman and Thomas Studies," *Child Study Journal* 24 (1994).

107 "If we apply some empathy . . . ." Other readings of such data can be found in Fowles, *The Case for Television Violence*; David Gauntlett, *Moving Experiences: Understanding Television's Influences and Effects* (London: J. Libbey, 1995); and Dolf Zillmann and Jennings Bryant, eds., *Responding to the Screen: Reception and Reaction Processes* (Hillsdale, N.J.: Lawrence Erlbaum, 1991).

CHAPTER 7. FANTASY AND REALITY.

117 "'Violence in our house . . . .'" *Frontline: The Killer at Thurston High*, documentary televised on Public Broadcasting System, January 2000.

118 "Every report of . . . ." See "Tragedy Hits Home," *Eugene Register-Guard*, May 24–June 2, 1998; and "Bound for Violence," *Eugene Register-Guard*, November 27, 1998.

125 Mike A. Males, *Framing Youth: 10 Myths about the Next Generation* (Monroe, Maine: Common Courage Press, 1999), pp. 280–281.

125 "Studies in other parts . . . ." Youth Vision, *Adult Attitudes Toward Youth* (Chicago: Youth Vision, 1995); L. Dorfman, K. Woodruff, V. Chavez, and L. Wallack, "Youth and Violence on Local Television News in California," *American Journal of Public Health* 87 (1997); Males, *Framing Youth*; and *Uniform Crime Reports for the United States* (Washington, D.C.: Department of Justice, 1997, 1998, 1999).

125 Mike A. Males, *The Scapegoat Generation: America's War on Adolescents* (Monroe, Maine: Common Courage Press, 1996); *Uniform Crime Reports for the United States* (Washington, D.C.: Department of Justice, 2000); and Elizabeth Donohue, Vincent Schiraldi, and Jason Ziedenberg, *School House Hype: School Shootings and the Real Risk Kids Face in America* (Washington, D.C.: Justice Policy Institute, 1998).

126 "Even youth advocates . . . ." "The Costs of Youth Violence," *San Francisco Chronicle*, April 4, 2001.

126 "What gets lost between . . . ." David Bender and Bruno Leone, eds., *Juvenile Crime* (San Diego: Greenhaven Press, 1997); Jonathan Kozol, *Amazing Grace: The Lives of Children and the Conscience of a Nation* (New York: Crown, 1995); U.S. Advisory Board on Child Abuse and Neglect, *A Nation's Shame: Fatal Child Abuse and Neglect in the United States* (Washington, D.C.: U.S. Congress, 1995); Donohue et al., *School House Hype*; and *Uniform Crime Reports for the United States*, 1999, 2000.

CHAPTER 8. THE COURAGE TO CHANGE.

129 "The keynote of Classical . . . ." See Harold Bloom, *Homer's Iliad* (New York: Chelsea House, 1996).

130 "The rise of science . . . ." This is a shorthand description of a long, complex shift in the relationships of the individual, violence, and society. It is placed in broader perspectives in Norbert Elias, *The Civilizing Process,* 2 vols. (New York: Pantheon, 1978, 1982); and Eric A. Johnson and Eric H. Monkonnen, eds., *The Civilization of Crime* (Urbana: University of Illinois Press, 1996).

131 "Plato, in imagining his . . . ." See Robert Mayhew, *Aristotle's Criticism of Plato's Republic* (London: Rouman and Littlefield, 1997).

131 "Although crime rates weren't yet . . . ." Ted Robert Gurr, ed., *Violence in America,* vol. 1, *The History of Crime* (Newbury Park, Calif.: Sage, 1989).

131 Michael Lesy, *Wisconsin Death Trip* (New York: Pantheon, 1973).

131 "During the buildup to . . . ." Anecdote taken from the displays of the Forbes Galleries in New York.

132 "A few years later . . . ." Charles Musser and Carol Nelson, *High-Class Moving Pictures: Lyman H. Howe and the Forgotten Era of Traveling Exhibition, 1880–1920* (Princeton: Princeton University Press, 1991), p. 266.

132 "And as we removed violence . . . ." See Jeffrey Goldstein, ed., *Why We Watch: The Attractions of Violent Entertainment* (Oxford: Oxford University Press, 1998).

133 "In fact, Hollywood's action movies . . . ." Data from Internet Movie Database (http://www.imdb.com).

133 "Nintendo and Play Station . . . ." Data from International Digital Software Association (http://www.idsa.org).

133 "The result has been an ideological . . . ." A less glamorous analogy than "war" was offered to me by Jeffrey Goldstein (see above), who compared the two camps of the media-aggression debate to an old married couple who have been having the same argument for so many decades that one is finally forced to think that they are invested not in the truth but in the argument itself.

134 "The first great modern conflict . . . ." Regarding dime novels in general, see J. Randolph Cox, *The Dime Novel Companion: A Source Book* (Westport, Conn.: Greenwood, 2000); Michael Denning, *Mechanic Accents: Dime Novels and Working-Class Culture in America* (New York: Verso, 1987). Regarding the furor against the novels, see Lydia C. Shurman, "Anthony

Comstock and His Crusade Against 'Vampire Literature,'" paper submitted to the Popular Culture Association Conference, Toronto, 1990; Evelyn Geller, *Forbidden Books in America's Public Libraries, 1876–1939* (Westport, Conn.: Greenwood, 1984); and Marjorie Heins, *Not in Front of the Children: Indecency, Censorship, and the Innocence of Youth* (New York: Hill & Wang, 2001).

136 "This was a medium dramatically unlike . . . ." See Robert Sklar, *Movie-Made America* (New York: Vintage, 1994).

136 "As the film historian . . . ." Jeanine Basinger, *A Woman's View: How Hollywood Spoke to Women, 1930–1960* (Middlefield, Conn.: Wesleyan University Press, 1995).

137 "Organizations such as . . . ." Leonard J. Leff and Jerrold L. Simmons, *The Dame in the Kimono: Hollywood, Censorship, and the Production Code* (New York: Grove Weidenfeld, 1990); Mick LaSalle, *Complicated Women: Sex and Power in Pre-Code Hollywood* (New York: St. Martin's, 2000); and Garth S. Jowett, Ian C. Jarvie, and Kathryn H. Fuller, *Children and the Movies* (Cambridge: Cambridge University Press, 1996).

137 "Many of the claims . . . ." Henry James Forman, *Our Movie-Made Children* (New York: Macmillan, 1934); Arthur Kellogg, "Minds Made by the Movies," *Survey Graphic* (May 1933).

139 "'It is apparent that children . . . .'" Kellogg, "Minds Made by the Movies," pp. 246–247.

139 "People who feel more invested in . . . ." For further developments of these ideas, see also Todd Gitlin's, "The Symbolic Crusade Against Media Violence Is a Confession of Despair," *Chronicle of Higher Education* (February 1994); and Heins, *Not in Front of the Children*.

141 "In 1982, Surgeon General . . . ." Quoted in "Surgeon General Sees Danger in Video Games," *New York Times,* November 10, 1982.

141 *Joint Statement on the Effects of Entertainment Violence on Children,* Congressional Public Health Summit, July 26, 2000.

141 "Some studies do suggest that . . . ." Craig A. Anderson, *Violent Video Games Increase Aggression and Violence*, testimony at U.S. Senate Committee on Commerce, Science, and Transportation hearing on "The Impact of Interactive Violence on Children," April 9, 2001. For the Inverness study, see Derek Scott, "The Effect of Video Games on Feelings of Aggression," *Journal of Psychology* 129 (July 1994).

143 "Entertainment relying on . . . ." Data from International Digital Software Association (http://www.idsa.org).

143 "In *The Uses of Enchantment* . . . ." Bruno Bettelheim, *The Uses of Enchantment: The Meaning and Importance of Fairy Tales* (New York: Random House, 1976).

143 "Once a group of parents . . . ." Richard Pollak, *The Creation of Dr. B: A Biography of Bruno Bettelheim* (New York: Simon and Schuster, 1997).

144 "At the peak of the dime novel . . . ." Denning, *Mechanic Accents*, p. 9.

146 "During the early 1930s . . . ." Michael E. Parrish, *Anxious Decades: America in Prosperity and Depression, 1920–1941* (New York: W. W. Norton, 1994); and Mike A. Males, *Framing Youth: 10 Myths about the Next Generation* (Monroe, Maine: Common Courage Press, 1999).

CHAPTER 9. VAMPIRE SLAYERS.

149 "Traditionally, women in action stories . . . ." See Molly Haskell, *From Reverence to Rape: The Treatment of Women in the Movies,* rev. ed. (Chicago: University of Chicago Press, 1987); and Yvonne Tasker, *Working Girls: Gender and Sexuality in Popular Cinema* (London: Routledge, 1998).

150 "The *Tomb Raider* game . . . ." Data from International Digital Software Association (http://www.idsa.org). See also Heather Gilmour, "What Girls Want: The Intersections of Leisure and Power in Female Computer Game Play," in *Kids' Media Culture,* ed. Marsha Kinder (Durham, N.C.: Duke University Press, 1999); and Justine Cassell and Henry Jenkins, eds., *From Barbie to Mortal Kombat: Gender and Computer Games* (Cambridge: MIT Press, 1998).

155 "These kids know about . . . ." See also Jeffrey P. Moran, *Teaching Sex: The Shaping of Adolescence in the Twentieth Century* (Cambridge: Harvard University Press, 2000); Valerie Walkerdine, Helen Lucey, and June Melody, *Growing Up Girl: Psychosocial Explorations of Gender and Class* (New York: New York University Press, 2001); and Lynn E. Ponton, *The Sex Lives of Teenagers* (New York: Dutton, 2000).

156 "Vampires have been overtly . . . ." See Nina Auerbach, *Our Vampires, Ourselves* (Chicago: University of Chicago Press, 1997).

157 "If Buffy were a parent's dream . . . ." See also Sharon R. Mazzarella and Norma Odom Pecora, eds., *Growing Up Girls: Popular Culture and the Construction of Identity* (Bern: Peter Lang, 1999).

158 "The arrival of sexuality is . . . ." See also Daniel J. Kindlon and Michael Thompson, *Raising Cain: Protecting the Emotional Lives of Boys* (New York: Ballantine, 1999).

159 "And, as many a culture critic . . . ." See, for example, Haskell, *From Reverence to Rape.*

160 "They envy girl power . . . ." See also Sherrie Inness, *Tough Girls: Women Warriors and Wonder Women in Popular Culture* (Philadelphia: University of Pennsylvania Press, 1998); and Cassell and Jenkins, *From Barbie to Mortal Kombat.*

163 "Watching a teenage boy . . . ." For more about the complexities of identification with a game-self, see Sherry Turkle, *Life on the Screen: Identity in the Age of the Internet* (New York: Touchstone, 1997).

CHAPTER 10. SHOOTERS.

166 "It's understandable that . . . ." *Joint Statement on the Effects of Entertainment Violence on Children,* Congressional Public Health Summit, July 26, 2000.

166 "In a powerful book . . . ." Lt. Col. Dave Grossman, *On Killing* (Boston: Little, Brown, 1995).

166 "Effective conditioning requires . . . ." B. F. Skinner, *About Behaviorism* (New York: Random House, 1976).

167 "Games have always been a part . . . ." See J. Huizinga, *Homo Ludens: A Study of the Play Element in Culture* (London: Routledge and Kegan Paul, 1949).

167 "After a decade of these games . . . ." See Jonathan L. Freedman, *Media Violence and Its Effect on Aggression: Assessing the Scientific Evidence* (Toronto: University of Toronto Press, in press).

167 "'The research on video games . . . .'" For more on Helen Smith's data, see her *The Scarred Heart: Understanding and Identifying Kids Who Kill* (Knoxville, Tenn.: Callisto, 2000).

167 "The contemporary style of the . . . ." Steven Poole, *Trigger Happy: Video Games and Entertainment Revolution* (London: Fourth Estate, 2000); and data from International Digital Software Association (http:// www. idsa.org).

168 "A few studies of adolescents . . . ." Craig A. Anderson, *Violent Video Games Increase Aggression and Violence,* testimony at U.S. Senate Committee on Commerce, Science, and Transportation hearing on "The Impact of Interactive Violence on Children," April 9, 2001; and Freedman, *Media Violence and Its Effect on Aggression.*

168 "The planned, systematic way . . . ." E. Pooley, "Portrait of a Deadly Bond," *Time* (May 10, 1999).

168 "Based on the data of . . . ." James P. McGee, "The Classroom Avenger," *Forensics Journal* 4 (1999); and Caren D. DeBernardo and James P. McGee, "Preventing the Classroom Avenger's Next Attack," *Center for School Mental Health Assistance Newsletter* (Fall 1999).

170 "'In video arcades . . . .'" Grossman, *On Killing,* p. 234.

170 "The games are becoming remarkably . . . ." See also Poole, *Trigger Happy*; and J. C. Herz, *Joystick Nation: How Video Games Ate Our Quarters, Won Our Hearts, and Rewired Our Minds* (Boston: Little, Brown, 1997).

170 "According to . . . ." Mihaly Csikszentmihaly, *Flow: The Psychology of Optimal Experience* (New York: Harper and Row, 1990); and Mihaly Csikszentmihaly and Reed Larson, *Being Adolescent* (New York: Basic Books, 1984).

171 "Gaming is becoming an increasingly . . . ." Poole, *Trigger Happy*; Steve L. Kent, *The Ultimate History of Video Games* (Rocklin, Calif.: Prima, 2001); and data from International Digital Software Association (http://www.idsa.org).

172 "Not surprisingly, then, gaming . . . ." See Jeanne B. Funk, "Girls Just Want to Have Fun," paper submitted to *Playing by the Rules: The Cultural Policy Challenges of Video Games*, conference at the University of Chicago, 2001 (Durham, N.C.: Duke University Press, in press). See also Heather Gilmour, "What Girls Want: The Intersections of Leisure and Power in Female Computer Game Play," in *Kids' Media Culture,* ed. Marsha Kinder (Durham, N.C.: Duke University Press, 1999).

172 "Studies show that if . . . ." Poole, *Trigger Happy;* Herz, *Joystick Nation;* and data from International Digital Software Association (http://www.idsa.org).

174 Craig Anderson's revelations were made at *Playing by the Rules: The Cultural Policy Challenges of Video Games*. My suspicion is that the e-mails were empty threats, a badly modulated form of fantasy violence; but they do suggest the tendency of some gamers to get lost in their own heads, for there could be no more ridiculous way to defend their games than to assault a prominent critic of entertainment violence with their hostility.

178 "Gory violence has many . . . ." See also Marsha Kinder, ed., *Kids' Media Culture: Console-ing Passions* (Durham, N.C.: Duke University Press, 2000); and Henry Jenkins, "Lessons from Littleton: What Congress

Doesn't Want to Hear about Youth and Media," *Independent School* (Winter 2000).

180–181 "'It's true that crime rates . . . .'" Fox News Channel, August 4, 2000.

181 "The 1924 Leopold and Loeb . . . ." Michael E. Parrish, *Anxious Decades: America in Prosperity and Depression, 1920–1941* (New York: W. W. Norton, 1994).

CHAPTER 11. MODEL, MIRROR, AND MENTOR.

183 "Senator Joe Lieberman . . . ." Quoted in "Protecting Children, Tempting Pandora," *New York Times*, June 27, 2001.

184 "Every bit of research . . . ." See, for example, D. J. Flannery and C. R. Huff, eds., *Youth Violence: Prevention, Intervention, and Social Policy* (Washington, D.C.: American Psychiatric Press, 1998); Monroe M. Lefkowitz, Leonard D. Eron, Leopold O. Walder, and L. Rowell Huesmann, *Growing Up to Be Violent: A Longitudinal Study of the Development of Aggression* (New York: Pergamon Press, 1977).

184 "Similar patterns hold true . . . ." See Ralph J. DiClementi, William B. Hansen, and Lynn E. Ponton, *Handbook of Adolescent Health Risk Behavior* (New York: Plenum, 1996).

186 "Mirroring is one of the basic tools . . . ." The therapeutic sense of mirroring was described by Alice Miller, *The Drama of the Gifted Child* (New York: Basic Books, 1981). I'm using the word here also to include some other related processes. See also Jerome Bruner, *Actual Minds, Possible Worlds* (Cambridge: Harvard University Press, 1986).

188 "The key, she said . . . ." Dr. Ponton's suggestions are developed further in her *The Romance of Risk: Why Teenagers Do the Things They Do* (New York: Basic Books, 1997) and *The Sex Lives of Teenagers* (New York: Dutton, 2000).

189 "In the 1970s, some spotty research . . . ." Mark L. Wolraich, D. B. Wilson, and J. Wade White, "The Effect of Sugar on Behavior or Cognition in Children: A Meta-Analysis," *Journal of the American Medical Association* 274 (1995).

194 "The limits of the media's instructive powers . . . ." Daniel S. Acuff and Robert H. Reiher, *What Kids Buy and Why: The Psychology of Marketing to Kids* (New York: Free Press, 1997).

195 "Of course, if a child's real world . . . ." See M. Hogben, "Factors Moderating the Effect of Television Aggression on Viewer Behavior," *Communication Research* 25 (1998).

195 "According to Stanford's . . . ." See Donald F. Roberts, "Media Templates," *Journal of Broadcasting and Electronic Media* 42 (1999).

196 "Jib Fowles of . . . ." See also his *The Case for Television Violence* (Thousand Oaks, Calif.: Sage, 1999).

200 "He has pointed out . . . ." See Robert Kubey and Mihaly Csikszentmihaly, *Television and the Quality of Life* (Hillsdale, N.J.: Lawrence Erlbaum, 1990); and Mihaly Csikszentmihaly, *Flow: The Psychology of Optimal Experience* (New York: Harper and Row, 1990).202   "Lynn Ponton told a story . . . ." Lynn Ponton, *The Romance of Risk: Why Teenagers Do the Things They Do* (New York: Basic Books, 1997).

CHAPTER 12. NOT SO ALONE.

206 "In her nationwide survey . . . ." See Helen Smith, *The Scarred Heart: Understanding and Identifying Kids Who Kill* (Knoxville, Tenn.: Callisto, 2000).

207 "Forensic psychologist . . . ." James P. McGee, "The Classroom Avenger," *Forensics Journal* 4 (1999).

207 "The late Dr. . . . ." Rachel Lauer, "Coercion in Schools: Depression and Violence in Youth," presentation at conference of New York City School Psychologists, Social Workers, and Educational Evaluators, Pace University, 1998.

208 "They may feel that their lives . . . ." See also William Damon, *Greater Expectations* (New York: Free Press, 1996).

210 "Music historian . . . ." Ricky Vincent, *Funk: The Music, the People, and the Rhythm of the One* (New York: St. Martin's, 2000).

210 "Ice-T recorded a rap . . . ." Lyrics by Ice-T, *Home Invasion* (1993), Emd/Priority Records.

210 "Both of those raps . . . ." Lyrics by Ice-T, *Home Invasion*.

CHAPTER 13. GROWING UP.

227 "They were an artist and a writer of . . . ." See also Gerard Jones and Will Jacobs, *The Comic Book Heroes,* rev. ed. (Rocklin, Calif.: Prima, 1996).

228–229   "It was, in part, a passionate arguments . . . ." Michael Chabon, *The Amazing Adventures of Kavalier and Clay* (New York: Random House, 2000).

Index